The Woollard Family
Of
Virginia, Kentucky, and Tennessee
Since 1650

and

Allied American Families:

Alston, Ashton, Burdett, Bysshe, Carlton, Cass, Charnock, Clarke, Clements, Cooke, Cotton, Cox, English, Fielding, Garner, Graves, Green, Hardy, Harris, Hinton, Jones, Keene, Kilgore, Lake, Lamkin, Lancaster, Laxton, Lillington, Malloy, Mathis, McGehee, McNeilly, Metcalfe, Mills, Mott, Newman, Palin, Presley, Price, Rucker, Rust, Shelley, Shippey, Sucre/, Sugar/Sugan, Thomas, Thompson, Turner, Walker, Williams, Yates, and others

Frances Forsythe Dean, PhD

Bernard Mathis Malloy, MD

Washington, DC

1992 / 2016

DEDICATION

To
Jennie May Mathis Malloy
1895-1969

CONTENTS

PREFACE

The material in this compilation represents the efforts of many people in various parts of the country who have been engaged in the Woollard search for more than a half-century. Like most genealogies, this one owes its existence to the determined efforts of a few people who diligently and conscientiously sought the truth. The search was begun in the 1920s by Jennie May Mathis Malloy; at her death in 1969, her sizeable collection of data was handed on to her son Bernard Mathis Malloy for completion.

Along the way, a number of people in several states contributed to the search. In addition to sources within the family, several professional researchers rendered assistance, as acknowledged here: In North Carolina, Ransom McBride and Mary H. Kerr; in Kentucky, Mildred H. Riedel and in Tennessee, Jane H. Fullerton, as well as many others. Colonial Virginia was researched by Frances F. Dean, who collaborated in the final compilation. Correspondence with contemporary family members James K. Wollard (Colorado), Mark A. Woolard (North Carolina), J.K. Wollard (Wyoming), and Charles C. Wollard (Missouri) helped to establish that Isaac Woollard was not of the North Carolina line (although laterally related).

Chiefly, the official records of the country have provided the vital statistics which are basic to any genealogical research: census records; colonial tax, militia, and tithable lists; county records of deeds, wills, inventories, settlements, and minute [order] books; and parish records of baptisms and marriages. Wherever possible the primary records have been consulted but, when not feasible, published transcriptions have served. Actually, published transcriptions and abstracts are accessible to more readers than their originals, which are on file in distant archives or courthouses. Also, this search included the numerous histories and compilations on the Revolutionary War, as pertained to military participation in the colonies of Virginia and North Carolina. At all times there was a need to study the history of a given place or era, for as the colonists moved ever westward, the old customs, rules, and laws were superseded by new guidelines as dictated by changing situations; citing local laws and customs always carries some risk because it is almost impossible to pinpoint the exact dates when amendments and local laws underwent modification.

In short, this was a thorough search. Nevertheless, no genealogical investigation can be considered to be "complete"—always there are gaps in the record (the surnames of wives are generally hard to find) and always there are additional details that could be added to round out the picture (cause of death, for instance). Perhaps it is this element of the unknown that accounts for the lure of genealogy. Therefore, it must be said that this record of family migration is no more than a collection of events arranged in chronological order by knowledgeable researchers for the purpose of linking the descendents to their ancestors, according to the evidence found.

Extreme care has been taken to avoid inaccuracies; even so, it must be acknowledged that uncertainty is an inherent feature of genealogy and consequently some errors cannot be ruled out absolutely. To the best of our ability, then, this account is factual; whenever speculation or conjecture is used in an interpretation, it will be pointed out by the researchers and supported by circumstantial evidence. Such occurrences are few, however.

All the Woollard findings represent original research, and the compilers accept responsibility for that section. However, the section on allied families, Appendix C, is based to a considerable extent on numerous previously published sources on the several family lines, rather than on our fully original research. Appendix C contains brief sketches on the Allied Families (spousal lines) according to existing published information, having thereby become part of the corpus of research. In some instances this section can be viewed as presentation of collected data which we are passing along but which are not to be regarded as completed at this stage of investigation.

Above all, it is hoped that other searchers will profit from all the information that is presented in this compilation.

Frances Forsythe Dean
Bernard Mathis Malloy
Washington, DC
December, 1992; September 2016

KEY TO USAGE, ABBREVIATIONS, AND REFERENCES

The major divisions of this compilation are sections, or "Parts," rather than chapters. Each section is a geographical category, proceeding from earliest family roots in England to successive locations in the colonies (from Virginia to Kentucky) and after the Revolutionary War to the several states (Kentucky and Tennessee).

Each individual is described in two ways. First, there is a narrative summary that interprets and relates the significant findings pertaining to that section. Next, the narration is followed by one or more "chronologies" to provide the proofs and sources on which the narration is based. The chronologies, for the most part, are notational rather than in complete sentences; all the standard abbreviations are used (months, states, Co for county, civil and military titles, etc.) but in addition there are some nonstandard abbreviations which are listed below. Surnames in the chronologies are spelled as they are in the record being cited.

Abbreviations Used in This Book

Titles & Honorifics	Esq, Gov, Col, Lt, Mr, Mrs, Sr, Jr, etc, but note that Mrs was used for females of quality whether married or unmarried
Family Relationships	The "maiden" name of a married woman will appear in capital letters; this departs from the accepted use of parentheses on the basis that it is her real identification and is in no way parenthetical.
h/o, w/o, wid/o, etc	For: husband of, wife of, widow of, sister of, etc
bro, sis, husb, g-father, g-g, father, g-son, g-ch	For longer words such as brother, sister, husband, grandfather, great-grandfather, grandchildren, etc, all recognizable
bnd, sur, or sec bnd/s, sur/s, etc (plur.)	For "bondsman," "surety," "security"; on marriage bonds, usage varied; usually a relative was bondsman – probably father or brother
Given names Wm, Ales, Jas, Jos, Geo Jno (John), Jon (Jonathan), Etc.; Eliz, Marg/Margt	Colonial writers abbreviated every male given name that could be shortened, some of them not used today (Fra for Francis and Xopher or Xpher for Christopher); In the chronologies, well known abbreviations for masc names (as shown) will be used, and some females names also lend themselves to abbreviation if readily recognizable.
County names Rich (Richmond), Loud (Loudoun), Madi (Madison)	First usage of county names will never be abbreviated; thereafter, long names will be shortened to a meaningful segment as shown in the examples. To avoid confusion, longer abbreviations will be used as necessary: Northamp (Northampton) and Northumb (Northumberland).
Grants, patents, deeds	These instruments abounded in abbreviations; some examples are shown:
Ck, R., Sw, Br, etc	For Creek, River, Swamp, Branch; also many lesser known

	designations
N, E, S, W; Sly. Eward	For compass directions; Sly or Eward, for southerly, eastwardly, etc
a. For acre or acres	Land measurements were also described as "poles" or "perches"
adj; trnsp	For: adjacent/adjoining; transport/ transported/ transportation
<u>Legal & Official</u> DB, MB, OB, RB (or Rec Bk), WB for Deed/Marr/Order/ Record/Will Bk	Unfortunately, county records cannot be cited with uniformity and consistency because every jurisdiction used its own system, so the researcher must abide by local titles. Where possible, the abbreviations will be used as shown. NOTE: The county name will not be repeated if the context of the reference makes the meaning clear.
min, MG	minister or Minister of God (used in marriage records)
Extr/Extrx/Extrs	Executor," "Executrix," and plurals (used in Wills)
dep/s	"Deponent," sometimes plural; also, "deposed," "deposition"
Cns/cns; Ndx/ndx	For "census"; for "index"
H/H, H/h; also Hh, hh	For "Head of Household"; for " household" (used with census data)
P/A. D/G, B/S	For Power of Atty, Deed of Gift, Bill of Sale
Ct/Pleas & Qtr Sess	For Court of Pleas & Quarter Sessions; also Co Ct (County Court);
Circ Ct, Min Bk	For Circuit Court, Minute Book, etc (rec Bk for Recorded Book
wit. /wits.	Witness/witnessed; the noun sometimes pluralized
<u>Volume/page numbering</u> Rich Co WB 3:98	Arabic numbers are used for volumes (also for designations such as Part, Section, book, etc); when volume number is followed by the colon (:), it indicates page numbers, as in the example: Richmond County Will Book No 3, page 98.
<u>Dates</u> 11 Feb 1723/4 is to be interpreted as 1724	Names of months will be abbreviated to three letters; before 1752, dates from Jan 1 to Mar 25 were generally "double dated." (See appendix for explanation of the Julian and Gregorian Calendars in respect to colonial records.)
c1755	"Circa" is indicated by lower case <u>c</u> immediately (i.e., unspaced) preceding the date.
< 1755 or > 1755	Carets preceding a date mean "before" (prior to, earlier than, etc) or "after" (later than)

<u>Miscellaneous</u>

w/ or w/out	Means "with" or "without"
dsp	decessit sine prole (died w/o issue)
b., d., m., dcd	born, died, married, deceased
m.(1) or m.(2), etc	used to indicate more than one marriage of any individual
x, as in: John x Doe	Lower case <u>x</u> in a signature indicates the signer's "mark (not an initial of the name)
&, as in "John & Mary"	Used in the Chronologies to indicates a married relationship

The above abbreviations are used throughout; however, whenever a unique abbreviation occurs (usually in quoted material) the usage may be self-explanatory (otherwise, an explanation will be supplied in brackets, as here). Finally, brackets also indicate editorial commentary or supplemental information.

References Used in This Book

The bibliography, under the heading **References Listed Alphabetically by Author and Short Title,** is a listing of all the sources referred to in this publication. It also includes some of the many other sources that were examined in the course of this genealogical search – but not all, for doing so would require too many pages. It should be stated, however, that the search went far beyond what is listed, if only to provide a better understanding of the scope of the search. Also, "negative" findings can be genealogically significant; if Woollards are not found in the early records of various counties, one can be fairly confident that those counties can be eliminated from the search.

Although most works will be referred to by author's name alone, when there is more than one work by the author, the publication date will be cited, as shown: Boddie-1958, Boddie-1948, etc.

Many other works will be cited by a "short title,' acronym, or initials. If an author's name is long and lends itself to shortening -- Hof for Hofmann or Hoc for Holcomb __ that may be the solution resorted to. All such short titles, etcetera, are to be found in the **References** and are cross-referenced there.

References to census records will cite page numbers when that information is available. Also, Family and/or Dwelling numbers (if available) will be identified by "#." All the standard indexes of the United States census records have been used --gratefully, for they are indispensable timesavers. Census indexes will not be cited individually under the name of the compiler unless there is reason to do so (conflict, discrepancy, misspelling, etcetera). Instead, the names of compliers of census indexes are listed here to acknowledge their contribution to the field of genealogy:

Elizabeth Petty Bentley
Madeline W. Crickard
Mary M. Morgan
Helen C. Marsh &
   Timothy R. Marsh
Augusta B. Fothergill &
   John Mark Naugle
Bradley W. Steuart

Deane Porch
Dorothy Williams Potter
Alvaretta Kenan Register
Jeanne Robey Felldin &
   Gloria Kay Vaniver Inman
Ronald Vern Jackson &
   Gary Ronald Teeples
Nettle Schreiner-Yantis &
   Lowell M. Volkel

Maxine E. Wormer
Ann T. Wagstaff
Byron Sistler &
   Barbara Sistler
James V. Gill &
   Maryan R. Gill
Florene Speakman Love

The Appendices

Each **Appendix** provides additional information, including historical notes on customs of long ago. Tables, figures, and charts; copies, samples, and other marginalia that might be insightful or interesting for the reader are found in **Appendix A.**

Appendix B is titled "Other Woollards." This includes the information on Sea Captain William Woollard of seventeenth-century Isle of Wight county and the Woollards of North Carolina who are descendants of the Richmond County family, as well as miscellany not shown to be connected to the family of this study.

Appendix C, "Allied families," provides brief narrative descriptions of the family lines of *spouses* (usually the wives) of Woollards. They appear in chronological order (not alphabetical or geographical) to correlate with the generations of Woollards as shown on Chart 1. In most instances, full chronologies are not included because space does not permit a fuller treatment; in other cases, precise sources may not be available for this publication because our information has been compiled from one or more already published family histories (with references if direct quotes are used). As stated before, the very brief family profiles of Appendix C are *not* the result of original research for this book.

INTRODUCTION

The central figure of this family saga is Isaac Woollard who lived in Western Kentucky for about thirty years (from c1775 to c1810). He was descended from English ancestors who had arrived in Virginia in 1650 and settled in a part of the colony known as the Northern Neck, which was a small peninsula of land lying between the Rappahannock and Potomac rivers as they flowed southward into the Chesapeake Bay. After a century of residence in that part of the Neck that later became Richmond County (where Woollards still reside), the father of Isaac – William – migrated to newly created Loudoun County (1757) in the northwestward extension of the Neck. From Loudoun County, son Isaac moved on to the Kentucky territory and over time, his sons dispersed to form new lines in Tennessee, Indiana, and Illinois; the particular focus of this research is the family line that was established in Tennessee. [See Appendix A, p 77 for description of the Northern Neck of Virginia and its counties.]

The tradition. By the twentieth century, however, Isaac's origins had been obscured by the passage of time; the descendants of Isaac Woollard of Kentucky knew him only according to handed-down tradition. According to family lore, the first Woollard came over from England to Virginia under appointment from the King. From Virginia, they went to North Carolina, then to Hardin County, Kentucky, then to Hickman County, Tennessee, then to where Springfield, Illinois is now located. The exception was William S. Woollard who married the day the rest of his family left Hickman County – the day he was 19 years old. His wife was Harriett Lancaster, also of North Carolina.

Even though this family record does not specify personal names, dates and places for any of the early Woollards, it does provide a basic framework. As will be seen, the findings of contemporary genealogical research eventually conformed to all salient points—with interpretations supported by historical events.

The Evidence. The search for Isaac Woollard was begun by Jennie May Mathis (Mrs John Cyril Malloy) who assembled a basic collection of evidence; after her death in 1968, her son Bernard Mathis Malloy took on the unfinished task. At that time, the documentary proof went back to Isaac's sons, William and Samuel and their younger brother Isaac, who had traveled together in the early 1800s from Kentucky to Hickman County, Tennessee, where they stayed for a few years.

In 1827, the brothers packed up once again and headed north into Illinois and Indiana. William Woollard settled in Spencer County, Indiana; Samuel Woollard and Isaac Woollard, Jr eventually moved on to various places in Illinois, both settling in Shelby County. One member of the family chose to remain in Tennessee-- Samuel's son, William S. Woollard, spent the rest of his life in Hickman County, and it is the search for his lineal descent from Isaac Woollard that produced this genealogy.

The immediate challenge for William's descendants, then, was to establish the connection between Samuel, William, and Isaac the younger with their supposed father, Isaac Woollard of Hardin and Green Counties, Kentucky. That objective was fulfilled, making it possible to identify three earlier generations of the Woollard family in America.

The Search. Using tax records, we were able to document Isaac's residence in Hardin and Green Counties between 1795 and 1810. Earlier than that, however, the trail was cold—there was no way to tell where Isaac had come from because of several political and historical factors that presented obstacles to research, factors that were peculiar to this particular time and place.

The Revolutionary War. Probably the most significant barrier was the Revolutionary War, a period of some five years of upheaval that commanded the attention and consumed the energies of the Virginia government, taking precedence over all else. Just before the outbreak of war, Virginia's western settlements had already reached a point of saturation, and the colony was looking to its Kentucky territory for expansion; Daniel Boone had penetrated beyond the Allegheny Mountains, opening the way for orderly development. Unfortunately, official development was curtailed by the war; the impetus for migration, however, was too strong to be controlled, so the migratory movement continued on its own -- and the Land Office was unable to process and record all land transactions, with the result that today there is no complete list of early Kentucky deeds, grants, and bounties.

Jurisdictional Changes. Another problem for the genealogist is the series of name changes in this part of the colony. Between 1738 and 1792, present-day Kentucky was known as Augusta County, Fincastle County, Transylvania, and Kentucky County, all in the colony of Virginia. In 1780, the Division of Kentucky was converted to three new counties – Fayette, Jefferson, and Lincoln; four years later, Jefferson County spawned Nelson County (still in Virginia). Then in 1792, Kentucky was admitted to the Union, and in the same year Green and Hardin Counties, Kentucky were created from Nelson, the parent county. This adds up to almost a dozen different jurisdictional identities for the researcher to cover. Isaac's trail led backward in time from Green, Hardin, Nelson, and Jefferson Counties, documented in the official records of those counties, but few records remain for the earlier jurisdictions.

The Dividing Line. Yet another research problem was the uncertainty over "the Dividing Line" between the Virginia and North Carolina colonies that would later constitute the state line between the newly created states of Kentucky and Tennessee when they were severed from the parent states of Virginia and North Carolina. Although Virginia and North Carolina had mounted a joint commission to survey the land, it proved to be a difficult task that was sidelined before fully completed. As a result, a strip of no-man's land existed between Kentucky and Tennessee; one contemporary report said that "the gore of land between the two lines was not claimed by either state and it went by the name of the Free State …. The settlers here paid no taxes, and in fact were subject to know [sic] law […and] remained independent for thirty years or more." (VMH, 7:242) Legally, the inhabitants could consider themselves to be either Virginians or Carolinians. An example of this ambiguity is Davidson County, North Carolina, lying along "the line," which eventually became Davidson County, Tennessee. Contiguous with it and just across the line to the north was Jefferson County, Kentucky, the lower edge of which might mistakenly have been considered to be in North Carolina. Indeed, it became known to Isaac's researchers that on one occasion Isaac Woollard had identified himself as a resident of Jefferson County, *North Carolina*; inasmuch as there never has been a county in North Carolina named Jefferson, this finding is only intelligible when considered in light of the confusion about the Dividing Line.

Missing Records. Many official records of this era are simply missing. Original records of Kentucky County, Virginia, 1776-1780, were lost in a fire in the nineteenth century. Federal census records of Kentucky for 1790 and 1800 are nonexistent – they were burned in Washington, DC as a casualty of the War of 1812. The 1800 census records for the states of Illinois, Indiana, and Tennessee are also missing, as well as for census year 1810 except for Rutherford County, Tennessee. Finally, the courthouse of Hickman County, Tennessee was burned during the Civil War, obliterating record of Woollard activities in that county for half a century. Handicapped by these known gaps in the record – as well as a myriad of unknown lost records – the genealogist treasures each item of information, no matter how small, that can be retrieved from the distant past.

The Woollard Surname. As compensation for the disadvantages listed above, the Woollard name itself provided certain advantages. According to surname frequency counts, "Woollard" seems to merit the term "unique" on at least two counts. First, the earliest colonial occurrence of this surname was restricted to Virginia, found almost entirely in Richmond County (indicating a single family); up to 1686 when cadet lines moved into the Albemarle region of North Carolina (just south of the Virginia line), the Virginia Woollards of Richmond County are virtually the only ones of that name in all the American colonies.[1]

Next, there is the graphic form of the name. The two-L spelling remained a Virginia feature although the North Carolina branch metamorphosed to the one-L Woolard, and also began showing up as Wollard. Today, the name as written in the Midwestern states (and their spinoffs throughout the rest of the country) also occurs most frequently as Wollard; nevertheless, many of these can be traced back to the Virginia Woollards of the seventeenth century.

The Northern Neck. Another advantage for the researcher was found in the geographical and sociopolitical features of the Northern Neck of Virginia. This part of the colony had been explored by Captain John Smith in 1608 but was always off the beaten track, well outside the perimeter of earliest settlement along the James River.

---

[1]A very few mentions of Woollards occur in the earliest records of Essex County, from which Richmond County later was separated. Also, Capt. John Woolard appeared in Isle of Wight County 1666 to 1672, at which time he contended legally with Col. Nathaniel Bacon to share the estate of deceased Justinian Cooper, Gent. (See Appendix B-1, "other Woollards," based partly on Boddle-1938, pp. 563-6 and VLR, 167-70.)

Surrounded by water, this hundred-mile extension of land was no more than thirty miles in width; thus, nature had provided the Neck with insulation and isolation from the mainland. As a result, social stability prevailed, and changes came more slowly than in other parts of the colony.

Moreover, the Neck differed in its political orientation, for it was a proprietary rather than a royal colony, a fact that exerted subtle but important influences on its inhabitants. In addition, the Northern Neck was administered by a "ruling class" of extraordinary men – the most widely known being the Washington, Lees, Masons, Monroes, Carters, and numerous others of outstanding ability. All of these factors combined to produce a cohesive community whose overall characteristics allow the genealogist to make certain inferences with more reliability than in other locales where social stability and conformity are not notable features. [See Appendix A, p 77, "The Northern Neck of Virginia."]

Results of the Search. All in all, this genealogical inquiry was gratifyingly rewarding, for it established a logistical and reasonable framework to account for the presence of the earliest Woollards in the New World, with acceptable linkages to their descendants who migrated into other parts of the country. It is to be expected that over a period of three and a half centuries many records will have been lost, and such was the case with the Woollard search. Nevertheless, enough crucial records remained to produce a clear picture of this family's continuum across the years and the miles, from 1650 to 1988, despite the missing details – knowing the surnames of wives, for example, would most definitely have produced a full, complete, and "perfect' family history.

THE DEVELOPMENT OF COUNTIES ALONG THE RAPPAHANNOCK RIVER

The Northern Neck is a small peninsula, an extension of land into Chesapeake Bay, between the Potomac River on the northeastern shore and the Rappahannock along the southwest riverfront. Since 1634, a number of name changes have occurred. Here is the "genealogy" of that part of the Northern Neck that became Richmond County.

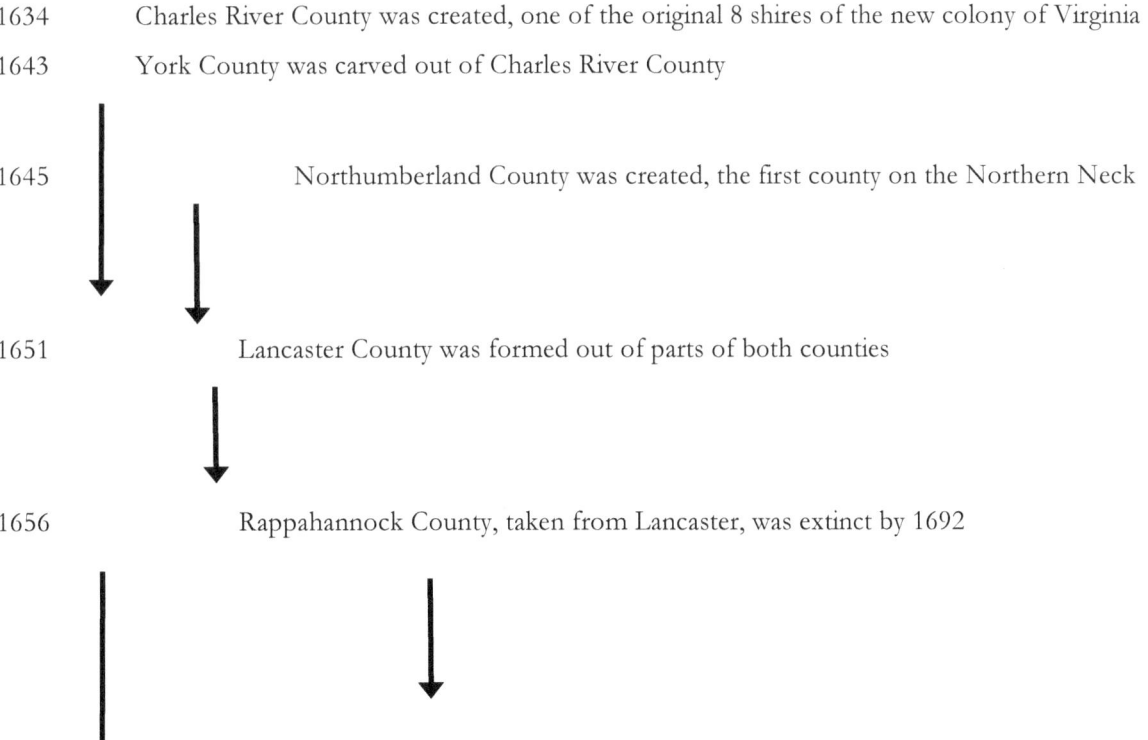

1634   Charles River County was created, one of the original 8 shires of the new colony of Virginia

1643   York County was carved out of Charles River County

1645   Northumberland County was created, the first county on the Northern Neck

1651   Lancaster County was formed out of parts of both counties

1656   Rappahannock County, taken from Lancaster, was extinct by 1692

1692   Essex County and Richmond County were separated by the Rappahannock River, replacing "Old Rappahannock County"

See also Appendix A, p 77, "The Northern Neck of Virginia."

This map of the Northern Neck shows
its six counties as they are today

PART I

ENGLISH BACKGROUND

PART I

ENGLISH BACKGROUND

<u>The Anglo-Saxon Period.</u> The English surname "Woollard" originated in Anglo-Saxon times and is therefore among the oldest still in use. At that time, people had only one name – a "given" name that was purposely unique, selected because it was not used by anyone else in the vicinity.

Many pre-Conquest names were compounds. According to all authorities, "Wulf" is translated as "wolf" (never as "wool") and "weard" as "guard." Hence, the combination of wulf and weard yields the surname Woollard (Woolard, Wollard, and other variants), meaning ""guardian [against] the wolf" (Matthews, 336-73). According to another analysis, Woolard/Woollard derived from Anglo – Saxon "Wulfheard," interpreted as "strong wolf" (Barber, 280) or perhaps "strong [as a] wolf."

In the year 931, King Atheistan, celebrating the feast of St Martin, rewarded a young thegn named Wulfgar for his services with a grant of land. The original copy still exists and with it Wulfgar's will. His wife was named Aeffe, and he was the son of Wulfric and grandson of Wulfhere; they were "old landed gentry from these parts [Devon] and had held estates here for nearly a century" (Michael Wood, 108-09).

<u>The Early Norman Period.</u> It wasn't until after the Norman Conquest of 1066 that surnames were used. At that time, King William mandated an accounting of his newly acquired lands – a truly monumental undertaking that resulted in what came to be known as the "Domesday Book." This is the earliest register, or roll book; it lists all landowners and is the earliest "official" sourcebook of English names, compiled in 1086 but retroactive to 1066, which William used as basis for establishing "rental" values.

The earliest date attributed to Woolard is an appearance in the Domesday Book with the date 1066, with other listings in 1188 and 1199 and five occurrences between 1206 and 1279, in Suffolk, Surry, and Kent (Reaney, 360). The purpose of the Domesday Book, of course, was to establish seigneurial rights, chiefly with respect to military service and tribute to the king.

<u>The Middle Ages.</u> Surnames continued to evolve and during the early medieval period became increasingly important. Edward I (1272-1307) established primogeniture as the basis of inheritance, thereby increasing the importance of a surname. As of 1275, the Hundred Rolls enumerated landholders in each district or "hundred." Some early listings of this name "from some long forgotten Wolfgard or Wolfhard" (Bardsley, 826) show its presence in Cambridge, Somerset, Huntingdonshire, Warwichshire, and Worcestershire as well as in Kent and Suffolk, bearing such familiar Christian names as Reymund, Geoffrey, Thomas, Walter, William, and Michael (see Bardsley).

Up to this point, the significance of these listings is that they identify landholders, for at that time England's social classes were sharply stratified, with several layers of peasantry in the ranks of the landless. In 1381, however, Richard II decreed a Poll Tax that taxed everyone over the age of fourteen. At this time, names that had never before been written down came into the pool of names; this helped to "fix" surnames.

For this period, Bardley and Reaney are the foremost scholars. Their research in surnames was based on etymology, and, hence, their examples are solidly authentic. However, their sampling were of necessity random; furthermore, they do not extend beyond 1317, which leaves a gap in the record several hundred years.

The Reformation (1538 – 1660). At the time of the Reformation in England, many institutional practices underwent changes. As one result of the upheaval, the first Parish Registers were started in 1538, initiated by Henry VIII. From this date, personal record-keeping began to be available to contemporary researchers.

The foregoing discussion serves to establish the antiquity of the name Woollard by demonstrating its Anglo-Saxon roots. Further research might or might not prove familial connections among these various individuals whose presence in England during the Early Norman period can be documented; obviously, many of them were of the same lineal descent – a common-sense probability that is reinforced by the comparatively small distribution of this particular surname. Regardless, these early occurrences have significance. Rupert Furneaux's assessment says it best:

> No one alive today can establish direct descent, by legal process, from a companion of the Conqueror [William of Normandy]. Registration of birth, marriage, and death did not become compulsory until 1533, and up to then, except perhaps in the case of people nationally prominent, the only records were those of ownership of land and summoning to military service. Nonetheless, many people … can reasonably claim to belong to families that may have been founded in the eleventh century, especially if their names are the same as those then recorded …. based on the recorded presence for centuries of men of [the same surname] living in the same district and bearing the same Christian names and coat of arms until … decent can be established by documentary record. As in many families, there is a break in continuity for some years after 1349, when two-thirds of the population was wiped out by the black death.

(Furneaux's *Invasion 1066*-198-99)

Natural Disasters. Natural events in England have from time to time caused the loss of public records, creating breaks in the chain of information on which the genealogist must rely. Between 1603 and 1665, 160,000 people died of plague in the city of London. Daniel Defoe's *Journal of the Plague Year* was based on the plague of 1665, the last outbreak. In 1666, the Great Fire of London may have helped to eradicate the disease (with other factors that also played their parts); however, four-fifths of the city was destroyed by the flames, with the consequent heavy loss of public documents. Thus, many family lines are interrupted by the loss of documentation due to the ravages of natural disasters.

The Chronology that follows is an incomplete listing of Woollards whose names were recorded officially over a period of seven hundred years, up to 1650 when the first Woollards ventured across the Atlantic Ocean to Virginia. Notice the gap between 1279 and 1608 – a loss of more than three hundred years. By the 17th century, at which time the cities of England had undergone a period of great growth in population, many Woollards are found in London; twenty listings occur between 1610 and 1643, representing ten parishes. In Essex between 1608 and 1642 there were 25 entries of Woollards, according to the IGI parish abstracts. It can be seen readily that modern spellings – Wollard, Woolard, and Woollard – had stabilized by this time.

Chronology: Woollards in England, 931 AD to 1650

12 Nov 931	Wulfgar, then of Devon, received a deed of land from King Athelstan; later, Wulfgar's will named wife Aeffe, father Wulfric, and grandfather Wulfhere (Michael Wood, pp. 108-09)
10 Oct 1066	The Battle of Hastings; William of Normandy became Wm the Conqueror of England
1066	Wiuuard, mentioned in Domesday Bk [DB] (Reaney, 360; this p. for all references)
1086	The shires [counties] of England were surveyed for the Domesday Book; data retroactive to the year 1066
1188	Wluerdus Legredere, Bury St Edmunds, Suffolk (Reaney)
1199	Martin Wiward, Feet of Fines, Cambridgeshire (Reaney)

<u>1206</u>	Richard Wulward, Pipe Rolls, Huntingdonshire (Reaney)
<u>1210</u>	Robert de Wlfward, Pipe Rolls, Warwickshire (Reaney)
<u>1212</u>	Engerram de Wolward, Curia Regis Rolls, Warw (Reaney)
<u>1212</u>	Robertus filius Wolfward, *Liber Feodorum*, Surrey (Reaney)
<u>1273</u>	Hlward Hutlawe, hundred Rolls [HR], Kent (Bardsley, 826; same page for all subsequent references to Bardsley)
<u>1273</u>	Reymund Wlward, HR, Kent (lbid.)
<u>1273</u>	Wulward, HR, Camb (lbid.)
<u>1273</u>	Thomas Wulward, HR, Camb (lbid.)
<u>1273</u>	Michael Woleward, HR, Camb (lbid.)
<u>1273</u>	Geoffrey Woleward, Exchequer Lay Subsidy in Somerset for Edw III (Kirby's Quest, p. 216; from Bardsley)
<u>1273</u>	William Woleward, Some (lbid.)
<u>1275</u>	Wulford ate Heghelonde, HR, Kent (Reaney)
<u>1279</u>	Robert Wlfard/Wulvard, HR, Oxforshire, Camb (Reaney)
<u>1317</u>	Ralph Wolford, Assize Rolls, Kent (Reaney)
<u>1318 – 1598</u>	During this 180-year period, no mention of the Wollards has been found; few records are extant for these years
<u>27 Oct 1588</u>	Roger Wollarde m. Mary Johnson, St Giles Cripplegate, London (IGI C-0515: 153, 00)
<u>1 Nov 1599</u>	John Wollard m. Judith Carr in Roxwell, Essex Co (IGI A-0454: 11908)
<u>29 May 1608</u>	Edw Wollard, s/o Agnis & John, chr at Great Chesterford, Essex (IGI A-0454, p. 11907)
<u>9 Nov 1610</u>	Katherine Woollard, d/o Thos Woollard, chr St Bartholomey Exchange, London (IGI #C-0515: 152,998)
<u>1 Sep 1611</u>	Eliz Woollard, d/o Wm, chr at Stepney, St Mary Whitechapel, London (IGI C-0151, p. 152,995)
<u>17 Mar 1615</u>	Marie Wollard, d/o Wm, chr at St Andrew Undershaft, London (IGI C-05151:152,998)
<u>28 Jan 1616</u>	Eliz Woollard m. Jas Adams, Widford, Essex Co (IGI A-0454:11907)
<u>30 Aug 1618</u>	Martha Woollard, d/o Lettis & Thos, chr St Andrew Undershaft, London (IGI C-0515 p. 152,998)
<u>27 June 1619</u>	Clarence Woollard, s/o Agnes & John, was chr at Little Chesterford, Essex (IGI # A-0454: 11907)
<u>28 May 1620</u>	Henry Wollard, s/o Lettis & Thos, chr St Andrew Undershaft, London (IGI C-0515, p. 152,996)
<u>30 Oct 1620</u>	Gilbert Wollard m. Rose Mathew, Great Burstead, Essex (IGI A-0454: 11907)

18 May 1623   John Wollard, s/o Lettuce & Thos, chr St Andrew Undershaft, London (IGI C-0515,p. 152,997)

10 Apr 1625   Frances Woollard, d/o Lettuce & Thos, Chr St Andrew Undershaft, London (IGI # C-0515:152,995)

21 Jan 1626   Henrie Wollard, s/o Lettuce & Thos, chr St Andrew Undershaft, London (IGI C-0515: p. 152,995)

7 Feb 1627   Thos Wollard, s/o Lettuce & Thos, chr St Andrew Undershaft, London (IGI C-0151: p. 153,001)

22 Feb 1628   Edw Wollard, s/o Eliz & Henry, chr St Mary Whitechapel, Stepney (IGI C-0515: p. 152,994)

17 Jul 1628   Anne Woollard, m. Rich Richardson, St Gregory by St Paul, London (IGI C-0515:p. 152,993)

25 Jul 1628   Alice Woollard m. Robt Jackson, Ashdon, Essex (IGI A-454:11907)

3 Oct 1628   Joane Woollard m. Nich Nodder, St Gregory by St Paul, London (IGI C-0515:152,997)

15 Jan 1629   Thos Woollard m. Collat Hargrave, St Peter Cornhill, London (IGI C-0515:153,001)

May 1634   John Woollard m. Mary Cooke, d/o Henry, Roxwell, Essex (IGI A-0454:11908)

22 Feb 1638   Eliz Wollard, d/o Priscilla & Thos, chr St Andrew Undershaft, London (IGI C-0515:p.152.995)

27 May 1638   Thos Wollard, s/o Wm, chr at Roxwell, Essex (IGI A-0454:11910)

24 Mar 1639   Wm Woollard m. Martha Strutt, Faulkbourne, Essex (IGI A-0454:11910)

25 Oct 1640   Matt Woollard, s/o Wm, chr at Roxwell, Essex (IGI A-0454:11909)

31 May 1642   Martha Woollard m. John Tebball, Faulkbourne, Essex (IGI A-0454:11909)

3 Sep 1643   Robart Woolard, s/o Nicholas, was chr at Stepney, St Mary Whitechapel, London (IGI C-0515:153,000)

4 Feb 1644   Sarah Wolurt, d/o Joane & Rich Wolurt, chr Blackmore, Essex (IGI A-0454:11909)

30 Apr 1648   Edmund Wollard, s/o Sarah & Thos, chr at great chesterford, Essex (IGI A-0454, p. 11907)

Using the data above, an isogloss map of England can be extrapolated; such a map would give a graphic display of Woollards in England, according to county location.

This survey of available data is based on two kinds of research. The earliest period, from 931 to 1317, draws from the oldest religious, official, and personal records – including the Domesday Book and the Hundred Rolls (based chiefly on the work of Bardsley and Reaney). These show the Woollard presence (nineteen occurrences) in ten counties; two clusters are evident – the Eastern counties of Cambridge and Suffolk and the Southeastern counties of Kent and Surrey. These four counties (of the total ten) account for twelve occurrences.

The second era, 1588 to 1650, is based on parish records that have been copied by the LDS for its international genealogical index (IGI). Only two jurisdictions have been examined for this inquiry – London and County Essex. This partial survey shows seventeen occurrences in London and thirteen in Essex.

A search of all the English counties would provide a more complete profile. However, a search of that magnitude (not a feasible reality) would still be inconclusive, although it would establish a tentative theory of the locales where Woollards lived.

MAP OF ENGLAND

Showing counties where the surname Woollard existed from AD 931 to 1650

PART II

THE WOOLLARDS IN VIRGINIA

PART II
THE WOOLLARDS IN VIRGINIA

IN RICHMOND COUNTY
SAMUEL[1] – JOHN[2] & MARY – JOHN[3] & ANNE – WILLIAM[4]

<u>The Seventeenth Century</u>. In 1650, the first Woollards arrived in the colony of Virginia, transported by Gervase Dodson, Gent. who on February 1 patented 1600 acres in Northumberland County in that part of Virginia called the Northern Neck. **George** and **Ann Woolard** and **Samuel[1] Wollard** were among a group of thirty-two persons in Dodson's party [see Appendix A, p. 81].

These people were Royalists, or Cavaliers, who fled England after the execution in 1649 of their sovereign, King Charles I, by Cromwell's Puritan tribunal. At that time, many Cavaliers escaped to the sanctuary of the Northern Neck. Virginia, an Anglican colony, was the natural haven for Anglicans in exile; in addition, the Neck was a proprietary colony (rather than a colony of the English establishment) and as such was administered differently from the rest of the Virginia colony, a fact that made it favorable for Cavalier refugees. [See Appendix A, p 77.]

Also, let it be noted that their arrival to the New World was a consequence of service *for* the King (in the English Civil Wars), thus conforming to the family tradition that their ancestor came "*in* service to the King."

Nothing else is known about Ann, George, and Samuel. Soon after their arrival, Northumberland County was divided, the first of a series of divisions that would create four new counties from the parent county: Lancaster, Rappahannock, Essex, and Richmond Counties. The Parish of North Farnham was created in 1663, and some of the parish's remaining records bear testimony to the presence there of the Woollard family. Presumably, they were descended from George or Samuel and most probably from Samuel, for during the next five generations the name "George" disappeared whereas "Samuel" continued to be used as a name for Woollard sons.

The next mention occurs in 1679, when **John[2] Woolard** returned to Virginia from England as a headright of Dennis McCarty of Westmoreland County. John may have been a young man, perhaps unmarried; trips "back home" to England were not uncommon, and traveling at the expense of someone else (who thereby claimed the headright) was a common arrangement. We surmise that John was the only (known) son of Samuel Wollard who had arrived twenty-nine years earlier.

John and his wife Mary had five children, all of them christened at North Farnham Church between 1682 and 1696. The existing records of the Parish show five generations of christenings and marriages of Woollards. Mary and John lived on Totusky Creek "near the church road" by "the stake in a small Indian field." The connection with the Dodson family was still evident in 1694 when Mary witnessed a deed for Charles Dodson. John Woollard died intestate in 1699 (his estate administered by Rawleigh Travers), and his wife Mary died in 1762. They were survived by three daughters and two sons, John (whose line will be traced) and Richard.

Issue: Mary, 1682; **John³**; Rebekah, 1687; Richard 3, 1691-1764; Elling, 1696

John[3] Woollard (1685-1759) and wife Anne had six children; all survived to adulthood and left progeny, except Isaac who died young (his only child having predeceased him). Of the five surviving children named in John's will, four of them remained in Richmond County – John, Joseph, Samuel, and Anne Smith, wife of Thomas. Their son William[4] moved out of the county.

The Eighteenth Century. John Woollard's will devised land to his married sons Joseph and Samuel but left money (£105) to son **William[4]**, who at the time may have already left Richmond County. There is ample evidence in the county and parish records of William's brothers and cousins (the sons of Richard 3), but there is no mention of William. However, William reappeared in Loudoun County, northward from Richmond County on the Potomac River and newly created just a few years before his father's death.

At some point, one or more of the early Woollards had migrated southward into the Albemarle area of North Carolina. Up to this point, according to all remaining records, Richmond County was the only locale in the colony (and all other colonies except Carolina) where Woollards were living. Their descendants still live there. After 1760, however, there was a new household of Woollards in Loudoun County.

Issue: Isaac, 1720-48; John, 1725; Joseph, 1726-60?, **William[4]** 1729-87; Samuel, 1735-1787; and Anne, 1732

Chronology: Woollards in Richmond County, Virginia

1 Feb 1650	Gervase Dodson, Gent, patented 1600 a. in Northumberland Co, VA for transportation of 32 persons, including Geo Woolard, Ann Woolard, and Sam'1 Wollard (C&P 1:203-04; Greer, 369)
1651	Lancaster Co was created out of Northumberland Co
1656	Rappahannock Co was created out of Lancaster Co
1663	North Farnham Parish was created [adj Westm and Northumb Co's on SE, and adj Lanc and the Rappahannock R on S & W]
1651-1678	NOTE: here is a gap in the Woollard records of 27 years; also, nothing is found for 1679 to 1691 (see below)
21 May 679	Jno 2 Woolard was trnsp to VA by Dennis Carty [McCarty of Westm Col, who patented much land in Northumb Co] (VCA (2) 1:4)
1682 - 1696	John & Mary Woollard of N Farnham Parish, Rich Co, VA had five children christened; their two sons John and Rich [see below] are presumed to be progenitors of succeeding generations of Woollards in that parish (Headley, 5)
14 Apr 1685	Baptismal date of John 3 s/o John & Mary Woollard (N Farnham Parish records, cited in King-1966, 205-08; hereafter cited as "King")
22 Oct 1691	Baptismal date of Rich s/o John & Mary Woollard (King)
1692	Richmond and Essex Counties were created from Old Rapp Co
22 Jan 1693/4	Mary Wollard wit. Deed, Saml Travers to Chas Dodson, Essex Co (DB 2:4; VCA (1) 16:34)
4 May 1694	John Woollard bought 100 a. in Farnham Parish; Saml Travers wit. (DB 2:48; also in VCA (1) 16:48)
1 Oct 1695	Power of Atty by Mary w/o John Woollard (DB 2:38; VCA (1) 16:60)
"	Powell's deed to Partridge mentions "line of John Wollard" (DB 2:135; VCA (1) 16:60)

"	"John Woollard wit. P/A from Michal Powell to Wm Barber Jun (DB 2:137; VCA (1):16:60)
"	John & Mary Woollard signed deed to John Partridge for "13 a. adj Totusky Ch … by the Church Rd…" (DB 2:137; VCA (1) 16:60)
8 Sep 1698	Mary Woollard proved will of John Partridge (Headley, 4)
2 Aug 1699	John² Woollard d. Intestate, leaving wife Mary and five children: **Mary, John³**, Rich, Rebeccah, and Elling; Rawleigh Travers to be adm (OB 2:429, 432-33; Headley, 5)
1716-1736	Rich Woollard (d. <1744, his will pr 5 Mar 1744) & wife Sarah (d. 1764) had 3 sons, John, Rich, and Wm, and 6 daus (Headley, 86; King)

RICHMOND COUNTY LEGACY

The administration of John Woollard, 2 August 1699
North Farnham Parish, Richmond County, Virginia
Abstract and commentary

"At a Court held for Richmond County the 2th day of Augst, Anno 1699," the Justices granted administration upon the estate of John Woollard Dcd to Rawleigh Travers, who gave security, John having died without leaving a will. It is historically interesting that the next entry in the Order book pertained to a settlement by "Madam Mildred Washington, Mr John Washington, Exors of Capt John Washington, Extrx of John Washington, The exors of Ms Martha Hayward" –whatever that may have meant.

The following entry ordered that Mr Samuel Samford, Mr Charles Barber, Mr Edward Jones or any two of them before the next Court "do meet at the house of John Woollard Deced and then and there do inventory and appraise all and Singular the Estate of the Said Deced … and to Serve … also to Relict of the Said Deced for her True Discovery of the Said Estate."

Further, Mr Rawleigh Travers was ordered to take "1291 lbs of good tobacco in cash due by bill together with costs of suit" out of the Estate of John Woollard, Dcd. (Richmond County Order book 2:429). No other records on the estate of John Woollard have been found, except the will itself (see next page).

---

22 Mar 1718	Rich and John Woollard wit. Will of Job Hamon (Headley, 39)
1720 - 1735	John² & Anne Woollard had six children, five of them sons: Isaac, John, Jos, Wm, Saml; within three generations, ten males have descended from John & Mary (King)
20 Jan 1726	Mary Woollard died (King)
10 Oct 1729	Wm⁴ Woollard, s/o John & Anne, was christened (King)
4 Feb 1734	Rich Woollard wit. Will of John Wade, Farnham Parish (Headley, 73)
27 Sep 1738	John Woollard, Junr died (King)
5 Mar 1743	Rich Woollard's inventory (Headley, 86)
7 Oct 1744	John Woollard to be trustee over estate of John Mill (n)er (Headley, 88)
13 Apr 1745	Isaac Woollard was named extr of Henry Williams (Headley, 88)

15 Nov 1747   Isaac (b. 5 Aug 1720, d. 1748/9) & wife Catherine (m.c1770) had son Esau (King)

11 Feb 1748/9   Isaac Woollard's will named w Catherine, bro Joseph; father John to be extr (WB 5:569; Headley, 96)

3 Apr 1749   Inventory of Isaac Woollard (Headley, 97)

20 Jan 1749   Wm⁴ Woollard & wife Mary had one son Wm⁵ (King) [NOTE: Christening records of their other children not found at Farnham Parish; they may have moved away!]

29 Mar 1750   John Woollard was named extr of Samford Jones' will (Headley, 99)

1751 – 1752   John⁴ & Sarah Woollard had two sons: Wm b. 1 Nov 1751, John b. 7 Jan 1752 (King)

30 Nov 1752   John Efford's will named wife Frances, sons Wm and John, dau Eliz Woollard [w/o Rich?] (Headley, 111)

12 Feb 1755   Jos Woollard was extr of Jas Hind (Headley, 113)

1755 – 1766   Rich & Eliz Woollard had three children: Winifred b. 14 Apr 1755 and two sons: Jos b. 25 Feb 1758 and Rich b. 6 Oct 1766 (King)

20 Jul 1758   John and Rich Woollard were listed as voters for an election of Burgesses (Rich OB 14:264-68; MVG 25:20-22)

9 Mar 1759   John³ Woollard's will named wife Anne, sons Jos, Saml, John, Wm⁴; dau Anne Smith (w/o Thos); g-ch Anne and John Smith; g-ch Jos and Priscilla (of son John); wit. Wm Woollard (Rich WB 6:151-53; Headley, 118-19)

LAST WILL AND TESTAMENT OF JOHN WOOLLARD
Dated 9 March 1759, North Farnham Parish, Virginia
An Abstract

John Woollard's will dated 9 March 1759 is specific and clearly organized; he methodically bequeathed his land, Negroes, household furniture, and livestock according to those categories.

Sons Joseph and Samuel received land. They also received two Negroes each, as also did son John and daughter Ann Smith.

Joseph, Samuel, and Ann Smith each received a bed and its "furniture"; in addition, Joseph received a large oval table and Samuel a small oval table and large chest. All other furniture remained for the use of John's widow.

The livestock was given mostly to John, who received two cows, two yearlings, two ewes, and two lambs; Ann Smith received one cow and one yearling. The remaining cattle were to be divided between Joseph and Samuel, and the rest of the sheep and hogs were to remain on the plantation during the lifetime of wife Ann. Four grandchildren were named as heirs of their parents, John Woollard and Ann Smith.

Thus, all the real property was allocated. In addition, cash payments of current money were to be paid to son William Woolard by his three brothers. Three amounts are mentioned: £15 to be paid to William by Joseph; £45 to be paid him by Joseph; and £45 to be paid by Joseph and Samuel. "Son William Woolard" is referred to three times and it was specified that he receive payment before the other distributions were made. Obviously, John Woolard made his will when he was "in perfect sense and memory." He must have had an orderly mind with a special gift for organizing material into its component parts.

Unfortunately, for present-day readers of John Woollard's will, no explanation is given for William's whereabouts or why he received only cash; undoubtedly, no explanation was needed at the time, for everyone would have understood. However, since William received cash only – no land or moveable

7 May 1759   Inventory of John[3] Woollard estate (Headley, 119)

6 Jan 1760   Jos Woollard as extr of Chas Hinds was made guardian of orphan son Josiah Hinds (Headley, 120)

20 Apr 1760   Sarah Woollard was named as d/o Henry Williams in his will (Headley, 121)

5 May 1760   Inventory of Jos Woollard (Ibid.)

1763-1769   Saml Woollard (d.1786) & wife Mary Anne had at least three children: son John b. 28 July 1763, and two daus Eliz and Ann (King)

25 Jun 1764   in her will, Sarah Woollard (wid/o Rich) named children Rich, Wm, and Betty Anne Warner; g-son Wm Tillery; wit. Wm Efford   (Headley, 130)

7 Aug 1764   Inventory of Sarah Woollard (Ibid.)

9 May 1771   Will of Thos Smith mentioned his dcd f-in-l John 3 Woollard and dcd b-in-l Jos Woollard, son Jos Woollard Smith; extr Saml Woollard 9 Rich WB 7: Headley, 156-57; W&M (1) 17:194)

29 Jun 1774   Inventory of rich Woollard (Headley, 142)

3 Dec 1774   Saml Woollard wit. Will of Josiah Hinds (Headley, 142)

9 May 1781   Mr Saml Woollard was named extr in will of Rich Burrell; wit. John Woollard (Headley, 158)

1782-1792   Jos Woollard & Wife Winnefred had 2 children: John b. 4 Feb 1782 and Cathrine Williams b. 20 Oct 1792 (King)

3 Apr 1782   After the Revolutionary War, the Rich Co Court allowed claims against the Commonwealth under the act for "adjusting claims for property impressed or taken for public service", a list of about 50 names included Saml Woollard, Thos and Caty Jesper, Geo Harrison, Martin Bearcraft, and Benj Rust (Tyler 7:108-09).

    [NOTE: This item has interesting application to the Woollard lineage in various ways. Several Woollards intermarried with Jespers in Rich Co, and the name "Jesper Woollard" – sometimes "Jasper" – appeared among the NC Woollards for several generations, demonstrating a connection with Rich Co; as late as 1811, Rich Jesper was bnd for Jos Woollard Jr when he married Fanney Jesper in Rich Co. In 1803, Isaac Woollard of Loud Co m. Phoebe Barracraft. In 1888 a descendant of Wm married a descendant of this Rust family, Martha Jane Rust, whose gg-grandmother, a widow, had married (2) Geo Harrison of Rich Co, VA. In 1798, John Woollard of Rich Co was bnd when Saml Rust married Nancy Hammond. See King.]

1783   Eliz Woollard, Jos Woollard, and Saml Woollard are listed as Heads of Households in the First Census of the United States, in Farnham Dist on John Smith's list (AIS Index, 63)

1786   Saml Woollard's will named wife Mary Anne; sons John, Saml, Wm Jesper Woollard; daus Eliz Smith, Anne, Eleanor, Mary Anne, Hannah, Sarah; extrs included friend Thos Smith; mentioned his bro John and his father's land purchased of Wm Hammond (Headley, 167)

1787   Rich, Mary Ann, and John Woollard were listed as H/Hs on tax List C for Rich Co (Fothergill, 1282)

Feb 1788   Eliz Woollard's will named daus Caty, Winifred Davis; sons Rich, John, and Jos Woollard; g-dau Betty Woollard; extr Thos Smith (Headley, 168)

29 Apr 1788   John Woollard m. Jemima Redman, Westm Co (VCR (4) 4:94)

Descendants of Samuel[1] Woollard of Richmond County, Virginia

Samuel[1] Woollard: From England to Virginia in 1650, with Ann and George

John[2] Woollard, b North Farnham Parish, d 2 Aug 1699
m Mary (d/o William?), d 20 Jan 1726

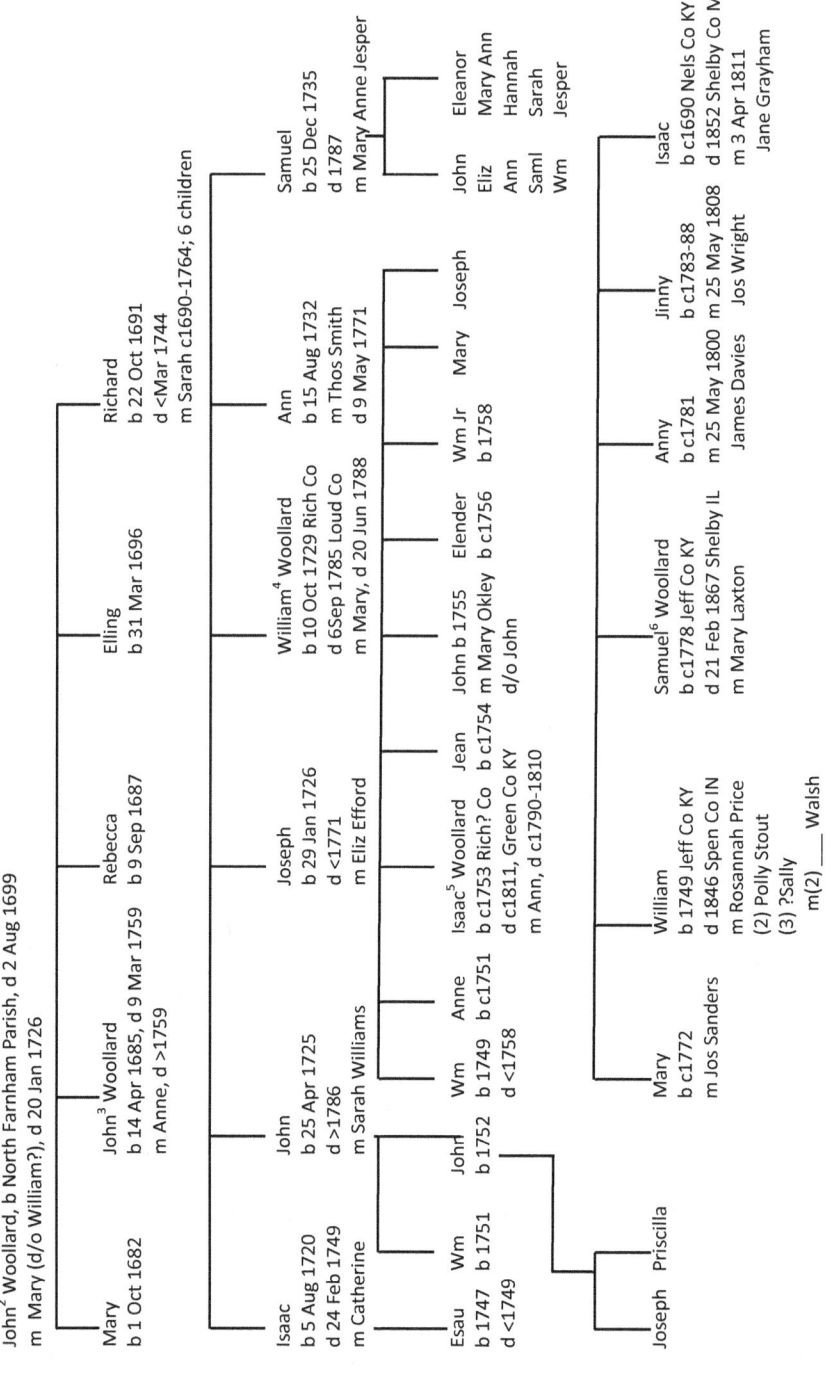

THE WOOLLARDS IN VIRGINIA
IN LOUDON COUNTY
WILLIAM[4] & MARY WOOLLARD OF SHELBURNE PARISH

In the decades before the Revolutionary War, Virginia's population was growing rapidly; the need for land was acute, and the only direction of growth was westward. New counties were created to handle the overflow, which generally followed the rivers. In 1757, Loudoun County was formed from Fairfax County and named for Virginia's governor, John Campbell, fourth Earl of Loudoun. Among its early settlers were **William[4] Woollard** and his wife **Mary** of North Farnham Parish in Richmond County.

In 1760, William Woollard acquired land from the Mercer family; this is the first mention but it is possible that he had been there as early as 1750 (at which time his name disappears from the records of Richmond County). It appears from the tithable lists of London County that there was a general influx from Richmond County to the new county upcountry. Middleton Wollard was listed in 1759; others were Charnuck and Presley Self, William and Matthew Rust, the Bearcraft (Barecraft/Barcroft) family, and Captain Willoughby Newton.

William was listed on most of the extant tithable lists between 1761 and 1782. Happily, these lists included the names of sons as they came of age at 16 years, so it is possible to approximate closely the birth years of William's son **Isaac[5]**, John, and William, Jr. The parish records are almost nonexistent; Cameron was the first parish, and then Shelburne Parish was created. Some of the vestry books "of the late 1700s" are in the Archives of the Virginia State Library, but the parish registers are missing. In 1775, William was listed as a tithable of Shelburne Parish.

The Order Books of the county include a few mentions of William Woollard: he sued to collect a debt (and won); he appeared in court as a witness for William Mason; he was appointed as surveyor of roads; and in 1783 his court action against Pollard was "discontinued." He farmed his own property with a white servant (indentured?) and a few Negroes, and in the process he and wife Mary reared six children.

William Woollard died intestate about 1785, and Mary was granted administration of his estate in September, 1785. Mary did not long survive her husband; her will is dated 20 June 1788, signed and sealed by Mary. She named son Joseph to be executor, which implies that her oldest son Isaac may not have been living in the county. In fact, that is exactly the case, for in October of that year Isaac "of Jefferson County in the State of North Carolina" sold his one-eighth share of his deceased father's land to his brother Joseph. This instrument was signed and sealed by Isaac and his wife **Ann.** [NOTE: This accounts for family tradition that placed Isaac in North Carolina, although in fact he was in a region that later would be part of the new state of Kentucky.]

Although a number of Woollards served in the Virginia Line during the Revolutionary War, Isaac apparently did not [see Appendix B, p. 87 on John of Loudoun County]. Twenty-five years after his death, the grandsons of William and Mary Woollard were still there – the US Census for 1810 named John and William Woollard, and Isaac and John Wollard. However, they were not listed in the 1820 Census for Loudoun County.

Issue: William (b.1749), Anne (b.c1751), **Isaac**[5] (c1753-c1811), Jean (b.c1754), John (b.1755), Elendar (b.c1756), William Jr (b.1758), Mary, Joseph

NOTE on "Issue": Wm b.1749 may have died young and his name was then given to a male child b. c1758 (who appeared as Wm Jr, a tithable of his father in 1774). This practice of naming a younger child for a deceased elder sibling was in the nature of a memorial and also a way to perpetuate family given names. Also note that "Jr" indicated a *younger* person, not necessarily a son – commonly, a nephew residing in the same community as his uncle.

Chronology: Woollards in Loudoun County, Virginia

<u>1757</u>	Loudoun Co was formed from Fairfax County
<u>c1759</u>	William[4] Woollard may have acquired his land in Loud Co even earlier than this date, but records are missing
<u>1759</u>	Tithable List included Middleton Wollard [Loud Co tithable lists have not been published; originally, they were not entered into bound volumes but submitted by the several militia officers on loose sheets of paper. These are at the courthouse in Leesburg and are boxed together but cannot be referred to by volume and page.]
<u>5 Sep 1760</u>	Wm Woollard leased 150 a. from Geo, John, and Jas Mercer by their atty; land originally granted to Geo Slayter from the Proprietors Office of Northern Neck of VA. The lease was for one year, Woollard "Yielding and Paying therefore one pepper Corn on and upon the Feast of Saint Michael the ArchAngel if demanded." (DB E: 179-85)
<u>1761</u>	Tithable List: Capt. Willoughby Newton Tithable List: Wm Wolerd, 1 tithable [self] on John Macklehany's list
<u>1762</u>	Tithable List for Cameron Parish: Wm Wollard[1]
<u>1762-1765?</u>	Wm Woolard vs Folke, for indebtedness; pltf won (OB B: 646)
<u>1763</u>	Tithable List: Wm Wollard (from "undated" folio; no list extant for year)
<u>1765</u>	Tithable List: Wm[1] Woolard
<u>8 Sep 1766</u>	Wm Woollard's re-lease of Mercer land, as above (DB E: 179-85)
<u>1767</u>	Tithable List: Wm Woolard, on the list of Francis Lightfoot Lee [This folio was labeled "1773-1779, Years inclusive" but here assigned to year 1767 on the basis of Woollard's not having tithable in addition to self]
<u>c1767-70</u>	Wm Wollard appeared in court as witness for Wm Mason (OB D:59)
<u>1769</u>	Tithable List: Wm[3] Woollard (Isaac Woollard, Negro Tom) on Craven Peyton's list [NOTE: Wm himself with son Isaac and Negro Tom added up to 3 taxables. Isaac was at least 16 years of age, suggesting 1750-53 as his birth year; also on this list were Nath, Saml, and Saml Laxton, Jr]

This "List of Tithables taken by Craven Peyton in the Year 1769" reveals the neighbors of William and Ann Woollard in Loudoun County, including the household of Charles Laxton (fifth down in right-hand column) whose tithables included Charles Junr and Nathl Laxton. The tithables of William Woollard (ninth from bottom of same column) included his son Isaac and Negro Tom. (From Loudon County Courthouse, Leesburg, Virginia; loose papers.)

1770 Wm[4] Woolard (Isaac Woolard, John Wooard, Benj Evans) [NOTE: This list was labeled "undated" and has been assigned to this year on the basis of the 4 tithables named]

1771 Tithable List: Wm[4] Woolard (John Woolard, Benj Evans, Negro Tom) on the list of Joslas Clapham, as also: John St Clair, (Isaac Woolard, Negros Jim & Cate)

1772 tithable List: Wm[4] Woolard (Isaac Woolard, John Wooard, Benj Evans)

1773 tithable List: Wm[4] Woolard (John Woolard, Benj Evans, Negroe Tomm)

1774 tithable List: Wm[5] Woolard (Isaac, John, and Wm Woollard, Jr; Ben Evans) on Clapham's list

1775 Tithable List: Wm[3] Woolard (Son Wm and Negroe Jane) on Shelburne parish list taken by Thos Lewis; also on list were Wm and Matt Rust

Tithable List: Isaac[1] Woollard   {these two men (by now married) were
Tithable List: John[1] Woolard   {on separate lists from their father.

Entries for the Woollards and Laxtons, from Peyton Craven's Loudoun County tithable list dated 1769 [Enlarged; see facsimile of full list on following page]

John St Clair, on Joslas Clapham's list, named Isaac Woolard as his "tythable" in 1774

Shelburne Parish List of 1775, taken by Thomas Lewis
(All from Loudoun County Courthouse, Leesburg, Virginia; loose papers)

<u>1777</u>	Tithable List: Wm[4] Woolard (John and Wm Woolard Jr, Negro Jean) on Clapham's list
<u>9 Sep 1777</u>	Wm Wollard was appointed surveyor of road "from Noland's Ferry to Hohn todhunter's" (OB G, Part 1:58)
<u>11 Dec 1778</u>	Wm Woollard (et al) was appraiser of estate of James Sanders (King, 24, 36)
<u>Aug 1779</u>	Tithable List: Wm Woolard[2] (Negro Jeannie; from the list of Wm Douglass)
	Tithable List: John Woolard[1]
	Tithable List: Wm Woolard[2]
<u>1782</u>	Tithable List: Wm Woolard[6] (negroes Tom, Isaac, Ned; 2 under six years of age; 6 horses, 14 cattle; from list of Josias Clapham)
<u>1783 – 1785</u>	Court action of Wm Woollard vs Pollard was "discontinued" (OB H: 152)
<u>c1785</u>	Wm Woollard d. interstate; left 8 heirs
<u>c1785</u>	Assembly of Virginia passed an act for intestate estates (See Hening)
<u>1785 – 1791</u>	Isaac[5] Wolerd, Military District of VA; listed as tithable of Nelson CO [KY? VA?] with one poll, 3 horses, 6 cattle (riedel's letter to BMM, 17 Jul 1979)
<u>6 Sep 1785</u>	Mary Wollard was granted admin. On the estate of Wm Wollard dcd (OB K:257)
<u>1787</u>	Wm Sr, Wm Jr, and John Wollard are on the tax list for Loudoun Co; also, Wm Woolhard was on Tax List C (Fothergill, 37, 69)
<u>10 Dec 1787</u>	Inventory and appraisement of Wm 4 Wollard's estate was returned into court and was received (OB K: 335)
<u>10 Dec 1787</u>	Inventory of Wm[4] Woollard estate named 3 "Negroe wenches Jane, Hannah, Sulla, and 3 boys James, Isaac, and Edward"; personal items of interest included "1 piece of Flowered Damask, Damask, 1 great Coat, a parcel of Woolen & flax thread, 1 pr shoes and Bucklesz" (WB C:105)
<u>22 Dec 1787</u>	"Wm Woollard sells to Isaac Larrowe 1/8th part of land left by Wm Woollard the older about 18 ¾ a., being an equal portion of the 150 a. left by Wm Woollard the older"; signed and sealed by Wm Woollard (DB R: 16-17)
<u>20 Jun 1788</u>	Mary Woollard, "being sick in body," made her will, son Jos to be extr; she left cash to children Isaac, John, Wm, Ann, Jean, and Elendar; dau Mary was given £4 cash, livestock and "6 pewter plates, 5 pewter basins, 1 pewster teapot, the spinning wheel, and clock reel; g-dau Eliz "that now lives with me" received £4 cash, a "feather bead & furniture," Calf, and 2 sheep; signed and sealed by Mary Woolllard (W B0: 12-13)
<u>8 Sep 1788</u>	Three men were appointed by court to settle Wm Wollard's estate "with the administratrix" (OB K: 489) [NOTE: Mary still living?]
<u>14 Oct 1788</u>	Estate account of Wm Woollard dcd was returned to court (OB L: 40)

ESTATE RECORDS OF WILLIAM WOOLLARD (d. Intestate)
Selected Portions from Loudoun County Courthouse

[handwritten: September 6, 1787]

[handwritten text]

257

[margin: Woolards admn]

6 September 1787 Mary Wollard was granted administration on the estate of William Woolard, dec'd (Loudoun Order Book K:257)

[handwritten: At a Court held for Loudoun County the 10th day of Decr 1787 This Inventory and appraisement of William Woolards Deceased Estate was returned into Court and ordered to be recorded   Teste Chas Binns Clk]

10 December 1787 Estate inventory and appraisement of William Woolard Deceased was returned to Court and ordered to be recorded (Loudoun Will Book C:311)

[handwritten: December 10. 1787.]

3

[handwritten text]

[margin: Woolards account]

10 December 1787 Estate inventory and appraisement of William Wollard dced was returned to Court and ordered to be recorded (Loudoun Order Book K:335)

[handwritten text]

[margin: Wollards Estat Acct to be settd]

8 September 1788 Administratrix and committee were ordered to settle the estate of William Wollard deced (Loudoun Order Book K:489)

22 Oct 1788   "Isaac Woollard of Jefferson Co, NC & Ann his wife sell to Jos Woollard of Loudoun Co. 18 ¾ a. being one eight equal part of land left by Wm Woollard, Sr dcd intestate and transferred to Isaac by Act of Assembly of Virginia … provided for interstate estates" (DB R: 163-64) [NOTE: There was no county named Jefferson in North Carolina nor in Virginia; Jefferson Co, Kentucky was formed in 1780. Document was signed and sealed by Isaac &Ann.]

22 October 1788   Ann & Isaac Woollard's transfer of land to Joseph, youngest brother of Isaac. On the death of William, his land had been divided among eight heirs; Isaac sold his share to Joseph, who had remained in Loudoun County. (Deed Book R:163-164)

9 Dec 1788   Probate of Mary Woollard's will; proved and recorded (WB 0:13)

9 Feb 1789   Inventory of Mary Woollard's estate (WB o: 13-14)

14 Apr 1789   Isaac Wollard & wife Ann's sale to Jos Wollard proved and recorded (OB L: 156)

In the eighteenth century, colonists who wanted to migrate westward generally formed a travel group for mutual self-help in surmounting the rigors to be faced. When Isaac and his wife Ann left for the Kentucky District of Virginia, sometime about 1776, they were among the vanguard who dared to test the unknown terrain. It is virtually certain that they did not go alone.

It is possible to speculate as to the names of other fellow travelers, for the record books of Loudoun County contain the surnames of families who later turned up in Green and Hardin Counties, Kentucky – whose children, in fact, later may have intermarried with the children of Isaac and Ann. These include Jonathan Price; Peter Graham; James, William and John Saunders; Barnet, Elijah and Evan Daviss; and the Laxtons.

In 1769, Samuel, Samuel Jr, and Nathaniel Laxton were neighbors of the Woollards in Loudoun County. All were listed on Craven Peyton's list of tithables for that year. See Appendix C, p. 90 for further discussion of the Laxtons.]

Did they all migrate together from Virginia to Kentucky? It is quite probable that they did.

PART III
THE WOOLLARDS IN KENTUCKY

PART III
THE WOOLLARDS IN KENTUCKY:

IN JEFFERSON AND NELSON COUNTIES, 1776-1793
ISAAC[5] & ANN WOOLLARD

Isaac[5] Woollard, son of Mary and William[4] Woollard, was born about 1753 in the colony of Virginia, probably in Richmond County but possibly in Loudoun. At age 16, Isaac was listed in the 1769 tax list of Loudoun County as a tithable of his father and likewise was listed as William's tithable for the years 1770, 1772, and 1774. According to these lists, Isaac was a year older than his brother John and five years older than brother William, Jr.

In 1771 Isaac Woolard was listed as a tithable of John St Clair (not yet identified). In 1775 Isaac (age 22) was listed as a head of household with himself as the only tithable and was no doubt married. This is in accord with the custom that men married at age 20 or 21. After that date, Isaac disappeared from the local tax lists although his father and brothers John and William were variously listed up through 1782.

It seems that about 1776, that momentous year, Isaac and his wife **Ann** joined the westward exodus of Virginians who were pushing into the Kentucky region. It is likely that they went with a travel party, as was usual, for it was a long and arduous trek into the unknown; men alone made the trip in shorter time, but traveling with a wife, children, and livestock increased the risks considerably. If they left in the spring, their departure preceded the declaration of independence and the ensuing war; no record of military service by Isaac exists.

They were headed for an unsettled land: in 1738 it was part of Augusta County; in 1774 it was known as Fincastle County; by 1775 it was called Transylvania; and in 1776 was renamed Kentucky County, all of these counties in Virginia. In 1780, the Kentucky lands were divided into three counties: Fayette, Jefferson, and Lincoln. There is no record of Isaac and Ann's whereabouts between 1776 and 1780, but it appears that they had located in Jefferson County.

In Jefferson County. In 1782, at a court held in Jefferson County, Isaac was listed as one of 62 persons designated to receive 400 acres from the county, by Act of the Virginia Assembly, and this is the earliest record yet found of Isaac in Kentucky. The purpose of this Act was to provide basic land grants to Virginia citizens who found themselves landless in Kentucky (presumably through no fault of their own but as a result of wartime conditions which impeded the land grant process). There were several other land recipients whose surnames link with the Woollards in one way or another and therefore should be mentioned: William Lagston, Samuel Sanders/Saunders, George Owens, Urania Merideth, and Meridith Price, Clerk.

Back in Virginia, Isaac's father died, leaving land that was divided among his other heirs. The word reached Isaac in Kentucky, and he soon sold his share to brother Joseph. In Loudoun County in 1788 a Deed of Sale conveyed the one-eighth share of land that had been the "property of William Woollard Sen Deceased" from "Isaac Woollard of Jefferson County in the State of North Carolina and Ann his wife" to Joseph Woollard. This deed was signed by Isaac State of North Carolina; however, there is a reasonable explanation. At that time, there was disagreement as to the exact location of the dividing line between the two colonies (North Carolina and Virginia) so that dwellers in the area of "the Gore" were free to designate themselves as residents of either colony. The significance of this curious fact is that it accounts for the family tradition that the Woollards lived in North Carolina after leaving Virginia.

To compound this confusion, Isaac also appears as a resident of the land just to the south of Jefferson County, Virginia [Kentucky] which had been designated a county of North Carolina when "in 1782 the Assembly of North Carolina recognized the new region [of Nashborough – settled by the followers of Judge Henderson] by the creation of Davidson County" (Hicks & Mowry, 98). A surviving Tax List for Davidson County in 1787 includes the name of Isaac Woollard.

Today this is in Tennessee, but in 1790 when Isaac Woolard, plaintiff, won his case there against Christopher Owens and Adam Hampton, it may have been regarded as belonging to North Carolina. This Isaac must be the same as Isaac from Loudoun County, for up to this time no other Isaac Woollard is to be found in any of the colonial records. Whatever the particular details may have been, these two references fulfill the family tradition that this Woollard line came to Tennessee from Virginia by way of North Carolina.

Nelson County. Kentucky's population was increasing all along so that in 1784 the southern part of Jefferson County was lopped off and given the name of Nelson County. For the next decade, Isaac's presence there is verified by county records.

In 1791, Isaac gave consent for the marriage of his daughter Mary to Joseph Sanders/Saunders in Nelson County; it appears that she was his oldest child and under 21 years of age. Isaac and Ann had at least six children; probably all but Mary were born in Kentucky. In 1792 and 1793 Isaac was listed for the last time as a taxable of Nelson County; thereafter, his name appears on the lists of Green and Hardin Counties. At that time, Isaac was about 39 years of age.

Issue: Mary; William, 1777-1853; **Samuel**[6], 1778-1867; Anny; Jinny; Isaac, 1790-1852

Chronology: Isaac Woollard in Jefferson and Nelson Counties, Kentucky

1776	Kentucky Co, VA was organized as a county; Isaac & Ann Woollard migrated from Loudoun Co about this time
1780	Jefferson Co, VA [later, KY] was created out of Kentucky Co
5 Mar 1782	"At a Court held for Jefferson … ordered that the County Surveyor lay off for the following persons, four hundred acres of land each agreeable to Act of Assembly passed May Last"; Isaac Woollard was among those named as recipients of 400 a. (Ct Min Bk A, 1780-81, p. 22) [NOTE: For explanation of Act, see Hening 10:431-321]
1782	Davidson Co was created by the NC Assembly (Hicks, 98) [NOTE: TN did not become a state until 1 Jun 1796]
1784	Nelson Co, VA [KY] was created from Jeff Co
1785 – 1791	A list of taxables for the "Military Dist of VA" in Nels Co during this 6-year period contains the name of Isaac Woollard
1787	Isaac Woollard on tax List for Davidson Co, NC [now in TN] (Clayton, 58)
22 Oct 1788	An indenture "between Isaac Wollard of Jefferson County in the state of North Carolina and Ann his wife of the one part & Joseph Woollard of Loudoun County and State of Virginia of the other part" conveyed for the sum of £15 Virginia currency "a parcel of Land or the Eighth equal part of a Tract of Land lying and being in Loudoun being the right And property one of William Woollard Sen. Deceased and transferred to me by an act of Assembly of Virginia made and provided for intestate Estates Containing by Estimation Eighteen acres & three Quarters with all houses, orchards, meadows, woods, ways, water, water Courses, and all the advantages whatever to the said … Isaac Woollard and Ann his wife … unto the said Joseph woollard …." Signed and sealed by Isaac and Ann Woollard, wit. By Thos Sanders, et al." (Loud Co Bk R; 163-64)
14 Jul 1790	Isaac Woolard, pltf, won his case agst Chris Owens and Adam Hampton, Davidson Co, "at the Courthouse in Nashville" and was awarded damages of "Eleven pounds" (Davi Min Bk A 1788-90, vol 2:325) [NOTE: In 1801 Wm Woolard bought land on Brush Ck from Owen Owens]

26 May 1791   Isaac Woollard gave consent for the marriage of dau Mary to Joseph Saunders (or Sanders) in Nels Co, VA (Stancliff 2:110).

1792   Hardin and Green Counties were created out of Nelson Co

1 Jun 1792   Kentucky was admitted to the Union as the 15th state

17 Oct 1792   Isaac Woollard appeared on a "Taxable Property List" for Nels Co as "white male above 21 [with] 3 horses, 6 cattle, 400 a." (*Nels Co, Ky Tax Bks, 1792-97; 1799-1810,* unpaged; in LDS Film #008178.

1793   Isaac Woolart was a List of Taxables, Nels Co, KY (Ford, 227)

1 Jun 1796   Tennessee became a state

7 Dec 1799   Saml Wollard and Thos Laxton signed the bond for Saml's marriage to Mary Laxton who was underage, and Laxton gave consent; wit. Jas Allen (Marr Bond #265; LDS Film #592673 "Bonds & Consents"; Nels MB 1:41; Scott, 59)

EARLY PLACE NAMES IN CENTRAL KENTUCKY

In 1738, Augusta County, Virginia was created; this vast western area was the parent county of today's western Virginia and the lands that would later later become Kentucky and West Virginia, undergoing numerous changes as shown below:

1774	Fincastle, Co, VA
By 1775	Transylvania, VA
1776	Kentucky Co, VA
1780	Division of Kentucky Co into 3 counties:

Fayette Co   Jefferson Co   Lincoln Co

1784   Formation of Nelson Co, VA | Between 1784 and 1792, 10 conventions were held about statehood for the "District of Kentucky."

1792   Hardin Co, KY   Green Co, KY

1792   On June 1, Kentucky was admitted to the Union as the 15th state

Map of Kentucky, 1780 to 1784:

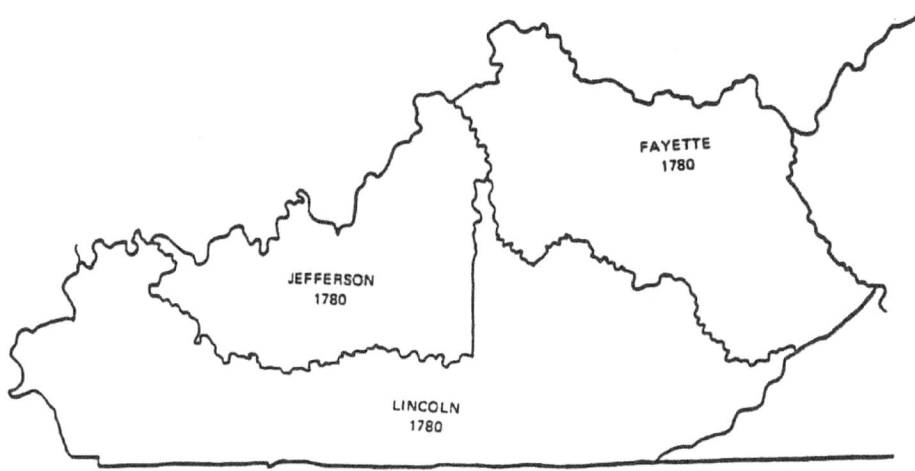

Map of Kentucky, 1792:

Kentucky's original counties were soon divided. From Nelson County (formed in 1785), Hardin County was formed in 1792. Green County was formed from Nelson County and part of Lincoln County in 1793.

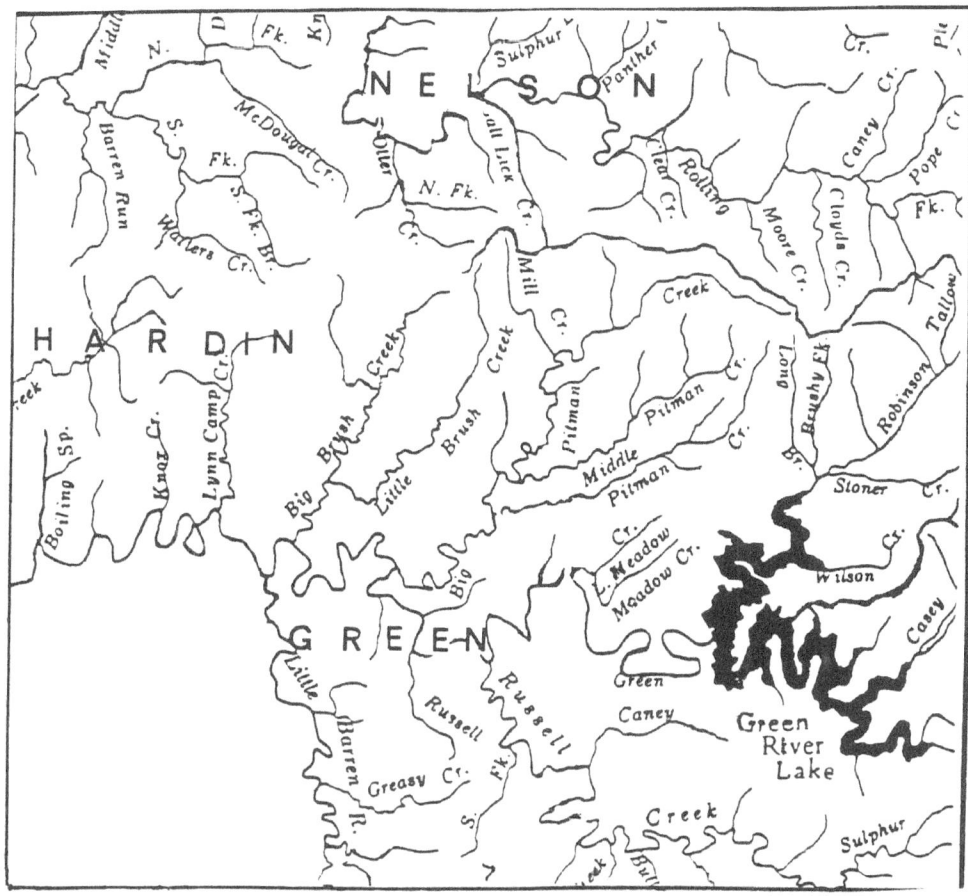

Stream Map Showing Region of Hardin and Green Counties: As late as 1830, Green and Hardin Counties were contiguous. As seen on this map Lynn Camp Creek, Big Brush Creek, and Little Brush Creek – where the Wooollards held land – are situated in the region where the two counties joined each other until 1830. (Reprinted with permission of the Kentucky Historical Society.)

THE WOOLLARDS IN KENTUCKY:

IN GREEN AND HARDIN COUNTIES: 1795-1819
WILLIAM AND SAMUEL[5] WOOLLARD, SONS OF ISAAC

After leaving Loudoun County for the Kentucky District, it appears that Isaac[5] Woollard and wife Ann were on the move between 1782 and 1793, but probably that is a misperception. As has been seen, the records place them in Jefferson County, Virginia and Jefferson County, North Carolina (assumed to be the same place). Next, Isaac apparently held land in Davidson County, North Carolina (later Tennessee); and then they were living in Nelson County, Virginia. However, it is possible that they were in the same location all along – somewhere between Lyncamp Creek and Brush Creek.

The year 1792 brought further jurisdictional changes – Kentucky attained statehood. Nelson County was subdivided into Green and Hardin Counties. The Woollards must have been on the county line, for during the next two decades their names appeared in the annals of both counties.

To the first Easterners who came there, Hardin County seemed a paradise. Audubon was there and reported seeing "immense legions of passenger pigeons."

But the weather could be cruel. The winter of 1779-1780 is remembered as "the bitter cold winter [when] game froze in the forest and domestic animals huddling close to the pioneer cabins froze their tracts [sic]." In 1811, a catastrophic earthquake made Hardin County seem more like Hell; beginning "about 2 o'clock in the afternoon of December 16th ... accompanied by thunder [it] was followed by complete darkness and saturation of the atmosphere with a queer sulphuric vapor ... and residents were tossed around like corks on an angry sea." For a while, both the Mississippi and the Ohio Rivers flowed backwards, and when it was all over left behind a newly created body of water, the Reelfoot Lake.

In 1814, an epidemic of unknown origin called "the cold plague" ravaged the county, causing many deaths. Two years later, 1816 earned a name as "the year without a summer." Frost and ice appeared in July, became even thicker in August, and in September the ice was a quarter-inch thick; the highest temperature in October was thirty degrees. At all times, Indians were a menace, and at one time a company of men called the "Yellow Jackets" was raised to fight the Indians.

Several small events cast their shadow across future political developments. In 1809, son Abraham was born to Tomas and Nancy HANKS Lincoln, and in 1813 a lawyer from Pennsylvania, James Buchanan, lived in Elizabethtown for several months. Thus, for a brief time the 15th and 16th presidents of the United States lived in the same small community. (All Hardin County descriptions are from Winstead, 1, 6.)

The younger children of Isaac and Ann came of age and married (eldest daughter Mary having married Joseph Sanders in Nelson County). William married Rosannah Price, Samuel[6] Woollard married Mary Laxton, and Isaac[6] married Jane Grayham; the girls Anny and Jenny married James Davies and Joseph Wright.

In 1795 Isaac Woollard's name appeared on the first tax list of Green County and continued on the tax rolls of Green or Hardin County for fourteen years, from 1795 to 1809. His sons William and Samuel were of age in 1799 (thus appearing on the tax list) and married. On the tax lists, the sons are readily identifiable by the acreage they held, William having 50 acres until 1813 and Samuel holding 156 acres until 1819.

With the Isaacs-- father and youngest son-- it is not easy to distinguish between them after Isaac Jr came of age, for the records do not identify them by acreage; the use of "senior" or "junior" was not yet an invariable practice. However, the tax records of 1808 and 1809 show that Isaac's household included one "White Male Over 16," which must be Isaac, Jr. This assumption is supported by the marriage of Isaac, Jr in 1811; hence, subsequent tax listings – 1812 through 1817 – are attributed to the younger Isaac. Son Isaac was taxed seven years – so that the name Isaac appeared in the county records for a period of twenty years.

When the country mobilized for the War of 1812, Samuel was in a militia company detached for active service. As for Isaac, Sr there is nothing that indicates what may have happened to him. He is not listed in the census of 1810; however, Samuel's census entry shows that one "White Male Over 45 years" was a member of his household, and the interpretation is that Isaac the elder was living with his son. If so, it appears that wife Ann was no longer alive. Isaac's age would have been 57 years. Thereafter, from 1811 and 1819, the record books of Green and Hardin Counties mention William, Samuel, and Isaac, Jr, but there is no further mention of their father Isaac. By 1820, the brothers have packed up their families and left Kentucky for Tennessee and "other parts."

Chronology: Isaac[5] Woollard and Sons William, Samuel, and Isaac[6]
In Green and Hardin Counties

<u>1792</u>	Green and Hardin Counties were formed from Nelson Co; Kentucky became a state
<u>29 Jun 1795</u>	Isaac Woolard was named on the first tax list of Green Co; he had 2 horses, 5 cattle; one son [Wm] was shown as over 16 but under 21 (KA 4:59)
<u>2 Mar 1798</u>	Saml Woollard was security for Chas Skaggs, Green Co (Marr Bond # 50)
<u>1799</u>	First appearance of Wm and Saml Woollard on tax list in Green Co
<u>3 Jan 1799</u>	Jas Laxtin m. Zelpha Mereda; Wm Mereda consented (Scott, 30; Marr Bond # 285)
<u>12 Dec 1799</u>	Saml Woollard m. Mary Laxton; bond Thos Laxton consented; min. Benj Lynn (Green Marr Bk A: 41; Scott, 59) NOTE: Marr bonds for this and next entry were dated 7 Dec 1799
<u>1800</u>	A list of "Sheriff's fees collected in Green Co included Saml Woolard and Thos Laxton" (GCR 2:3, Oct 1978)
<u>19 May 1800</u>	Will. Wollard m. Eliza. Belcher; bonds Wm Woolard, Ezekiel Davis; min. Stephen Skaggs (Green Marr Bk A: 82)
<u>25 May 1800</u>	Anny (Amy) Woollard m. Jas Davies; Jas Davies signed the bond; min. Benj Lynn (Green Marr Bk A: 40; KA 8 (4) 174, 182)
<u>5 May 1801</u>	Wm Woolard of Green Co bought 50 a. on Brush Creek from Owen Owens and his wife Jane of Campbell Co, VA (Green Co DB 2:268; LDS # 591335)
<u>20 Nov 1803</u>	Wm Woollard registered his earmark in Green Co, "to wit, an underbit out of each ear" (LDS # 551052)
<u>1804</u>	The county line was changed at the NW corner of green Co
<u>22 Jun 1807</u>	Wm Woollard was appointed overseer of the road from the land of Jeremiah Skaggs Sr to the Hard Co line (LDS # 5591333, 551052)

12 Dec 1807   Saml Woollard bought 156 acres from John Blanton of Shelby Co for the sum of & 45 (Hard Co DB 2:7, 8; DB C: 239; LDS # 182295)

23 May 1808   Jinny Woolard m. Jos Wright; bnd Wm Woollard, dated 23 May 1808 (Stanfill)

KY Cns 1810   Saml Woollard in Hardin Co, KY, age 26-45, had "1 male 45 and up," presumably his father Isaac; if this interpretation is correct, it implies that Isaac was widowed, perhaps ailing (his age 57), and living in the home of an elder son (#289, p. 226)

11 Oct 1810   Wm Woolard m. Polly Stout, bnds Wm Woolard, Ezekiel Davis, min. Stephen Skaggs (Steph and Thos were mins] (Marr Bk A:82)

1811 – 1819   Isaac's death and burial are not a matter of record; he may have d. in the year of "the cold plague" but almost certainly died by when sons Saml and Isaac moved to TN in the year 1819.

3 Apr 1811   Isaac Woollard [Jr] m. Jane Grayham, Green Co; bonds Isaac Woolard and Jas Skaggs (MB A:29)

THE NEW MADRID EARTHQUAKE

MAGNITUDE OF U.S. QUAKES

Measuring the area of greatest impact for major U.S. earthquakes.

North America's largest earthquakes occurred in 1811 and 1812 in New Madrid, Missouri along the Mississippi Valley. The effects reached into neighboring Kentucky and Tennessee.

The magnitude of the New Madrid earthquake was approximately the same as that of the San Francisco quake of 1906, but its area of damage was fifteen times greater. The seismic shock caused the earth to ripple in waves several feet high. The shock was felt in Savannah, and one thousand miles away in Boston, the church bells rang.

From an article on seismology by Robert L. Ketter
Published in The Washington Post (4 Dec 1988, L-3)

3 Aug 1813   Saml Woolard, pvt, was in Capt Ed Rawling's Co, Infantry of Militia Detached for 6 mos. To 8 Sep 1813, mobilized for War of 1812 (Clift, 220)

1816 – THE YEAR WITHOUT SUMMER

Many people died and many sickened from lack of food; crops and livestock died, the wild and domestic fowl froze. March of that year was cold and stormy, snow and sleet fell in May; July was cold and frosty. By August, almost a an inch of ice had formed "and killed every green thing in the United States… frost and ice were as common as butter cups usually are." New England was the hardest hit by this cold wave which extended to Great Britain.

It has been theorized that the "Year without Summer" was caused by the 1815 explosion in Java of the volcano Tambora; the spread of ashes into the stratosphere blocked solar radiation, and the pattern of wind currents carried the ashes across the United States. This account is based on a clipping from a 1979 farm cooperative

---

<u>1819</u>   The Woollard brothers migrated to Hickman Co, TN

<u>KY Cns 1820</u>   No Woollards are listed in Ky cns

WOOLLARDS ON THE TAX LISTS OF GREEN AND HARDIN COUNTIES
Compiled from Records in the Kentucky Dept of Libraries and Archives

Year	Name	Co.	Minors	Name	Co.	Acres	Name	Co.	Acres	Name	Co
1795	Isaac	G	1	(Wm 17?)							
1796	Isaac	G	2	(Wm 18?)			(Saml 17?)				
1797	Isaac	G	2	(Wm 19?)			(Saml 18?)				
1798	NA			(Wm 20?)			(Saml 19?)				
1799	Isaac	G		Wm	G		Saml	G			
1800	Isaac	H									
1801	Isaac	H		Wm	G		Saml	G			
1802	Isaac	H		Wm	G	50a					
1803	Isaac	H		Wm	G	50a	Saml	G			
1804	Isaac	H		Wm	G&H	50a	Saml	H			
1805	Isaac	G		Wm	G	50a	Saml	G			
1806				Wm	G		Saml	G			
1807	Isaac	H		Wm	G&H		Saml	H			
1808	Isaac	H	1				Saml	H	150a		
1809	Isaac	G		Wm	G	143a	Saml	H	156a	(Isaac Jr 17?)	
1810	*(Isaac >45?)	Wm					* Saml	H	156a	(Isaac Jr 18?)	
1811							Saml	H	156a	(Isaac Jr 19?)	
1812							Saml	H	156a	Isaac Jr	
1813				Wm	G					Isaac Jr	G
1814							Saml	H	156a	Isaac Jr	H
1815							Saml	H	156a	Isaac Jr	H
1816							Saml	H	156a	Isaac Jr	G
1817							Saml	H	156a	Isaac Jr	H
1818	NA			NA			NA				
1819							Saml	H	156a		
1820											

Key:

    G or H indicates Green or Hardin Co

Number 1 or 2 indicates "white males over 16"

Name and age in parens indicates the "white male over 16" interpreted as a son of Isaac

N/A for years in which the tax list is "not available"

Entries for Wm and Saml show number of acres

* 1810 cns shows "1 White Male Over 45," presumed to be Isaac, Sr.

PART IV

THE WOOLLARDS IN TENNESSEE

PART IV
THE WOOLLARDS IN TENNESSEE

SAMUEL[6] WOOLLARD OF HICKMAN COUNTY

Samuel[6] Woollard was born in Kentucky, probably in Nelson County, in 1778. He was "of age" in 1788 when he appeared as security for Charles Skaggs in Green County; the following year Samuel married **Mary Laxton** in what may have been a double wedding with her brother Thomas, who married Hannah Elkin on the same date. Mary was underaged, so Thomas gave consent for the marriage. [Probably this Thomas was either her father or brother.] The following year was Samuel's first appearance on the county tax rolls.

In 1807, Samuel Woollard bought 156 acres from John Blanton. According to the county tax lists, it was located on Lyncamp Creek. This was their home until 1819 when they left Kentucky for Tennessee.

In his later years, Samuel's father Isaac was probably living with Samuel and Mary. US census of 1810 showed a "white male over 45" in Samuel's household, and Isaac at that time was nearly 60. Samuel's militia regiment was activated for service in the War of 1812 in August of that year. At about this time, or earlier, his father died. Eventually, Samuel and his brothers moved out of the state; Samuel's last appearance on the Hardin County Tax List was in 1819. He and Isaac went to Tennessee, but older brother William moved to Spencer County, Indiana, where he died in 1846.

The brothers Samuel and Isaac acquired land in Hickman County – Isaac in 1824 and Samuel in 1827, according to existing records, both of them settling on Sulphur Fork of Beaverdam Creek. However, their stay there was brief; in 1827, they moved once again. On the day that the Woollard brothers left, Samuel's son William S. observed his nineteenth birthday; William did not migrate with the rest of the family but chose to marry Harriett Lancaster and settle in Hickman County.

This move took the brothers Samuel and Isaac to Johnson County, Indiana where they settled in Hensley Township. In 1827, 1832, 1833, and 1834 they received land in Sections 17, 18, and 27. According to one account, "Samuel Woollard was of the earliest settlers in Hensley Township" (Banta, 157). The Woollards lived here about two decades, and the children were growing to adulthood. Marriage records of Johnson County include those of Woollard grooms Samuel Jr. John, Isaac, John, Joel, and Jesse, as well as those of sic Woollard bridges, all of them children of Samuel or Isaac. The censuses show them there in 1830 and 1840, but at some time thereafter they moved on.

They next moved to Shelby County, Illinois, and the earliest indication of their presence there is Isaac Woollard's Power of Attorney in 1843 to Jas Pope to sell Isaac's Sulphur Fork land in Hickman County. By 1848 Samuel Woollard had land in Shelby County: 42.32 acres of Public Domain land; in 1850 he bought 162.46 acres; and in 1856 he acquired 53.24 acres, the total being about 258 acres. In addition, there are three other deeds to Samuel (1850 – 1856) that do not specify acreage. At the same time, his James and John also acquired land in Shelby County.

In 1852 Samuel was appointed administrator of the estate of his brother Isaac who died intestate, at the request of Widow Jane who relinquished her right as administratrix. In April of that year, Samuel's wife Mary died and was buried in the Price Family Cemetery; she was 70. Within a month, Samuel deeded land to his son Joel. Five years later, Samuel again deeded land to Joel and by census time in 1860 was living in Joel's household.

On 21 February 1867, Samuel died at the ripe age of 87. He was buried next to Mary in Price Cemetery. He had lived in Shelby County for nineteen years.

Issue: Five daughters, names unknown: six sons: **William S.**[7] (c1808-96); Samuel Jr (1812-85); James; John (b. 1807); Isaac; Joel (b.c1812) [Birthdates reconstructed from census records]

Chronology: Samuel[6] Woollard of Hickman Co, TN, Johnson Co, IN, and Shelby Co, IL

TN Cns 1820	No Woollards are listed
IN Cns 1820	Wm Woollard & wife (ages 26-45) were in Spencer Co (p. 101)
30 Jul 1824	Isaac Woolard received Grant #494 for 100 a. in Hickman Co, TN on the Sulphur Fork of Beaverdam Ck (Hick Roll #92, Landgrant 1:494)
1827	Isaac Woolard acquired land in John Co, IN, Hensley Township, Sect 17 (this and subsequent entries are in Bergen, 94)
1 Nov 1827	**Sam Woolard** received Grant #25523 for 25 a., same location as Isaac's, under signature of Gov Sam Houston (Gen Grants Bk CC: 783)
1827	Saml moved to IN, Leaving behind son Wm S. who m. Harriett Lancaster
IN Cns 1830	Saml (age 50-60), Isaac (40-50), John (30-40) were in John Co; Saml had 7 children (all on p. 84) Wm Woolard (50-60) was in Spen Co; he was #165 and #164 was Vincent Rust (20-30)
1830 – 1845	During this time frame, Saml's children are of marriageable age (some of Isaac's, too); names of the 5 daus of Saml not known; Jesse Woollard not identified; if not children of Saml (the likeliest possibility) then of Isaac, for most of them reappear later in Shelby Co, IL, where Saml and Isaac settled. [See box. P.351)
1832	John Woollard's land, Sect 17, Hensley TWP; Isaac's in Sect 18
31 Jul 1832	John Woollard wit. Will of John Schrum, John CO, IN (IN Source Bk 2:96-98)
By 1833	Saml Woollard was recognized as "one of the earliest settlers" in Hensley TWP, John Co, IN (Banta, 157)
1833	Saml Woollard's land, Sect 8. Sect 17; Jas Woollard's land in Sect 8, Hensley TWP
1834	Isaac Woollard's land, Sect 27, Hensley TWP
1837	Jas Woollard, Sect 17; Jesse Woolard, Sect 8, Hensley TWP
19 Aug 1839	John Wollard wit. Will of Saml Prewitt, John Co, IN (IN Source Bk 2:49-52)
2 Dec 1839	Jas Woollard acquired 80 a. in Shelby Co, IL of Public Domain Land; this is the earliest land grant to a Woollard (All such land sales following are from Archives Listing, p. 460)
IN Cns 1840	Saml and Isaac Woollard (p. 43) and Saml Woollard (age 20-30, p. 599 in John Co, IN
IL Cns 1840	Jas Woollard (age 60-70) in Shelby Co

3 Jul 1843	Jas Pope of Hickman Co, TN was given P/A to sell 100 a. tract of Isaac Woollard on Sulphur Fork of Beaverdam Ck, Entry #241 (Hick DB L:3640365, Roll 25)
3 Mar 1848	John Woollard bought 42.46 a. in Shel Co, IL
3 Mar 1848	Saml Woollard bought 42.32 a. in Shel Co, IL
29 Jan 1850	Saml Woollard bought 42.66 a. in Shel Co; on 26 May he bought 100 a.; on 8 June he bought 50 a. for a total of 162.46 a.
US Can 1850	Saml Woollard is not listed for either John Co, IN or Shel Co, IL
IL Cns 1850	Shelby Co, Beck's Ck Dist included: Isaac & Jane (ages 60); Saml & Cassandra (38,42); Jas & Rachel Wollard (45,43); John & Elizah Woolard (both 34); Daniel & Sarah (30,32); Wm & Suzannah (both 23); and J.C. & Milla Woollard (21,20) (pp. 43,154,890,895)

NOTE: Ages shown span 3 generations; birthplaces given as KY and IN fit the migration pattern. Sorting out these family lines in the 1850 and 1860 CNSes is difficult because by that time (40 to 50 years after the death of Isaac of Hardin Co, KY) his sons and grandsons had produced many male children, and every family included one each of the names Wm, Saml, Isaac, and John, and also quite a few Jameses. Nevertheless, in many instances the identification can be clearly seen.

Apr 1852	Mary LAXTON Woollard, w/o Samuel, died at 70 yrs; buried in Price Cemetery (Shel Co Cem NDX, v.6)
11 May 1852	Saml Woolard deeded land Joel Wollard (Shel DB 12:374)
23 Sep 1852	Isaac Woollard d. intestate and wid Jane relinquished her administration to Saml (Shel Probate Journal 3:385-86; 389-92)
16 Jun 1856	Saml Woollard bought 42.32 a. in Shelby Co (ILArch Public Domain)
27 May 1857	Samuel Woolard Seigner deeded to Joel Woolard 60 a. in Shelby Co; was not filed until 18 May 1867 (Shel DB 37:297-98)
IL Cns 1860	The household of Joel Woollard (age 48) included Wife Margaret (39), 2 children (4,1), and Samuel Sr (80); Samuel's group prop eval was 2000 (#108)
Feb 1867	Samuel Woollard, age 87, died and was buried beside his wife Mary in Price Family Cemetery (Shel Co Cem NDX, V.6)

Marriage Records of Johnson County, Indiana

Marriage Bonds   Marriage Returns

    17 Mar 1831 Isaac Woollard m. Elizabeth Butram, wid   3 May 1831

* 23 May 1833 Samuel Woolard m. Cassandra Kelso

    24 Nov 1836 Mariah [Marian S.] Woollard m. Moses Swain   24 Nov 1836

    28 Sep 1837 John Woollard m. Anna Roberts

* 20 Nov 1837 Samuel Woolard m. Sarah Roberts

* 9 May 1838 Sarah Woollard m. Joseph Craig   13 may 1838

    5 Jun 1838 Jesse Woollard m. Mary Titus   14 Jun 1838

* 21 mar 1839 Joel Woollard m. Margaret Titus   21 Mar 1839

* 31 May 1841 Mary Wollard m. Harvey Reaner [Keaner]   3 Jun 1841

    11 Feb 1842 Julia Emeline Woollard m. Wm Shanks

    6 May 1843 Mary Ann Woollard m. Francis M. Coleman   12 May 1843

* 8 Feb 1845 Rachel Wollard m. Harvey [Henry]

    From DAR *Marriages Recorded of Johnson Co, IN, 1830-2850, v.1* and *Johnson County Early Marriage Returns, 1830-1843*

  * Indicates those who later appear in 1850 and/or 1860 Cns of Shelby Co or in the deed records, together with or in proximity to Samuel, Isaac and Joel Woollard

On 7 September 1824, Samuel Woolard was issued a grant of 25 acres in the 8th District of Hickman County, West Tennessee. This land was on the SUlphur Fork of Beaverdam Creek in Range Seven, Section 7.

THE WOOLLARDS IN TENNESSEE

WILLIAM[7] S. WOOLLARD
FARMER AND MAGISTRATE OF HICKMAN COUNTY

William[7] S. Woollard was born in Hardin County, Kentucky about 1808, son of Mary LAXTON and Samuel[6] Woollard, and grandson of Isaac[5] and Ann who had migrated from Virginia just prior to the Revolutionary War. Although Isaac's residence was in old Jefferson County, Kentucky, by 1787 he had acquired land in Davidson County, North Carolina; later, this region became part of the state of Tennessee.

At some point after Isaac's death (c1812), Samuel moved his family to Hickman County, Tennessee (formed from Davidson County in 1807) and settled on the Sulphur Fork of Beaver Dam Creek in the Ninth District, which lies on both sides of Duck River. "The Line of 1784 runs through the Ninth District, crossing Beaverdam Creek at the Jack Malugin place and Sulphur Fork at the James Malugin place" (Spence, 288).

Fortunately, the old tales were collected; so that today quite a lot is known about this part of the world. Just across the Duck River were the Indians, who were encamped on Skull Creek, named by the earliest whites who found an ancient human skull there. Wolves were so numerous as to be a perilous nuisance; deer abounded and grazed among domesticated herds. The earliest known structure was built in 1808, so there were eyewitnesses to report destruction in that region from "the earthquake of 1811" [at New Madrid, Missouri] (Spence, 210). In 1833 a thrilling meteoric display' astounded all, so that thereafter this time was identified as "the year the stars fell" (Spence, 289).

Solomon Jones was a pioneer of this community, and his son John A. Jones farmed the south side of the river. John Cooper's location was later called the "Walker place"; a Cooper daughter married James Walkers. The Lancasters, and "an old family in Hickman County claimed … [descent] from the House of Lancaster in England, hence of Royal blood" (Walker).

Samuel Woollard and his brother Isaac stayed on Sulphur Fork for a few years and then moved on to northern parts, their sons accompanying them except Sam's son "Billy" who married and stayed behind. It was Billy's nineteenth birthday when his family left for Indiana; on that very day William took a bride – **Harriett Matilda Lancaster** (b.c1811, Spartanburg, South Carolina, daughter of **William)** – and they settled down in Sulphur Fork. Their six children grew up here. In 1838 William Woollard bought 200 acres in the same location; their home was first known as the Old Woollard Homeplace; when Nancy Jane Woollard married Robert B. Malugin it became the Malugin place until 1940's when it was acquired by Fred Mitchell.

William Woolard was among "the prominent men who located on Sulphur Fork at an early date" (Spence, 780). Later, he was a magistrate of the Ninth District, as also was John A. Jones (Spence, 284). It is assumed that the Woollards were members of Liberty Church (Primitive Baptist) which had been organized in 1827, the church being built on Blue Water Stream. Existing records show William's continued presence on Sulphur Fork throughout his lifetime.

Tragically, Harriett died young – she was only about twenty-seven. Walking in the apple orchard, she had stepped on a thorn that penetrated her heel, and tetanus developed. William reserved a tract of land for a family burial place; it was on a hillside, west of the residence, north from the spring and east from the garden, "cornering on an apple tree." Harriett was probably the first of the family to be interred here.

Soon remarried, William's second wife was Sarah "Sally" Cooper (b. 1818, Tennessee). Their nine children, born between 1841 and about 1860, brought the total to fifteen, all of whom survived to adulthood. In 1844

William Lancaster died, and William S. Woollard, guardian, represented the children of Harriett in settling his estate.

Many incidents of their life together are known and can be strung together to indicate the tenor of their existence. During the Mexican War (1846-1848), William's underaged son **James Monroe[8] Woollard** "ran away" to join up, along with his uncle Isaac Lancaster. After returning from the War, William's son James taught school in Centerville and is remembered as a popular and respected schoolmaster.

In 1850 another death occurred – the first-born child of Harriett and William, daughter Matilda died unmarried. Three years later, son James married Mary Alston Jones, daughter of another pioneer of the Ninth District, and the day they were wed left for Spring Creek in Western Tennessee, to begin farming in Madison County.

There was a progressive spirit in the community as evidenced by activities of William's sons. In addition to teaching school, young James also belonged to a Debaters' Club. Another group of young men formed a study group under the tutelage of Dr. Andrew J. Lowe; Samuel and John C. "Bud," William's sons, were members of the group during the winter of 1858-59. Later, both died in the Civil War.

In April of 1859, a hurricane 'of unparalleled violence … swept across the Ninth District from southwest to northeast, "destroying fences, orchards, outbuildings (Spence, 287). A tree fell across the roof of John A. Jones; situated on a high bluff, the house did not blow off into the river – saved, it was supposed, by the weight of the tree. Ominously, other storm clouds were forming which would wreak far greater damage on those who survived the hurricane. Secession and the Civil War were about to burst upon them.

During the Civil War, the Ninth District was occupied by the Federals. Sons James and Samuel formed a company in Madison County, serving as captain and lieutenant respectively, to fight with the Confederates; James was wounded at Shiloh and taken prisoner, and Samuel died during the War. These times were so painful that ever afterward the family avoided any mention of it.

For the next three decades, William S. Woollard's life is unrecorded except for purchases and sales of land. The last recorded deed was executed in 1895, a year before his death. In this deed, the burial plot was carefully described and was excluded from the sale. He died without a will in 1896, at the age of 88 years; T.B. Walker administered his estat.

Issue of William S. Woollard and (1) Harriett Matilda LANCASTER: Matilda J. (1830-1850, dsp); **James Monroe[8]** (1831-1906); Mary Agnes (b.1833, m.Will Edwards); Elizabeth (b.1835, m. Green Leeper); Rachel Carolina (b.1836, m. Rocky Lancaster); Samuel J. (1837-65, d. in Civil War)

Issue of William S. Woollard and (2) Sarah Cooper: Ellen (b.1841, m. Hay Taylor); John C. "Bud" (b. 1842, m. Mary Jane Walker); William F. (b.1844, dsp after Civil War; Isaac Taylor (1847-1911, m. (1) Mary Thompson, (2) Sally Cooper?; Martha H. (b.1848, m. Bob Murrey, who lost an arm in the Civil War); Emmaline (b. 1849, m. James McColium); Nancy Jane (1852-1935, m. Bob Malugin); David T. "Dock" (1853-1899, m. Mary Murphree); Sarah Narcissa "Sis" (b. 1856, m. Elias G. Pickard) NOTE: Birth dates are taken from the 1850 cns.

Chronology: William[7] S. "Billy" Woollard
b. c1808, Hardin Co, KY – d. 1896, Hickman Co, TN

<u>1808</u>	Wm[7] S. Woollard, s/o Mary LAXTON & Saml Woollard, was born in Hardin Co, Ky (date derived from 1850 Cns; all cns records give KY as birthplace)
<u>c1819</u>	His father and uncle Isaac Woollard migrated to Hickman Co, TN; they acquired land, both settling on Suphur Fork of Beaverdam Ck, but moved on after a brief stay
<u>1 Jun 1827</u>	Liberty Church (Primitive Baptist) organized, located on the Flowers place on Blue Water Stream; it is assumed that this was the Woollards' church (Spence, 275)
<u>c1827</u>	Wm S. Woollard m. Harriett Matilida Lancaster (b. c1811, Spartanburg, SC, d/o Wm & Martha); this was his 19th birthday and also the date of departure of his father Samuel and siblings, John and Jim specifically named (From old family letter)

TN Cns 1830	Wm Wollard (p.279; Hodges gives his age as 24)
1830 – 1837	Six children born during these years: daus Matilda J., Mary Agnes, Eliz A., and Rachel Carolina and sons Jas Monroe and Samuel J.
4 Mar 1831	Son **James Monroe**[8] **Woollard** b. Hick Co, TN (m. c1852, d.19060
10 Sep 1838	Wm Woollard bought 200 a. from D.G. Jones on S side of Duck R. and both sides of Beaver Dam Ck crossing Sulphur Fork; wits. Caleb and Wm B. Murfree; recorded 14 Mar 1840 (TN Arch, Roll 25, Hick DB K: 285-86)
c1838	Harriett Woollard, about 27, died of tetanus ("lockjaw"), caused by a thorn in her heel, stepped on while walking in the apple orchard (Handwritten notes of Jennie Mathis Malloy, cited hereafter as Recollections of JMM)
c1840	Wm Woollard m. (2) Sarah "sally" Cooper (b.c1818, TN d/o John & Nancy LOVE Cooper) as entered in the Cooper-Pinkerton Bible (WPA # 465-44-3-115, "Bible, Family , and Tombstone Records," pp. 54-56)
TN Cns 1840	Not found
1841	Birth of Ellen, eldest child of Wm & Sally Woollard
21 Apr 1844	Heirs of Wm Lancaster, dcd were wid Martha; dau Matilda, w/o Lewis D. Lowe; son Isaac; Wm Woolard, guardian of Wm Lancaster's g-children by his dcd dau Harriett; Eliz Murphree. The lands of Wm Lancaster, lying on the E side of Beaver Dam Ck were distributed by lot, Wm Woolllard receiving Lot No. 3 (19 a.) and also cash (TN Arch, Roll 1a, Hick Min Bk:331-35)
25 Feb 1845	Wm Woolard purchased from John C. & Louisa Thornton a tract of land W of the Sulphur Fork of Beaverdam Ck adj Woolard's tract and that of Marg Golightly (Tn Arch Roll 23, Hick Bk M:16)
Jun 1846	Wm Woolard as guardian of his children (Mitilda J., James M., Mary A., Eliz A., Rachel C., and Saml J.) reported to Hick Co Ct on their inheritance from Wm Lancaster (WPA #165-44-6999, "Rec of Hick Co Guardian & Adm Settlement," 1844-46, p.39)
Jul Term 1846	Lewis D. Lowe, et al petitioned to sell slaves of Wm Lancaster, dcd, namely: Danl & wife, Jemima, Eliza, and Hannah (TN Arch Roll 1a, Hick Min Bk: 436-37)
Aug 1846	Isaac Lancaster, adm of Wm Lancaster, dcd reported to court on behalf of Eliz Murphree, Wm Woollard, Martha Lanceaster, "heirs of Moses Lancaster" (WPA # 165-44-6999, p. 45)
May 1848	Report of Wm Woolard, guardian of Matilda i.[sic], Jas M., Mary A., Eliz A., aml I.[sic; in cursive penmanship, capital I and J were very similar (WPA # 165-44-6999, Vol D, 1847-52 p. 16)
Oct 1849	Guardian report of Wm Woolard showed that his dau Matilda was dead and identified him as "Father of said Matilda" (WPA # 165-44-6999, Vol D:65)
TN Cns 1850	Wm Woolard (age 42), Sarah (320, Matilda (200, Eliz (150, Caroline (14), Saml (13), Ellen (8), John (7), Wm (6), Taylor (3), Martha (3), Emaline (1) [NOTE: Son Jas M. was living with A.M. Williams] 9Hick Co # 1078)
9 Feb 1856	Wm S. Woollard wit. Deed of John W. Walker to L.D. Lowe and Isabelle Woollard, a tract in Distr 9

of Hick Co for 46 ½ a. adj J.M. Woollard's 100 a. tract (TN Arch Roll 26, Hick Bk D:217-18)

TN Cns 1860 — Wm Woolard (52) & Sarah M. (42), children Ellen (19), John C. (18), Wm F. (15), Isaac T. (13), Martha H. (12), M.E. (f 10), Doctor T. (6), Sarah N. (4), and Sophronia (1) in Hick Co, 9th Dist (p. 307)

2 Dec 1867 — Wm Woolard bought from Jas O. Morgan 500 a. on Blue Water Ck adj G.D. Leeper and Green Pickard; wit W.F. Woolard [s/o Wm S.] (TN Arch Roll 27, Hick DB R:208-08)

28 Dec 1869 — Wm Wollard sold to Isaac Coble, colored, a tract of 500 a. on Blue Water Ck adj G.D. Leeper and Green Pcikard; D.L. Wollard was wit. (TN Arch Roll 27, Hick Bk R:501)

TN Cns 1870 — Wm Woolard (62) & wife (52), E. (17), D.L. [Doctor T.] (16), and S.M. Sarah N.] (14) in 9th Dist of Hick Co (Hh #34)

10 May 1878 — Wm Wollard purchased from C.W. Russell 100 a. on both sides of Beaverdam Ck adj Wm Wollard's 200 a. tract, S. Murphey's corner (TN Arch Roll 28, Hick DB t:604-05)

TN Cns 1880 — Wm Woollard (72), dau Nancy J. (28), son D.T. (26) & wife Mary H. (22) with children Gertrude (3) and Claud (1), Hick Co, 9th Dist (p. 334)

25 Apr 1886 — N.G. [Nancy J.] Woolard m. R.B. Malugin, Hick Co; she was the dau who would reside in William's "home place," his last surviving dau (Leeper, K. *Hickman Co Ct Minutes*)

27 Sep 1895 — Wm Woolard deed to W.S. Wollard 220 a. [described below under date 20 Dec 99]; signed "Wm Woolard (W. Samuel Woolard)" (DB H-1:375)

2 Mar 1896 — T.B. Walker was appointed adm of Wm Woollard, dcd of Hick Co (TN Arch Roll 17, Hick Min Bk:431)

6 Jun 1899 — T.B. Walker's settlement report named the following: W.S. Woollard, D.T. Woollard, W.M. Baxter, Hattie E. Thompson, S.N. Pickard, N.J. Malugin, J.M. Woollard, Lillie E. Stephens, Sallie Weathersppon, Mary Edwards, D.H. Woollard, Willie & E.J. Woollard, E.A. Leeper (TN Arch Loose Papers File)

20 Dec 1899 — W.S. Woollard sold to R.T. Pinkerton 220 a. at "the corner of the original Jones tract on the E ban of Beaverdam Ck… below the mouth of Sulphur Fork… near where Mrs. D.T. Wollard now lives," also adj J.H. Barber, B. Chandler, John W. Walker's tract deeded to Wm Woollard, S. Murphree, W.S. Woollard, "with the exception of a tract of land 300 feet square for which I reserve as a Burial place for the Wollard family… being on the hill some 150 yrds west of my residence and about 200 yds north from the Spring and just east of what is now the garden cornering on an apple tree running north with gharden 30 feet to corner, thence east 300 feet to a corner, thence south 300 feet to corner, eat to the beginning." (Hick DB H-I:376)

19 Jan 1900 — Settlement report of T.W. Walker, adm of Wm Woollard, dcd, named same people as in earlier report, with some variations: Mrs. Mary Edwards, Mrs. Green Leeper, Wm Lancaster heirs, Mrs. E.G. Pickard, R.B. Malugin, and Wm Woollard's heirs; filed 3 Apr 1900 (Loose Papers File)

21 Mar 1904 — R.T. Pinkerton sold his purchase of the W.S. Woollard tract to R.L & wife M.T. Flowd, "except a burial place for the Woollard family 300 feet Square" (DB L-1:212)

Directions to home of William Woollard, Route 1, Centerille, TN 37033

(Home of Austin McNabb as of 2 September 1979)

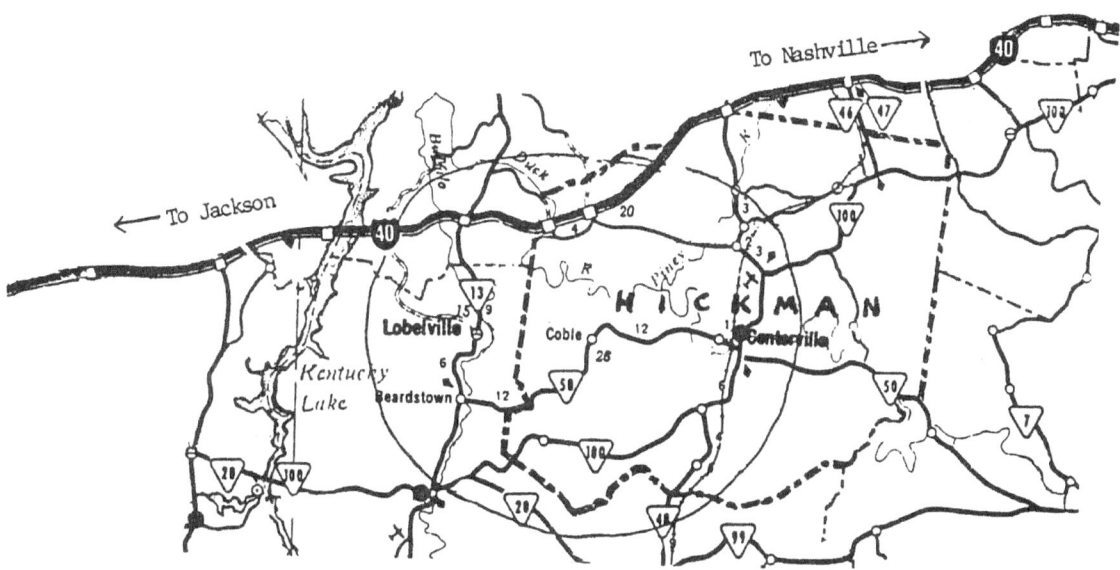

I-40 West to Exit 143

TN State #13 South to TN State #50 (14.5 mi.) to Bearsdtown

TN State #54 East over Buffalo River, (13.1 mi.) through Coble (TN State Marker 3031 on right described in *Tennessee Historical Markers*, Nashville, TN, 1972, p. 157)

Right on Beaver Dam Road (unpaved, 0.5 mi.)

Left on narrow bridge (0.7 mi.); keep to main road which curves to the left

William Woollard home on the right; Austin McNbb is the name on the mailbox to the left.

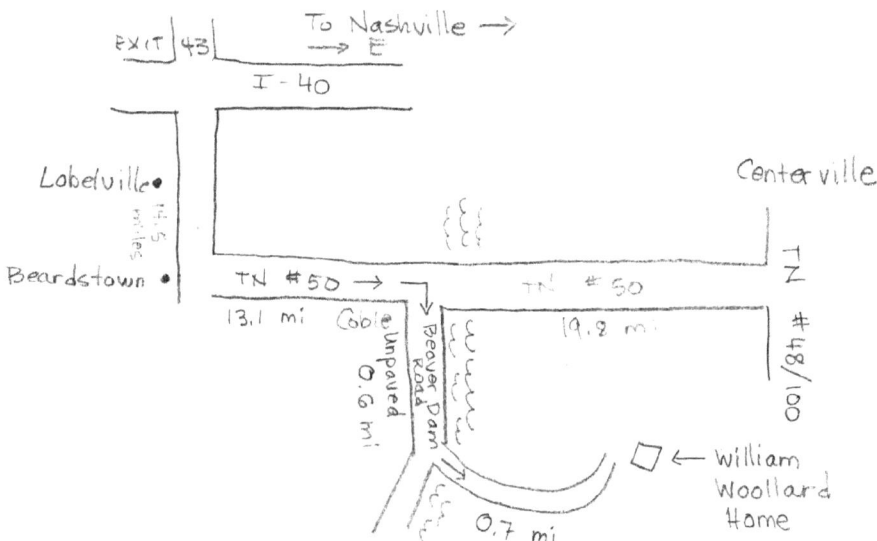

Outline map showing the migration of the Woollards 1650-1860

The Woollards in Tennessee

Capt James Monroe[8] Woollard, CSA
Soldier in Mexican War
Planter, Cotton Broker, and Magistrate of Madison County

<u>In Hickman County.</u> **James Monroe[8] Woollard** was born in Hickman County, Tennessee on March 4, 1831. His parents were Harriett LANCASTER and William[7] S. Woollard; his father was a farmer and magistrate, his mother from a family of Baptist preachers. He was the oldest of six children. When he was about seven years old, his mother died of tetanus. His widowed father married Sarah Cooper; they had ten children, so Jim was part of a very large family.

When Jim was fifteen, war was declared against Mexico; a year later, too young to enlist, he "ran away " with his Uncle Isaac Lancaster to Nashville, where they joined up for the duration and were sent to Mexico. Jim became ill at Molino del Rey and did not see a battle action. When the war ended, Jim and his Uncle Ike were discharged at Memphis, Tennessee.

Back home again in Centerville, Jim was a veteran but still not a man; only seventeen, he followed bookish pursuits – he joined the Debaters' club, taught school, and in 1850 was listed in the census as "clerk." As a school teacher, he made a name for himself as one who could not be outwitted by prankish pupils. On one occasion, two boys propped a chair at the door so that it would turn over when the door was opened; the young schoolmaster entered the room and amazed the class by going straight to the pranksters, paddling first one and then the other, surprising everyone by knowing exactly who the culprits were.

By his twenty-first birthday, James Monroe had received an inheritance from his grandfather William Lancaster and had married. With his bride **Mary Alston JONES** (daughter of **Susan McNEILLY** and **William A. Jones),** he left for West Tennessee to settle there and begin farming. An old slave went with them.

<u>In Madison County.</u> They acquired land at Spring Creek in Madison County. Four children were born – two girls and two boys. Their land records have not been found, but in 1854 Mary Woollard received a considerable inheritance from her father **William A. Jones** of Hickman County; in 1856, he paid $2000 for 100 acres on Beaverdam Creek near his Lancaster relatives. These land documents show that James M. used a seal ring, which indicates that he traveled back to his Middle Tennessee homesite on the occasion of each deed transaction.

At some time, Jim Woollard began keeping a daily journal; three of these day books survived (now in the possession of James Woollard Malloy), for the years 1860, 1867, and 1868. The first book conveys very well the routine tenor of Mary and Jim's tranquil existence. The 1860 journal of this young family man is particularly poignant in light of the impending days of wartime soon to come upon them and blight their lives forever. In addition to keeping a log of daily farming activities, he made entries of other matters, including his magisterial function of taking depositions and his attendance at school board meetings. On the social side, there were visits and visitors, attendance at debates, and attendance at Masonic events. The family attended various churches – they went to Lebanon for church (there is mention of "the first Sunday School at Lebanon"), to Providence for church, to Oak Grove Church, and to the Presbyterian Church in Jackson when he spent the night there. Thanksgiving and Christmas Day did not appear to be viewed as nearby Spring Creek.

Especially touching are his entries that commemorated the anniversary of his little son's death. On April 7 he wrote that "this morning 12 mo ago Billy got up sick and kept getting hoarse all the time that he lived. Stayed at home all day, no person came. Warm and Spring like. This night 12 mo ago sent for Dr Johnson to see Billy." The following entry begins, "This day 12 mo ago Billy was very sick – sat up with him all night and had to Stimulate him to keep him alive till day." On Tuesday, April 10 he wrote, "This morning 12 mo ago sent N.N. May after Dr Rogers to see Billy – he can't do him no good. He died at 6oclk evening. Went with Mary and Mrs Burton to Spring Creek. Took dinner with R.N. Hill." On the following morning he "sent N.N May after Shroud for Billy, buried him about 4oclk afternoon."

Four days later, on the 15th, he wrote: "Boy baby borne this morning at 5oclk. Dr. H. with Mary ... women stayed all day." On the 18th, he noted that it had rained "last night. Planted some Cotton at Home field. Went to Fishers and Attkisons after Dinner. Saw Mrs Adams and Mrs Burton, then talked about my boy." They had lost a son and a year later gained a son.

On October 23, Jim wrote that he "went to Jackson to hear Douglas speak. Stayed with him in his room 1 ½ hours. Made good speech. He [Douglas] went from Jackson to Memphis to speak." Jim's entry for Tuesday the 6th of November was: "election day/Went to Election [at] Spring Creek, "took depositions of E.A. Clark and A. Jones for Murphrey case. Heard Lincoln was Elected President."

Jim's younger brother Samuel J. Woollard also moved to Madison County. When war became inevitable, James and Samuel organized a company of men from Spring Creek and Jackson. On 15 May 1861 Jim was appointed Captain of Company E, 6th Regiment, Tennessee Infantry Volunteers, and Sam was one of his lieutenants. They went to New Madrid, Missouri where three months later their unit was transferred from State Service status to the Army of the Confederate States. [Samuel died of measles during the war; buried at Union city, Tennessee.

In her husband's absence, Mary JONES Woollard had all responsibilities of the family and homestead. During an epidemic of yellow fever, Mary nursed a sick slave; her little boy Willis Banks Woollard died of the dreaded fever, and three months later Mary too succumbed to it. Jim's sister Mary Agnes Woollard was sent for to take over the care of surviving daughters, **Susan9 Matilda Woollard** and Isabella May Woollard. Aunt Mary Woollard rode horseback from Centerville to Madison County, fording the Tennessee River as part of the arduous journey. It would be five years before she returned to her home in Middle Tennessee.

"Shiloh, Bloody Shiloh." The battle of Shiloh took place on April 6 and 7, 1862 near the little church of that name. It began on a sunny Tennessee morning – the petals of peach blossoms littered the ground of a nearby orchard, and when a Union officer shouted, "The Rebels are out there thicker than fleas on a dog's back!" ... "the astounded Yankees dropped their Sunday breakfasts and grabbed their muskets" (Catton, 124).

The Confederate attack was led by Generals Albert Sidney Johnston, P.G.T. Beauregard, and Nathan Bedford Forrest against Union forces commanded by Generals Grant, Sherman, and Lew Wallace. "The peculiar horror of Shiloh" – in the words of Bruce Catton – was that this battle, the biggest in the national history up to that time, was fought by untrained boys on both sides. The Peach Orchard, the Bloody Pond, the Sunken Road, and the Hornet's Nest lived on in the legend of "Shiloh, bloody Shiloh." The battle resulted in the loss of 13,000 Federal and over 10,000 Confederate troops.

General Johnston was shot in the furious Sunday afternoon battle at the Peach Orchard; he bled to death while waiting for his staff physician, who was treating the Federal wounded. Also wounded in the Peach Orchard, Captain Woollard was shot in the knee; he dragged himself to a small creek of Bloody Pond and put mud on the wound to stop the bleeding before he was taken a prisoner of war. He had kept his pistol, and when a Union medical officer wanted to amputate his leg, he threatened to kill "if he touched his leg." Needless to say, no amputation was performed; for the rest of his life he was lame and walked with a cane.

Military Prison at Alton. Captain Woollard was sent with other Confederate prisoners to Alton, Illinois. Like all other Civil War prisons, the one at Alton was ill equipped and inadequately staffed, and its inmates suffered in every way. Food was meagerly supplied, disease and infection were rampant, and in winter the poorly clothed Confederates were exposed to bitterly cold weather. A letter by Colonel W. Hoffman, Commissary-General of Prisoners, dated 4 December 1862, called attention to "certain matters connected with the Alton Prison which occasion much confusion and detriment to the service. It is reported to me that recently 273 prisoners arrived at the prison about 10 o'clock of a dark and bitter cold night. No rolls or papers of any kind were sent with these prisoners ….” (*War of the Rebellion: Official Records of the Union and Confederate Armies* (Series 2), vol. 5, p. 25; cited hereafter as "off Rec"). Another report protested "the ignominious, cruel, and barbarous practices" at Alton (Off Rec (2) 8:347).

James Woollard's length of time as a prisoner of war has not been determined; a search of Alton records at the National Archives did not find any mention of him.[2] Because the date of his exchange or discharge has not been found, it is impossible to fill in James Woollard's activities and whereabouts during the three years between April 1862 and April 1865.

Many years later, Captain Woollard's granddaughter Jennie Mathis Malloy wrote her recollections of him and recalled that his abhorrence of war, based on his own experiences, was so strong that he avoided mention of it if he could. He never went to reunions or talked over war experiences. She wrote that his imprisonment was somewhat mitigated by the intervention of Catholic nuns, who delivered tobacco, candy, and fruit sent to him by his relatives. These were the Sisters of Charity. Their ministrations were not welcomed by the Union Army, who viewed them as a nuisance due to the necessity to provide "the renting and furnishing [of] a house for them and the ire of a servant," as Colonel Hoffman put it when he wrote that "their continued employment at the hospital is not approved" (off Rec (2) 7:221). After the War, James Woollard showed his deep gratitude to the Sisters by sending his little daughters to them for a year of schooling.

Post-War Years. At the end of the War, James M. Woollard made his home in Jackson where he owned and operated a furniture store. On the first day of January 1867, according to his journal, he was aboard the "Sam J. Hale," traveling from Cincinnati, Ohio to Columbus, Kentucky, returning to Jackson after a buying trip to stock his store. In February on another trip, he went by sleeping car to Cincinnati, mentioning Louisville and Bowling Green.

In 1868 James Monroe Woollard married Julia R. Blake Myler who was recently widowed; his diary for 1868 records his devoted courtship. Childless herself, she helped him bring up the girls. Throughout her lifetime, she was active in church affairs and helped achieve notable advancements in the local religious community; their home on Church Street in downtown Jackson was a landmark for many years.

Fortunately, the city of Jackson became a commercial center for cotton shipment, and Captain Woollard was one who profited from the opportunity. He became a successful cotton broker and was prosperous. As a long-time magistrate of Madison County, he was widely known and respected.

In January of 1888, on a day of sleet, James Woollard slipped and fell, breaking his left hip. At age 58, he never regained his former mobility, living the last eight years of his life severely incapacitated. His daughter Sue and her husband helped take care of him.

Julia Woollard died in 1905, and James died the following year (age 75). They are both buried in Jackson, Tennessee in Riverside Cemetery, which formerly had been the family burial ground of the Lancasters, his mother's family [donated by the Lancasters to the city].

Issue of Mary Alston JONES and James Monroe Woollard:

Susan[9] Matilda Woollard (1854-1933)

William Andrew Woollard (b.4 Feb 1856, d.10 Apr 1859)

Isabela May Woollard (b.1859, m. WG Kimmons of Corinth, MS)

Willis Banks Woollard (b.15 Apr 1860, d. 15 May 1861)

---

[2] The likeliest categories of microfilmed records were searched, nine rolls in all, as shown: m-598/10-31—8/#5092/Roll 82; Roll 17, vol 43; R13:22:23; R14:27-28r15:29-30; R16:31,32,33,34

Chronology: James Monroe[8] Woollard
1832, Hickman Co, TN, to 1906, Jackson, TN

4 Mar 1831   Jas Monroe[8] Woollard, s/o Wm S. & Harriett LANCASTER, was b. Hickman Co, TN in the Ninth District

1838 – 1839   When Jas was about 6 or 7 yrs of age, his mother died of a tetanus infection; he was the oldest of six children

TN Cns 1840   His father's cns listing has not been found

13 May 1846   USA declared war on Mexico; Jas M. Woollard was underaged for enlistment

17 Sep 1847   With his uncle Ike Lancaster, JMW "ran away" to join up for the Mexican War; he enlisted at Nashville and was mustered in 30 Sep 1847, serving as private in Capt Fowlke's Co K, 3rd Rgt, TN Inf Volunteers "for the duration of the War" (All Mexican War data are from Natl Arch and TN Arch)

Oct 1847   JMW and Isaac Lancaster wrote a letter from Nashville; this letter was preserved and eventually was sent to Jennie MATHIS Malloy by C.S. Hunt of Linden, TN (Hunt's letter dated 5 Dec 1953)

Dec 1847   JMW's company was stationed at the "City of Mexico" where on Dec 30-31 he was reported sick

23 Feb 1848   By January, JMW was stationed at Molino del Rey; he was "left sick" on this date

30 Apr 1848   JMW was still at Molino del Rey; Mexico

24 Jul 1848   JMW was mustered out at Memphis, TN, having served honorably for 10 mos and 7 days; he did not participate in any battles, according to his pension application in 1894

28 Aug 1848   JMW wrote to the Commissioner of Pensions to claim a land bounty "under the 9th section of the Act of the 11th of February 1847"

Back in Hickman Co after the war, JMW taught school in Centerville; he was "greatly interested" in the Debaters' Club to which he belonged (Handwritten notes of Jennie MATHIS Malloy, cited hereafter as recollections of JMM)

1 Oct 1849   JMW's inheritance from g-father Wm Lancaster was administered by his father Wm Woollard as guardian (WPA#165-44-6999, "Hick Co Guard & Admin Setlments, Vol D, 1847-52, p.65)

TN Cns 1850   James M. Woollard (19) was listed as a clerk and was living in Hick Co with A.M Williams, merchant (#657, p.47)

4 Mar 1852   Jas M. Wollard m. **Mary Alston JONES** (b.1834), d/o **Susan McNeilly** and **Wm Andrew Jones** of Jones Ck (where the Jones family operated a grist mill), Hick Co (Letter of Winfield Scott, Commissioner, US Dept of Interior, to Miss Jennie M. Mathis, dated 29 Jan 1927)

They left for Spring Ck, West TN in Madison Co on the day they were married, to begin farming; an old slave went with them; their four children were born in Spring Creek (Recollections of JMM)

22 Sep 1854   **Susan Matilda[9] Woollard** was b. Madi Co, TN; other children were Wm Andrew, Isabella May, Willis Banks (US Pens Off Form 3-173, 8 Jan 1901)

17 Oct 1854   Jas M. Woolard & wife, et al petitioned for division of slaves in the estate of her father Wm A. Jones,

dcd whose estate was in settlement 1845-53, at which time 22 slaves had been held in reserve for Jones' minor children: Jas & Mary Woolard received Geo, Priss, Feby, Bob, Henry, Sarah, Joe, Dosha, Gabe, Charity, Pat, Benj, Sindy, and Andrew, as well as cash (WPA #465-55-3-115, "Hick Co Min Bk, 1844-55," pp. 404, 439-40)

4 Feb 1856	Birthday of son Wm Andrew Woollard (JMW Journ, 1860)
9 Feb 1856	A deed of John W. Walker to L.D. Lowe and Isabella Woollard describes a tract as "adj J.M. Woollard's 100 a. tract" (TN Arch Roll 26, Hick Bk D:217-18)
21 Jun 1856	Wm P. Whitson of Hick Co sold to Jas M. Woollard for $2000 a tract of 100 a. on the east bank of Beaverdam Ck adj "Lewis D. Lowe & wife's share" from estate of Wm Lancaster, dcd, and adj Isaac Lancaster; also an entry "immediately west of Skull Ck" (TN Arch Roll 26, Hick DB P:293)
4 Dec 1856	Mary A. Woolard, Eliz A. Leeper, G.D. Leeper, Rachel C. Lancaster, John S.J. Lancaster, and Samuel J. Woolard transferred to Jas M. Woolard a parcel of 14 a. from the estate of Wm Lancaster, dcd in Hick Co, east bank of Beaverdam Ck [Martha Lancaster is named as wid/o Wm] (TN Arch Roll 26, Hick Bk P: 344-5; Hick DB 0:344)
25 Mar 1858	Jas M. Woollard conveyed to Wm H. Smith a tract of 286 1/7 a. on Beaver Dam Ck adj "Lewis D. Lowe & wife's distributive share" in the land of Wm Lancaster, dcd; these deeds were signed and sealed by Jas M. Woollard (TN Arch Roll 27, Hick Bk Q:21-22)
10 Apr 1859	Death of Wm Andrew Woollard, "Billy" (JMW Journ)
28 Apr 1859	Birth of dau Isabella May Woollard
3 Mar 1860	Election returns for Madi Co showed that James W. Woolerd voted in the Spring Ck precinct of the 12th Dist (Fam Findings, Oct 1973:102,105)
15 Apr 1860	Birth of son Willis Banks Woollard (JMW Journ)
TN Cns 1860	Jas M. Woollard (29), planter & Mary (27), dau Susan (5), Isabella (3) and Willis (4 mos); also in their household were Mary A. Woollard (23) [sis/o Jas M.?] and Drucilla [Priscilla] Jones (19); taken Aug 18 in 11th Dist (John T. Walker's letter, dated 10 Jun 1929)
< Civil War	Jas m. and bro Saml J. moved to the Jackson, TN Vicinity before the War; they formed a company from Springcreek and Jackson for the Confederate Army, with the brothers as capt and lieut respectively in the same company (John T. Walker's letter, dated 10 Jun 1929)
14 Jan 1861	J.M. Wollard of Madi Co and Lewis D. Lowe of Hick Co jointly held a tract formerly held by Lowe and Wm Lancaster, dcd and a tract in the name of M.L. Fowlkes on Skull Ck and by this covenant agreed to redistribution; registered 20 May 1861; signed and sealed by both parties (TN Arch Roll 27, Hick Bk Q: 534-5)
15 May 1861	Jas M. Woollard, age 30, was appointed captain of Co E (Woollard's), 6th Rgt TN inf Volunteers by A.W. Campbell at Jackson, TN, organized for State Service, to serve for a term of 13 months (Military files, Natl ASrch and TN Arch)
cJun 1861	Left to manage the family affairs, Mary Woollard nursed one of her slaves who was ill with typhold fever; she became ill herself and also her infant son Willis, for whom it was fatal; she died 3 mos later (Recollections of JMM)

<u>11 Aug 1861</u>	Mary A. JONES Woollard d. in Madi Co, TN; she was buried in Springcreek (date of death from letter of Winfield Scott, cited above)
<u>1861 – 1866</u>	After Mary's death, the two little daughters had no one to care for them, so their aunt Mary Woollard (sis/o JMW) was sent for; she rode horseback from Hick Co, fording the TN River en route, and remained with them until the end of the war (Recollections of JMM)
<u>1861 – 1865</u>	The Civil War Years: All Civil War data are based on military records on file at the Natl Archives, Washington, DC, and the TN Archives, Nashville, TN
<u>12 Aug 1861</u>	Muster roll of this date shows JMW encamped at New Madrid, MO and transferred to service of the CSA, in Co E, 6th Rgt TN Volunteers
<u>6 Apr 1862</u>	JMW's company was engaged in the two-day Battle of Shiloh, one of the great battles of the war; at the Peach Orchard, JMW was wounded and taken prisoner
<u>17 Apr 1862</u>	Must report of this date shows JMW wounded in action, 6th and 7th of April near Shiloh, TN; he was taken as prisoner of war to the Military Prison at Alton, IL where the Sisters of Charity helped the prisoners; date of release not known

[April 1864 to 1866: No evidence of JMW's activities during this time; military records at the Natl Archives show that a Capt Jas M. Woollard was engaged in action at Oxford, MS on 1 Feb 1864; he requisitioned forage for the horses on Gen Nathan Bedford Forrest's Scouts; however, this may have been another man of that name who later served as Mayor of Lebanon, TN]

<u>1 Jan 1867</u>	"On board Sam J. Hale, traveling from Cincinnati 0 to Columbus Ky … passed Smithland at noon … Little Girls got my New Year's gift …." (JMW Journ for 1867)
<u>1 Jan 1868</u>	JMW was living in Jackson, operating a place of business and engaged in building plans for the "factory" (JMW's Journ for 1868)
<u>4 Mar 1868</u>	Notation in diary: "37 years old today … I hope we may marry before another Birthday rolls along" (JMW's Journ for 1868)
<u>21 May 1868</u>	Prenuptial agreement between Jas M. Woollard and Mrs Julia B. Myler (TN Arch Roll 13, Madi Bk 26:52-3; also JMW Journ)
<u>21 May 1868</u>	JMW m. Julia R. BLAKE Myler (b.24 Apr 1835, Raleigh, NC), d/o Mr & Mrs N.O. Blake, wid/o Mr _____ Myler; wit. Saml C. Lancaster; W.H. Leigh, MG (Madi Co Marr Records, 1866-1900 – WPA# has been lost)
<u>22 Sep 1869</u>	J.M. Woolard's receipt for shipment from W.C. Dowell, Trenton, TN by Southern Express Co (Original)
<u>22 Jan 1870</u>	J.M. Woolard's receipt for shipment from R.H. Hammerly, Tupelo, MS by Southern Express Co (Original)

A COMPLETE Table of Stamp Duties

AS AMENDED MARCH 3, 1865.

AGREEMENT, or CONTRACT, not otherwise specified; any appraisement of value or damage, or other purpose; for each agreement, or for each sheet of each agreement, &c., or renewal of same.... $0.06

ASSIGNMENT, or TRANSFER, of mortgage or policy of insurance, or renewal or continuance of agreement, contract, or charter, same stamp as the original instrument.

BANK CHECK, DRAFT, or ORDER for the payment of any sum of money drawn upon any bank, banker, or trust company, or for any sum exceeding $10, drawn upon any other person, companies, or corporations, at sight or on demand........... .02

BILL OF EXCHANGE, (Inland,) DRAFT, or ORDER, for the payment of money, not at sight or on demand, or any PROMISSORY NOTE, (except bank notes issued for circulation, and checks made and intended to be forthwith presented, and which shall be presented to a bank or banker for payment,) or any memorandum, check, receipt, or other written or printed evidence of money to be paid on demand, or at a time designated, for every $100 or part thereof........... .06

BILL OF EXCHANGE, (Foreign,) or LETTERS OF CREDIT, drawn in but payable out of the United States:

If drawn singly or in duplicate, same as Inland bills of Exchange.

If drawn in sets of three or more, every bill of each set, for every $100, or the equivalent thereof, in any foreign currency in which the bill is expressed............ .02

BILL OF LADING, or RECEIPT, (other than charter party,) for any goods &c., exported to a foreign port.......... .10

Rates of Postage.

LETTERS TO ANY PART OF THE UNITED STATES, 3 cents for each 1-2 ounce or part thereof.

DROP LETTERS, 2 cents per each half ounce.

ADVERTISED LETTERS, 1 cent, in addition to the regular rates.

VALUABLE LETTERS may be registered on application at the office of mailing, and the payment of a registration fee not exceeding 20 cents.

TRANSIENT NEWSPAPERS, Periodicals, Pamphlets, Blanks, Proof Sheets, Book Manuscripts, and all mailable printed matter, (except circulars and books,) 2 cents for each and every 4 ounces. Double these rates are charged for Books.

UNSEALED CIRCULARS, (to one address,) not exceeding 3 in number, 2 cents, and in the same proportion for a greater number.

SEEDS, CUTTINGS, ROOTS, &C., 2 cents for each 4 ounces or less quantity.

ALL PACKAGES of Mail Matter not charged with letter postage must be so arranged that the same can be conveniently examined by Postmasters; if not, letter postage will be charged.

No PACKAGE will be forwarded by mail which weighs over 4 pounds.

ALL POSTAGE MATTER, for delivery within the United States, must be PREPAID by stamps, except duly certified letters of soldiers and sailors.

WEEKLY NEWSPAPERS, (one copy only,) sent to actual Subscribers within the County where printed and published, free.

LETTERS TO CANADA and other British North American Provinces, when not over 3,000 miles, 10 cents for each 1-2 ounce. When over 3,000 miles, 15 cents. Prepayment optional.

LETTERS TO GREAT BRITAIN or IRELAND, 24 cents. Prepayment optional.

LETTERS TO FRANCE, 15 cents for each 1-4 ounce. Prepayment optional.

LETTERS TO OTHER FOREIGN COUNTRIES vary in rate according to the route by which they are sent, and the proper information can be obtained of any Postmaster in the United States.

Title page and end papers of Captain James M. Woollard's Journal for the year 1867.
Each of his journals was bound in black leather with his name and the year imprinted in gold lettering.

Receipts of J. M. WOollard in 1869 and 1870
from the Southern Express Company, for express forwarding of freight

TN Cns 1870	J.M. Woolard (39) in Madi CO (p. 328)
1 Aug 1870	J.M. Woolard's deed to John H. Lanier, Sr, a tract of 208 a. in Madi Dist #12 (TN Arch Roll 14 , Madi Bk 28:99-100)
TN Cns 1880	J.M. Woolard (50, cotton broker) & Julia (46, wife), dau Sue M. (22) and 3 boarders, residing at Liberty & Church Sts in Madi Co (#355)
1887	By this date, several firms of cotton brokers "mad connections with east and south and shipped directly to spinners and exporters"; Jackson became a major cotton market, and J.M. Woollard was a prominent broker (Williams-1946, 361)
12 Jan 1888	JMW's dau Sue Matilda Woollard m. **Luther E. Mathis,** Jackson, TN
16 Jul 1888	JMW fell, breaking his left hip; already handicapped by his Civil War injury, he was now permanently disabled at age 58 (Natl Arch, Mex War Pens Records)
25 Jan 1895	JMW's g-dau **Jennie May[10] Mathis** was born in Jackson, TN
< Mar 1896	Death of JMW's father Wm S. Woollard, Hick Co
6 Jun 1899	Estate settlement of WSW mentioned J.M. Woollard (TN Arch, Loose Papers)
19 Jan 1900	Final settlement of WSW estate in hick Co; JMW was named as an heir (Ibid.)
TN Cns 1900	John (Jas] M. Woollard (69) & Julia (64) lived in Jackson, Mad Co at 274 Church Street (#274)
30 Jul 1905	Julia BLAKE Woollard, "beloved wife of Capt. J.M. Woollard… died after a week's illness," funeral services at the First Meth Eips Church by the Rev. T.F. Saunders of Middle Ave Meth Epis Church which she helped found (Two obits dated 31 Jul 1905, newspapers not identified, found in vertical file at TN State Lib)
18 Dec 1906	Jas M. Woollard d. and was buried in Riverside Cem, Jackson, TN beside wife Julia; this cemetery was formerly (since 1830) known as Lancaster Graveyard but was renamed later when Saml Lancaster gave it to the county in 1850 (*The Jackson Sun*, May 1984, pp 106-108) NOTE: Although his headstone shows birth year as 1832, JMW gave 1831 on censuses and pension papers.
19 Dec 1906	Robt H. Cartmell wrote in his diary: "Capt J.M. Woolard was buried in Jackson today, about 75 or 76 years of age. Had been in declining health for a year or more but the immediate cause was pneumonia. He was a soldier in the Mexcian as also in the great war of 61-65. Long a citizen of Madison Co, a magistrate for 10 or 12 years." (TN State Lib, R.H. Cartmell Papers, vol xxiii, 19 Dec 1906)

Descendants of Samuel[6] Woollard in Tennessee
William[7] S. Woollard, 1808-96, Hickman Co
m1 Harriett Lancaster, d. c1838

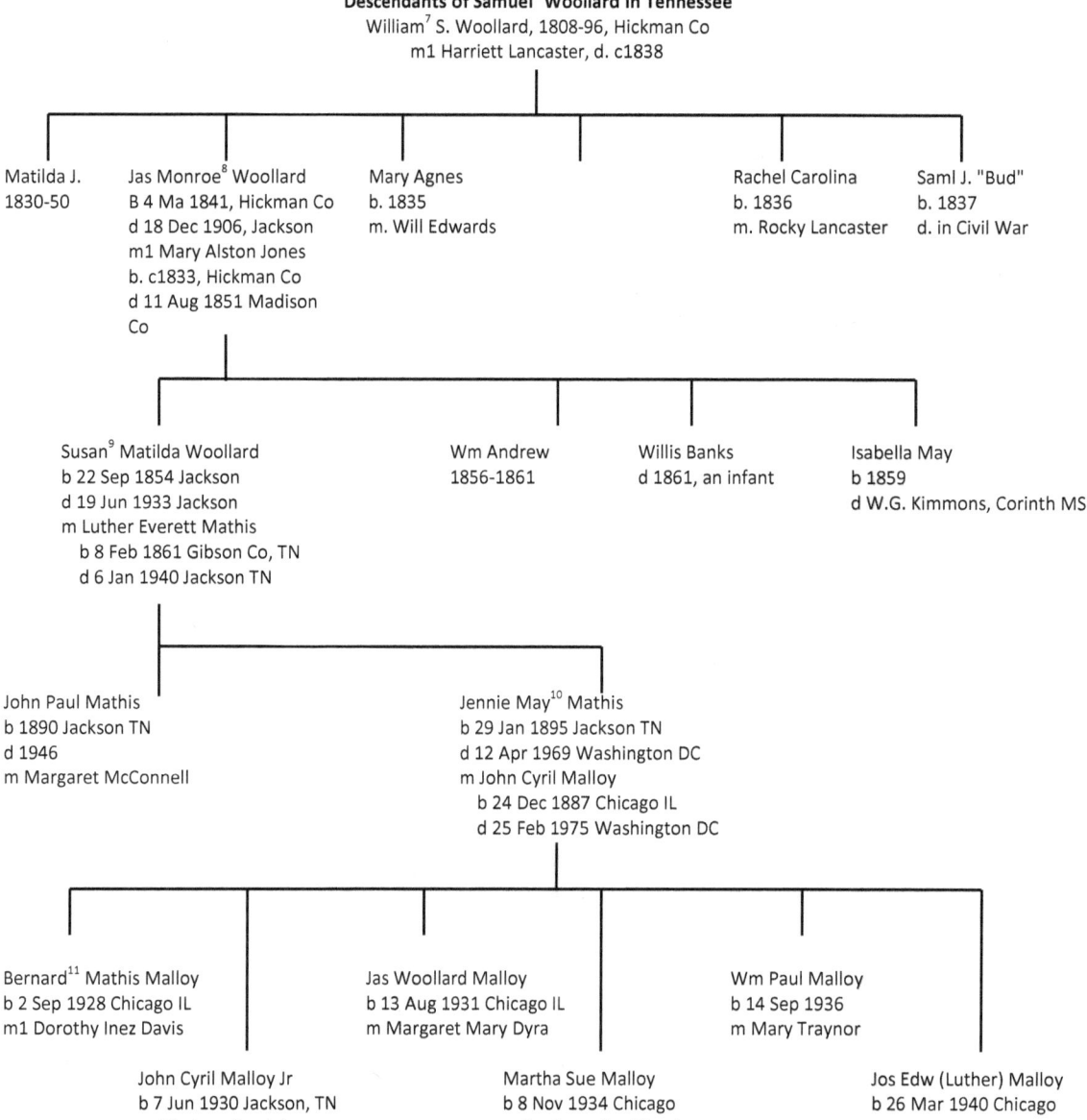

Matilda J.
1830-50

Jas Monroe[8] Woollard
B 4 Ma 1841, Hickman Co
d 18 Dec 1906, Jackson
m1 Mary Alston Jones
b. c1833, Hickman Co
d 11 Aug 1851 Madison
Co

Mary Agnes
b. 1835
m. Will Edwards

Rachel Carolina
b. 1836
m. Rocky Lancaster

Saml J. "Bud"
b. 1837
d. in Civil War

Susan[9] Matilda Woollard
b 22 Sep 1854 Jackson
d 19 Jun 1933 Jackson
m Luther Everett Mathis
    b 8 Feb 1861 Gibson Co, TN
    d 6 Jan 1940 Jackson TN

Wm Andrew
1856-1861

Willis Banks
d 1861, an infant

Isabella May
b 1859
d W.G. Kimmons, Corinth MS

John Paul Mathis
b 1890 Jackson TN
d 1946
m Margaret McConnell

Jennie May[10] Mathis
b 29 Jan 1895 Jackson TN
d 12 Apr 1969 Washington DC
m John Cyril Malloy
    b 24 Dec 1887 Chicago IL
    d 25 Feb 1975 Washington DC

Bernard[11] Mathis Malloy
b 2 Sep 1928 Chicago IL
m1 Dorothy Inez Davis

Jas Woollard Malloy
b 13 Aug 1931 Chicago IL
m Margaret Mary Dyra

Wm Paul Malloy
b 14 Sep 1936
m Mary Traynor

John Cyril Malloy Jr
b 7 Jun 1930 Jackson, TN
m Marlene Oradel

Martha Sue Malloy
b 8 Nov 1934 Chicago
m Jos Cornellus Murphy

Jos Edw (Luther) Malloy
b 26 Mar 1940 Chicago

IN REPLY REFER TO
Law Division.
Mex. War Surv. Ct. 20,141,
James M. Woollard,
Co. K, 3 Tenn. Inf.

UNITED STATES
DEPARTMENT OF THE INTERIOR
BUREAU OF PENSIONS
WASHINGTON   January 29, 1927.

Miss Jennie M. Mathis,
173 East Deaderick Ave.,
Jackson, Tenn.

Madam:

    Receipt is acknowledged of your letter of
inquiry, relative to the service and family history of the above-named soldier.

    In a report from the records of the War
Department, now on file in this bureau, it appears that one James Woollard enrolled on September 7, 1847, and was mustered into service on
September 30, 1847, at Nashville, Tenn., and
served as a Private in Co. K, 3d Tennessee Infantry, and was honorably discharged on July
24, 1848, at Memphis, Tenn. It appears in papers
filed in the claim on May 6, 1901, that the soldier alleged that he was first married in 1852,
in Hickman County, Tenn., to Mary A. Jones, who
died in Madison County, Tenn., on August 11, 1861,
and two children were born of this marriage, namely, Sue, born on September 24, 1854; and Mary,
born on April 28, 1859. He married, in May, 1868,
Julia R. Blake, at Jackson, Tenn. In the paper
filed on May 23, 1892, the soldier alleged that he
was born in Hickman County, Tenn., on March 4, 1831.
The soldier drew a pension, based on the above-
named service, until the date of his death in December, 1906.

                    Respectfully,

                    Winfield Scott

                    WINFIELD SCOTT,
                    Commissioner.

FRM/mep

General Winfield Scott's 1927 letter of reply to Miss jennie M. Mathis:
A biographical summary of James Moneroe Woollard based on his military service during the Mexican War.

THE WOOLLARDS OF TENNESSEE

SUSAN MATILDA[9] WOOLLARD
b 24 September 1854, Madison County, Tennessee
d 19 June 1933, Jackson, Tennessee

Susan Matilda[9] Woollard was the eldest child born to Mary Alston JONES and James[8] Monroe Woollard. They lived near Spring Creek in Madison County, Tennessee; Susan's brother William Andrew, called Billy, was born in 1856. In April of 1859, three-year old Billy died, and eighteen days later Susan's sister Isabel la May was born.

A few glimpses of Susan's childhood are provided by her father's diary for the year 1860 when Susan was not yet six years old. In the spring of that year, her mother's sister Priscilla was living with them. They received lots of guests – many for overnight at their rural home; among these were W.W. Myler and "his Lady." On the 29th of March her father wrote that Susan was sick; the following day she was "some better" in the morning and, later, "some better this evening." In April he wrote that "Little May is kind of sick." A new member of the family arrived on the 15th of April – baby brother Willis Banks Woollard. In October "Susan went home with J.W.G. Jones to stay two or three weeks." [John Willis G. Jones, a cousin of Mary JONES Woollard, was a descendant of Ruth BANKS and Willis Jones, who was a brother of Mary Woollard's grandfather, Solomon Jones.] On November 2, her father "started to Lexington after Susan," and on the 5th wrote that he "brought Susan & May home with me." That year, Thanksgiving Day was on Thursday the 29th, but the family observance was not noted in the diary. Likewise, Christmas Day (on a cloudy Tuesday) was a quiet day – "nobody came, Mary went to Bob's to stay all night." However, on the 31st they went to Springcreek and "stayed to a Dancing Party at night" on this "last day of the year 1860."

In May of the following year, Tennessee was on the brink of secession (which occurred on 8 June 1861), and the men of Spring Creek and Jackson began organizing regiments; Susan's father was elected Captain of Company E of the 6th Regiment of Tennessee Infantry Volunteers and very soon left for active military duty. The next twelve-month period was surely the saddest in the entire life of seven-year-old Susan: yellow fever came to their community and claiming Susan and younger sister May without either parent. In April their father was wounded at the Battle of Shiloh; taken prisoner, he was sent to Alton, Illinois to a Union Prisoner of War encampment. Their Aunt Mary Woollard, traveling by horseback, came from Hickman County to stay with them for five sorrowful years until their father returned from the war.

At some point after his return, Captain Woolard sent his two daughters to Alton to be educated by the Sisters of Mercy. These Catholic nuns had ministered to the Southern prisoners during the war, and out of gratitude he sent his little girls to be taught by them. However, Sue and May were lonely and homesick, of course, and returned to their home before the schooling was completed. On 1 January 1867 Sue's father wrote in his diary that he was "on board 'Sam J. Hale," traveling from Cincinnati, O, to Columbus, Ky. Passed Smithland [KY] at noon. "Little girls got my New Year's Gift."

Susan's father had settled in Jackson; she was fourteen in 1868 when her father married the widow Julia BLAKE Myler. The new Mrs Woollard was a very active laywoman and succeeded in founding Trinity Methodist church in Jackson; Sue shared her religious commitment.

In 1869 and 1870 Susan Woollard was a student at the Memphis Conference Female Institute (MCFI), where she studied for two years. The MCFI Catalogue for 1869 listed Miss Susie M. Woolard as a member of the Junior Class. Later, she also taught there.

Susan had suitors and selected **Luther Everett Mathis** (b. 1861, d. 1940) of Gibson County, Tennessee, whom she married in 1888. Throughout their forty-five years of marriage, she called him " Mr Mathis" and he called her "Miss Sue." In personality she was reserved and dignified but always kind. It was her custom to rise early and take care of duties and household affairs during the morning hours; afternoons were for social calls, according to the Victorian standards of the time.

Susan and Luther Everett Mathis had two children, son Paul Jones and daughter **Jennie May[10] Mathis**. The family also included Susan's mother-in-law, **Martha Jane Rust Mathis** (widow of **Alexander Littlejohn Mathis)** who lived with them. Many years later – after her children had married and left home – the household of Miss Sue and Luther Mathis once again included a child, their small grandson **Bernard[11] Mathis Malloy.** He was the son of Jennie May and her husband **John Cyril Malloy.** The Malloys lived in Chicago and had four children under five years of age; out of concern for daughter Jennie May, who "had her hands full," the Mathises took little "Barney" to live with them.

Susan Matilda WOOLLARD Mathis died 19 June 1933 and was buried in Hollywood Cemetery in Jackson, Tennessee. Her husband died 6 January 1940 and was also buried there.

Resolutions of respect to Mrs L.E. Mathis were adopted by the General William H. Jackson Chapter of the United Daughters of the Confederacy. Excerpts show their high regard for her: "The life of this splendid woman speaks for her, a eulogy that cannot be expressed in words. Born in a southern community, the daughter of a Confederate soldier, Sue Woolard Mathis was the embodiment of the spirit of the Old South, and throughout her life she was loyal to its ideals and traditions … a gracious, gentle woman …."

Issue: Paul Jones Mathis b.1890, Jackson, TN, m. Margaret McConnell, d. 1946)

Jennie May[10] Mathis (b.29 Jan 1895, Jackson; d.12 Apr 1967, Wash., DC)

Chronology: Susan Matilda[9] Woollard
b.1854, Madison Co, TN – d.1933, Jackson, TN
m. Luther Everett Mathis, 1888

24 Sep 1854	Birth of Susan Matilda Woollard, d/o Mary Alston JONES & Jas Monroe Woollard, Springcreek, Madi Co, TN; she was named for both grandmothers, Susan Mc NEILLY Jones and Harriett Matilda LANCASTER Woollard
1861 – 1865	Separated from both parents during war years; her mother died of yellow fever (1861); her father was taken away as prisoner of war, and Aunt Mary Woollard came to live with Susan and her sister May until their father returned from the war
Post-War	At the end of the Civil War, Capt Woollard, out of gratitude, sent Susan and sister May to the Sisters of Mercy in Alton, IL for schooling; exact date not known
1 Jan 1867	Sue and May received New Year's gifts from their father (JMW's Journal, 1867)
21 May 1868	Susan's father Jas M. Woollard m. (2) Julia R. BLAKE Myler, wid/o W.W.(?) Myler (JMW's Journal, 1868)
1870 & 1871	Susan attended school at Memphis Conference Female Institute (MCFI); taught at MCFI, no details known (FF 6:147, 149; FF 7:33)

<u>12 Jan 1888</u>	Susan Woollard m. Luther Everett Mathis of Gibson Co, TN; they lived in Jackson where he owned a grocery store
<u>1890</u>	Birth of son Paul Jones Mathis, in Jackson, TN
<u>29 Jan 1895</u>	Birth of daughter Jennie May 10 Mathis, in Jackson, TN
<u>1931</u>	Grandson Bernard Mathis 11 Malloy (b.1928, Chicago, IL) to Jackson, TN to stay with grandparents Susan & Luther Mathis
<u>19 Jun 1933</u>	Susan Matilda WOOLLARD Mathis d. in Jackson, bur in Hollywood Cem; age 79 yrs
<u>6 Jan 1940</u>	Luther E. Mathis d. in Jackson, bur in Hollywood Cem; his age also was 79

THE WOOLLARDS IN TENNESSEE

JENNIE MAY[10] MATHIS
b.29 January 1895, Jackson, Tennessee
d.12 April 1969, Washington, DC

Jennie May[10] **Mathis** was the only daughter of Susan[9] Matlida WOOLLARD and Luther Everett Mathis. She was born in Jackson, Tennessee, where her grandfather Captain James Monroe Woollard (widowed) had been a long-time magistrate of the county and veteran of the Mexican War and Civil War.

After graduating from Jackson high School in 1912, Jennie May attended Miss Mason's at the Castle in Tarrytown, New York, for finishing school. On returning to Jackson, she continued her education. In July 1917 she studied voice at Memphis Conference Female institute (MCFI) where her mother before her had been a student. Then she enrolled at Union University in Jackson, receiving her Bachelor's degree in 1925. After graduation, she began her career as an elementary teacher (first grade). She also attended Columbia University as a postgraduate student during her summer vacations.

Her first teaching positions were at College Street School and Whitehall School in the city of Jackson. During summers, the young lady teachers would take jobs at Marshall Fields and spend their vacation in Chicago (properly chaperoned, of course). In Chicago she met her husband-to-be, **John Cyril Malloy** (b.24 December 1887, Chicago, d.25 February 1975, Washington, Dc). Jennie May's father had never approved of her suitors – they were never quite good enough for his daughter – so she made her own choice, an "Irish Catholic Yankee" (in the words of that Yankee's son).

The Malloys had six children . When their eldest son, **Bernard**[11] **Mathis,** was a very active five-year-old with three younger siblings, Jennie May's doting parents feared that her strength was not up to all the family demands (although her health was good), so "Barney" went to Jackson to live with his Mathis grandparents.

Later, after John Cyril Malloy's retirement, the family moved to Jackson in 1943. Her parents were both dead, and Jennie May resumed her teaching career, this time at Brown's Church, a county school, and at the First Presbyterian Church School in Madison. As a teacher, she practiced the highest values of education; over a period of about twenty-five years, she taught three generations of fortunate students and is still remembered for her educational contribution to the community. She has been described as "indomitable."

Jennie May Malloy was an active member of the First Methodist Church. She was interested in genealogy and began collecting family data. She wrote an account of her grandfather Woollard's experiences, cited herein as "Recollections of Jennie Mathis Malloy") Recollect. Of JMM). She was an active member of the United Daughters of the Confederacy (UDC) and also the Daughters of the American Revolution (DAR).

While attending a meeting of the DAR in Washington, DC, she was taken III and died there on 12 April 1969, at age 74. She was buried in Hollywood Cemetery, Jackson, Tennessee. Her husband, John Cyril Malloy, also died in Washington (at 87 years of age). He is buried in Calvary Cemetery in Evanston, Illinois.

Issue: Bernard[11] Mathis Malloy

John Cyril Malloy, Jr (b.7 Jun 1930, Jackson, TN, m. Marlene Oradei)

James Woollard Malloy (b.13 Aug 1931, Chicago, m. Margaret Mary Dyra)

Martha Sue Malloy (b.8 Nov 1934, Chicago, m. Jos Cornelius Murphy)

Wm Paul Malloy (b.14 Sep 1936, Chicago, m. Mary Traynor)

Jos Edw (Luther) Malloy (b.26 Mar 1940, Chicago)

Chronology: Jennie May[10] Mathis
b 1905, Jackson TN – d 1969, Washington DC
m. John Cyril Malloy, 1927

29 Jan 1895	Birth of Jennie May Mathis, d/o Susan Matilda WOOLLARD & Luther Everett Mathis, in Jackson, TN
1912 – 1914	Attended Miss Mason's at The Castle, Tarrytown, NY
1914 – 1918	After finishing school, Jennie May Mathis returned to Jackson and continued her education
July 1917	Jennie May Mathis studied voice at MCFI (MCFI Bulletin, not dated)
May 1927	Received her Bachelor of Arts from Union Univ; began teaching at the College Street School and also the Whitehall School (Graduation program of Union Univ)
1925 – 1927	During her summer vacations, Jennie May attended Columbia Univ, NYC for post-graduate studies. Later, her summer vacations were spent in Chicago, where she and other unmarried teachers took jobs at Marshall Fields; on one of these trips she met her future husband.
8 Feb 1927	Jennie May Mathis m. John Cyril Malloy, Chicago, IL
1930 – 1940	The Malloys lived in Chicago; their 6 children were born during this period
1943	John Cyril Malloy retired and moved his family to Jackson, TN
1950s – 1960s	Jennie May Malloy resumed her teaching career, at Brown's Church in Mad Co and at Firsit Presb Church School in Jackson
12 Apr 1969	Jennie May MATHIS Malloy d. suddenly, Washington, DC; her age was 74; interment at Hollywood Cem in Jackson, TN
25 Feb 1975	John Cyril Malloy also d. in Washingtion, DC (age 87); Bur Calvary Cemetery, Evanston, IL

Miss C. E. Mason's School
The Castle
Tarrytown-on-Hudson
New York

February
Twenty-sixth
1 9 1 8.

To Whom It May Concern:-

Miss Jennie May
Mathis of Jackson, Tennessee, is a graduate
of "The Castle" school at Tarrytown, New
York.

We found Miss Mathis
an earnest student, and if she passes the
Civil Service Examinations, she will do her
work earnestly, conscientiously, and thoroughly.

The enclosed report will
give her standing for the two years of her
student life and residence at The Castle.

Very truly yours,

C.E. Mason

Miss Mason's Castle School was situated on Castle Ridge, Tarrytown, New York. The school was fashionable and highly esteemed. Miss Mason instilled social charm and poise; French was spoken at the dinner table. Miss Mason insisted on the highest ideals and emphasized the dignity and rights of women. Founded in 1895, the school closed in 1933 after the death of its headmistress. (From Canning & Buston's *History of the Tarrtowns*, Harbor Hill Books, Harrison, NY, 1975.

Mrs. Jennie Malloy

Services for Mrs. Jennie May Malloy will be at 3 p.m. Wednesday in the chapel of Griffin Funeral Home with Rev. Jimmy Moore and Dr. Paul Lyles officiating. Burial will be in Hollywood Cemetery.

Mrs. Malloy died Saturday in Washington, D.C., while visiting her son.

She was a retired school teacher, having taught both in Jackson and Madison County school systems. She taught most recently at the Presbyterian Day School and the Huntersville Private School.

She was a delegate to this year's Continental Congress of the National Society of D.A.R. She was a member of the First Methodist Church, and a member of the Wesleyan Service Guild.

Survivors are her husband; John Cyril Malloy Sr. of Jackson; five sons, Dr. Barney Malloy and Capt. Luther Malloy, both of Washington, D. C., John Malloy Jr. of Miami, Fla., James Malloy and William Malloy, both of Chicago, one daughter, Mrs. Joe Murphy of Chicago and 19 grandchildren.

Active pallbearers are to be David Murray, Robert Willet, Jack Holland, Billy Holland, Roger Murray and Russell Rice.

Honorary pallbearers include John Nickias, Russell Woodard, Petty Gray, Reggie Smith, Nando Jones, L. L. Fonville, Dr. Lamb Myhr and Mayor Bob Conger.

Jackson Sun, 14 April 1969

THE WOOLARDS OF TENNESSEE

BERNARD MATHIS[11] MALLOY, MD
OF WASHINGTON, DC
b.2 September 1928, Chicago, Illinois

The eldest child of Jennie[10] May MATHIS and John Cyril Malloy was **Bernard Mathis[11] Malloy,** called "Barney." Barney was born in Chicago, Illinois on 2 September 1928. His grandparents were Susan Matilda WOOLLARD and Luther Everett Mathis, and, on his father's side, **Mary CASS** and **John Cyril Malloy.** In time, Barney's family would include four brothers and one sister: John Cyril (b.1930), James Woollard (b.1931), Martha Sue (b.1934), William Paul 9b.1936), and Joseph Everett (b.1940). Barney spent part of his early years – from age five – in Jackson, Tennessee with his maternal grandparents, the Mathises. Later, his father retired and all the family moved from Chicago to Jackson. Bernard Mathis Malloy's scholastic and professional resume includes the following:

Education	B.A., Lambuth College, 1951
	M.D., Vanderbilt University, 1954
	Diplomate, American Board of Psychiatry & Neurology, 1961
Military	U.S. Army, Sgt; 1946-48

Internship, Residency, and Fellowship –

Vanderbilt University Hospital, Nashville, TN (1954-56)

Payne Whitney Clinic, The New York Hospital, NY, NC (1956-58)

National Hospital for Neurological Diseases, Queen Square, London (1958)

Instructional	Vanderbilt University; Cornell University (Instructor)
	Cornell University (instructor)
	Georgetown University (Assistant Clinical Professor)
Memberships	American Medical Association
	American Psychiatric Association
	American Psychoanalytic Association
	Southern Psychiatric Association (vice president, 1988-89)
	Phi Chi
	Sons of the American Revolution
	Society of Colonial Wars

On 1 July 1958, Bernard Mathis Malloy married **Dorothy Inez Davis** (b. 7 August 1935 in Memphis, Tennessee, daughter of **Sara Inez WHALLEY** and **Claud Everett Davis)** in Decatur, Georgia. Children, born in Wash., DC:

John Davis Malloy, b. 30 December 1961; BA degree, Vassar College

Bernard Mathis Malloy, Jr. b. 23 September 1965; BA, Swartmore College

Elizabeth Grace Malloy, b. 30August 1967, BA, Harvard-Radcliffe College

On 6 March 1982, in Washington, DC, Bernard Mathis Malloy married (2) **Patricia APPEL Davidge**.

APPENDIX A
HISTORICAL NOTES – SOCIAL AND POLITICAL

The Calendar year

Certain conventions of colonial usage are generally unfamiliar to contemporary readers; the calendar is an example. Up until the mid-eighteenth century, England used the Julian calendar, named for Julius Caesar who ordered it in 46 BC, according to which March 25 was the first day of a new year. This calendar was reformed in 1582 by Pope Gregory XIII, for whom the new version was named; among other alterations, the Gregorian calendar's starting point was the first day of January. It was adopted by the Roman Catholic nations of Europe, but most of the Germanic states continued using the Julian calendar until 1700.

England, however, did not adopt the Gregorian calendar until mid-eighteenth century; in the interim – as a form of compensation – England resorted to "double dating" as a sort of functional compromise. Under this system, all dates between January 1 and March 25 were written with both the current year and the upcoming year, as shown here: 23 February 1748/49, using a slash, would be 23 February 1749 according to our reckoning. In 1752, England switched to the Gregorian calendar so that thereafter "double dating" was not necessary.

In this publication, the vagaries of this calendar confusion show up in the **Chronologies** where the reader needs to be aware that it is not an error when, for example, a December date precedes a January date even though both are in the same year.

Spelling, Punctuation, and Abbreviations

As for spelling, there was no such thing; words were written as they sounded, and it was not until the end of the eighteenth century that "correct" spelling became important. Above all, spelling was <u>not</u> an indicator of literacy – actually, English officials of the 16th and 17th centuries were skilled at writing in Latin as well as in English; in their system, it was Latin rather than English that demanded punctilious observation of all grammatical rules. This compilation retains original spellings in all quoted materials [without using sic].

In colonial times, punctuation was much simpler than it is today. Internal punctuation (comma, semicolon, colon) was practically nonexistent, and sentences flowed along in what we would call "run-on" style. On the other hand, end punctuation (period, question mark, etcetera) was not always used either; sometimes, individual style prevailed – for instance, the clerk who made extensive use of a "dash" in lieu of all other punctuation. Capitalization of certain common nouns within a sentence was also a feature of colonial English writing, comparable to present –day capitalization of nouns in German.

Abbreviations were quite acceptable even in formal documents, unlike today's view of abbreviation as suitable only for casual, business, or notational writings. Indeed, our ancestors of that era were most inventive in their use of abbreviations. Probably the most used were "ye" for "the" and "do" for "ditto," and the ampersand (&) for "and." Contractions of suffixes and final syllables were standard practice; usually, the final consonant was written as a superscript over one or two dots (marks), as shown in the following examples.

testmt for testament	Imprs for Imprimis	Exor for Executor
Depont for deponent	JanY for January	Saml for Samuel
Condr for Commander	Agst for Against	Magd for Madalene
Vizt for Videlicet	sd for said	Currt for Current [money]

The reader must be prepared to encounter unexpected but usually understandable abbreviations. If you were writing with a quill pen – which couldn't have been easy – perhaps you also would gratefully shorten long words wherever feasible.

About Dates and Discrepancies

In genealogical writings, it is quite common to find more than one date for the same event; as this pertains to birth, marriage, and death (all of which are "personal" rather than "official"), there simple, logical explanations, and it is helpful to be acquainted with such explanations.

In colonial Virginia and Carolina, the Anglican church had the responsibility – as an arm of government – of recording births and baptisms, banns and marriages, and deaths and burials. Even after achieving independence there was no governmental system for keeping accurate personal records of individuals, neither at the state level nor the federal level. Until the twentieth century, there was no law mandating that births and deaths were of importance only to the families involved, so it was up to the families to keep their own records; most families has a "Family Bible" in which this information could be entered, but even that custom was not widespread during colonial times. As ever, the possibility of "human error" always existed.

Birth, baptism, and christening. Colonial parish records, for the most part, vanished long ago. There was no uniform format for the parish priest to follow, so those records that have survived and quite varied. In many of them, two dates can be found: the date of birth and the date of christening. Either of these dates must be accepted as valid.

The banns and marriage. In earliest times, a marriage intention was announced to the community from the pulpit by the priest who "published" the banns on three successive Sundays to the congregation; non-Anglicans had to put up a bond in lieu of the banns. The primary concern, of course, was responsibility – to spare the community any possible future expense by reason of desertion or fraud (someone would have to look after the widow and orphans). Perhaps the banns were also recorded in writing, but this writer has never found references to such evidence. Marriage bonds were customary in North Carolina also; in Virginia at a later date, after the church of England was disestablished, marriage bonds were obtained from the local authority as a preliminary to marriage. The groom-to-be announced his intention to wed, naming his bride and paying a sum of money as security in the event of fraud or failure on his part to provide for his family. The bond also required the signature of a bondsman, in some locales referred to as the security or surety (abbreviated throughout this work as "bnd, "sec," or "sur"); frequently, the bondsman was a brother of bride or groom or father of the bride. Some records also include information about the actual solemnization of the marriage, including the date and the officiant (written usually as "Min" or "MG" for Minister or Minister of God). Thus, two dates could exist for same event, both of them being valid.

Death and burial. Here, again, it is possible to find two dates or even three dates for the demise of an individual. First, the actual date of death may differ from the date on a headstone. And later, after death certificates became part of the official record – after the turn of the nineteenth century – the date of the Death Certificate could be used as proof of death, thus providing a third possible date for the same event.

The Last Will and Testament. More than one date can be ascribed to a single event. The date of the will may be accepted as a death date, although actually the instrument may have been drawn up at a much earlier date – sometimes years earlier. The date of probate proves that the individual's death has occurred, but sometimes the proving of a will could be delayed, so in many instances there is no way to ascertain the actual date of an individual's death.

The significance for genealogists is that in all three of these personal events there is the possibility of reasonable discrepancy. Whenever slight variations are found, there is no cause for perturbation, for as shown above they can be resolved in the context of historical reality. In this compilation, a single date is generally used unless the situation requires all known dates for the sake of clarification.

Social Rank

Present-day American notions about "being democratic," "unassuming and unpretentious," "elitist," or "nonbigoted" simply did not apply in the seventeenth century, not in England nor in any part of Europe. Class distinctions were taken for granted; individuals always knew which class they belonged to and there was almost unanimous acceptance of one's place on the social scale.

In England, however, unlike the rest of Europe, there was a certain degree of fluidity in what might be called the middle range. People in this group were "the gentry," membership accruing them by right of birth. They were below "the nobility" (although they might have marriage connections with members of the peerage, in which case that connection was factored into the total picture). The peerage included duke, marquess, earl, viscount, and baron.

Members of the gentry were below the peerage, and their status was indicated by the use of honorifics attached to their name. These included, in descending order, the following: knight (prefixed by "Sir" (; squire ("Esquire" or "Esq." following the name); and gentleman (prefixed with "Mr" and /or followed by "Gentleman" or "Gent.'). The wife and daughter of the gentry were addressed as "Mrs" ("Mistress"), regardless of age (little girls having the same form of address as their mothers). Today, "Mr" merely indicates gender, but in colonial America it identified rank; conformance was strictly enforce, along with other law respecting the rights and privileges of caste.

In addition, military titles of rank implied social status as well as military rank. In colonial America, militia titles were a man's for his lifetime. Burgesses and justices also acquired honorary military titles which were permanent; they always indicated a man's standing in his own community. Education also qualified a man to be called "gentleman," and members of the clergy were in that same category.

Some occupations also implied status; besides the clergy (designated as "clerk," perhaps) a man's name would be followed by distinctions such as "merchant,' "Doctor of Physicks," or "Chirurgeons" (surgeon). Mariners were called "Captain."

Honorifics serve the genealogist as markers, along with the designations "Sr" and 'Jr," for men who commonly had one given name, handed down through successive generations. Without middle names (initials), it is often difficult to distinguish between generations of men with identical names, all living at the same place in the same time period.

The Northern Neck of Virginia

The site. The coastline of Virginia, along the Chesapeake Bay, is deeply indented by the four rivers which drain into the Bay. Each indentation forms a slender peninsula – or neck of land – that protects into the Bay. There are three of these "necks."

First, of course, there is the broad, deep James River where in 1607 the English established their headquarters at James Towne, or James Citty as it was also called. They settled up and down the James on both sides until the region began to fill up. Then they began to move northward up the Bay, occupying virgin lands as they progressed.

Just north of the James River was the York River, and the peninsula between the rivers was soon settled. This neck of land has always been known to Virginians as "the Peninsula."

Beyond the York was the Rappahannock River, an Indian name meaning "Quick-Rising River." The colonists began moving into that part of the colony by the 1640; this was the second or middle colony.

Finally, above the Rappahannock flowed the fourth of these tidewater rivers, the Potomac, down from its origin in the mountains to enter the Chesapeake waters. Its Indian name meant "River of Swans." Because its peninsula is the northernmost of the three formations, it came to be known as the Northern Neck. It was visited in 1607 by Captain John Smith; he explored it and produced the first map that shoed it existence. He thought that "heaven and Earth" could not aspire to a better place of habitation, for it had "hills, plaines, valleys, rivers, and brooks all running most pleasantly … [a] fruitfull and delightsome land." It has been assumed that from earliest times it was referred to as the Northern Neck, but the earliest written reference to it as such is dated 1677.

The Neck is about a hundred miles in length but only fifteen to twenty miles wide. The society that flourished there was defined by it remoteness from the rest of the colony. Because of the geographical compactness of that part of Virginia, the socio-political system of the Northern Neck necessitated a spirit of civic coordination on the part of all; in this cultural atmosphere there developed a cohesive network between its inhabitants and those who governed them locally. In doing so, it acquired distinctive characteristics.

However, there was another feature that set it apart: instead of being directly under royal control like the rest of the colony, the Northern Neck was under proprietary contral, [laced there by Charles II in 1650.

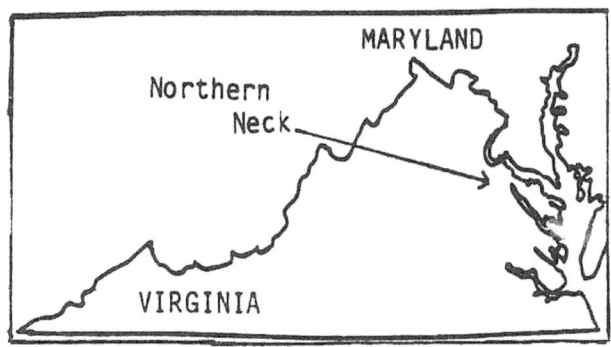

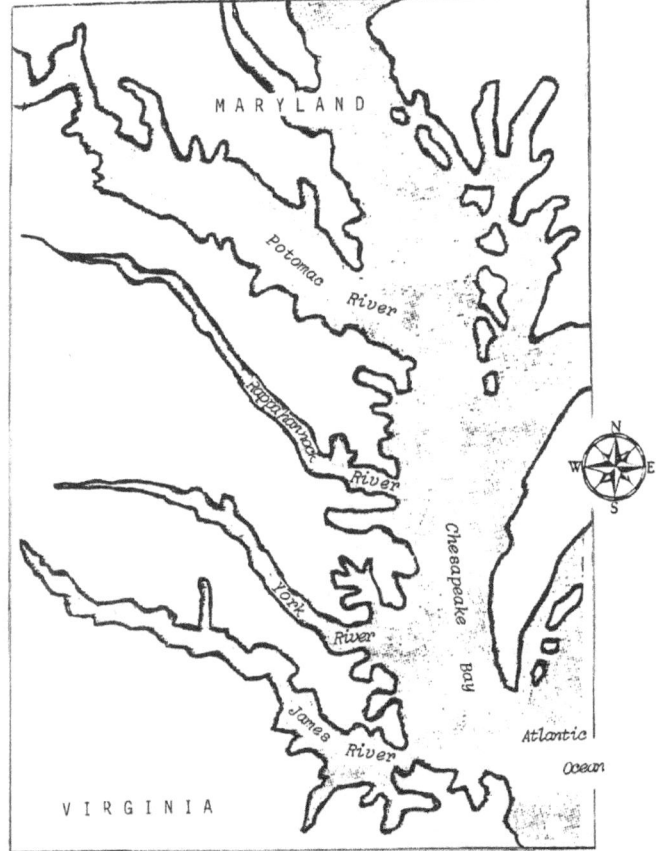

Virginia's tidewater shoreline along the Chesapeake Bay, showing the three necks of land formed by the James, York, Rapahanock, and Potomac Rivers

Because of the geographical compactness of that part of Virginia, the socio-political system of the Northern

Neck necessitated a spirit of civic coordination on the part of all; in this cultural atmosphere there developed a cohesive network between its inhabitants and those who governed them locally. In doing so, it acquired distinctive characteristics.

However, there was another feature that set it apart: instead of being directly under royal control like the rest of the colony, the Northern Neck was under proprietary control, placed there by Charles II in 1650.

Formation of counties. In the New World, population from the outset was moving ever inland from the earliest coastal settlements. Population growth was continuous, and as areas filled up with people, new shires (counties) were created to accommodate the growth. In the Northern Neck, the earliest settlement was at Chicacoan on the Coan River by John Mottram who in 1640 had crossed the Potomac from Maryland, escaping the religious clashes occurring there among Anglicans, Puritans, and Roman Catholics. Mottram was soon joined by like-minded Englishmen; among them were Giles Brent, Henry Fleet, Gerrard Fowke, Thomas Keene, William Metcalfe, Robert Newman, William Presley, and Richard Thompson. And this was the start of English occupation along the Potomac River. They simply crossed the river and started occupying that wild strip of verdant, unoccupied land.

This map of the Northern Neck shows its six counties as they are today

The Virginia Assembly accepted their presence there by creating a county – Northumberland – and taxing the county's residents; that was in 1644. Population growth was so fast that a new county, Lancaster, was carved out in 1651, followed by the establishment of Westmoreland County in 1659. Thereafter, other counties were created: Rappahannock in 1656; Stafford County in 1664, King George County in 1720, and Essex and Richmond Counties in 1692. Connected to mainland Virginia by a narrow isthmus, the Neck remained fairly separated from the mainland – as recently as 1927. Only one bridge crossed the Rappahannock River giving other access to the Neck. Additionally, at that time the Neck had no railroads or airports.

The Proprietary. In 1650 Charles I of England was beheaded, his family was banished. And the Kingdom of England was declared a commonwealth. Charles II, exiled in France, rewarded some of his supporters by giving them possession of land of Virginia – "all that entire Tract, Territory, or porcon of Land situate, lying and being in America, and bounded by and within the heads of the Rivers of Rappahannock and Patawomecke … and said Rivers." Charles was in exile for ten years, but when he returned to the English throne in 1661 he recorded the patent which literally gave the Northern Neck to seven new owners, the Proprietors. Two effects were, first, that landholders now held titles which were no longer valid (even though the charter required the Proprietors to honor all land holdings which had been take up previously under the headright system); and, second, the former landowners had become tenants, obligated to pay annual quit rents to the new owners – a worrisome development for the original landowners. Actually, the land was as much theirs [the landowners'] as property today belongs to the "owners" – as long as they pay the real estate taxes on them. The quit Rents to the proprietors can be viewed as property taxes.

There were also socio-political effects, of course. The purpose here is not to analyze them fully but rather to call attention to them in order to make the point that the Northern Neck, as a proprietary, was "different" from the rest of the colony even though they were all subject to the same laws that governed the colony. "Isolation" is too strong a word, but the Neck was always "apart" from the rest of the colony, even though it was in every other respect a part of Virginia's colonywide jurisdiction.

Of the seven court favorites whom Charles II had named as the Proprietors, only Thomas 2nd Lord Culpeper actually went to Virginia; upon his death in 1689 the Northern Neck descended to his daughter Catherine. She married Thomas fifth Baron Fairfax of Cameron, and their son Thomas the sixth Baron held the land thereafter. Later, the young George Washington was commissioned as a surveyor for "the Right Honorable Thomas Lord Fairfax, Baron of Cameron in that part of Great Britain called Scotland, Proprietor of the Northern Neck of Virginia." The Revolutionary War changed everything, but it was not settled finally until 1816 when the Supreme Court of the United States ruled against the claims of Lord Fairfax's current Heir at Law and Devisee.

MR GERVASE DODSON, GENT.
SURVEYOR & PLANTER
b.1621, England – d. 1661, Virginia

[Gervase Dodson is the man who in 1650 brought the first Woolards from England to Virginia]

Gervase Dodson was born in England in 1621. As a young man during England's Civil Wars, 1642 to 1650, he was involved militarily, serving as "a soldier several years in Ireland and England," by his own account. His statement was ambiguous, however, for he says that he was "for the King and Parilament,'til the death of King Charles I, when he left all and came into this country [Virginia]." That sounds as if he was a Royalist – why else would he have come to the Northern Neck, an Anglican stronghold? However, it is certainly possible that he may have supported both causes, at some point having changed sides.

In 1650, after the defeat of the Royalists, Gervais Dodson, thirty years of age, left England for Virginia. He brought with him a group of thirty-two persons as headrights, for which he received 1600 acres in Northumberland County upon the mouth of Upper Machodic River where it empties into the great Potomac River. His patent was recorded on 1 February 1650. Among those listed as headrights were George Woolard, Ann Woolard, and Samuel Wollard.

The next patent of record for "Jarvos" Dodson for transporting seven persons is dated 14 May 1653 and granted him 350 acres in Northumberland County, adjoining his own land and that of Stephen Norman, located on Peter Phypond's Neck. Two months later he received 1300 acres "in Northumberland, now Westmoreland" on the Upper Machodic for land transactions, buying, selling, and assigning property all along Northern Neck – not only in Northumberland and Westmoreland but also in Stafford, King William, and Lancaster Counties.

As a surveyor, Mr Gervase Dotson's status in the community was one of importance. Some of the records refer to reports filed by him; one of his chain carriers remembered [at a later date, after Dodson's death] working for him when he surveyed the Glebe lands. For the government he surveyed the Indian lands and located their boundaries. He seemed to enjoy at all times the respect of his fellow colonists.

This was the period of the Commonwealth, when back in London Oliver Cromwell headed the government. The Anglican religion was no longer the Church of England, so the Dissident practiced. In Virginia and Maryland – especially in Maryland – Puritans clashed with Anglicans and Roman Catholics, and soon this struggle was joined by the Quakers. Virginians were forbidden by law to use their Book of Common Prayer but did so anyway – the authorities had no means of enforcement, and the Northern Neck was far enough away from Jamestown to escape notice. Typically, Virginians looked on this period as "the usurpation of Cromwell." One of those who joined the Quakers at that time was Gervase Dodson.

In 1660, however, there was another change in the head of state, for Charles II was brought back to the throne; this occasioned yet another reversal in religious matters. Those who had executed his father – called the Regicides – were punished; others were allowed to petition for amnesty from the new king by signing an oath of loyalty. On 9 March 1660, Mr Gervas Dodson, "acting under the Royal Proclamation of pardon ... petitions for the benefit of the proclamation." He stated that "he ever loved the King's person and posterity, and only opposed that [which] the parliament said ruined him and the country – evil Counsel." That was the standard excuse used by all – they rationalized that the King himself was a blameless person who had been corrupted by his "evil Counsel."

A short while later, Gervase Dodson was punished for his religion. He had met with other men at the home of David Dussin to practice their Quaker beliefs, "contrary to law.' The punishment was twenty lashes. This occurred on the 26th of June 1660. He was bout forty years of age.

Chronology: Gervase Dodson, Gent.
b. c1621 – d.1661, Virginia

<u>1621</u>	Gervase Dodson was born in England
<u>1 Feb 1650</u>	Gervase Dodson, Gent received 1600 a. Northumberland Co, Ely on Potomeck R., Sly on mouth of Upper Machotiq R. for tr of 32 persons, including Geo Woolard, Ann Woolard, and Saml Wollard (C&P 1:206)
<u>14May 1653</u>	Jarvis Dodson received 350 a. in Northumb Co adj Stephen Norman on Peter Phyponds necke, for tr 7 persons (C&P 1:236)
<u>13 Oct 1653</u>	Mr Gervase Dodson received a patent for 1300 a. "in Nothumberland, now Westmoreland on the upper Machoticke Necke," adj Palmer Hinton, Mr Christopher Boyce, Mrs Townshend for tr 16 persons (C&P) 1:235)
<u>1653 – 1654</u>	Gervais Dodson was a surveyor; these years were identified by word of Abra Joyce (Northumb Bk 16:93; Fleet 1:521)
<u>1653 – 1659</u>	[Exact date not given] Gervase Dodson sold 200 a. to Geo Ball; wit. John Dodman Peter Knight (Westm Rec 1653-57, p. 24; cited in Fleet 1:52
<u>8 Mar 1654</u>	Jno Jenkins of Westm Co, planter, assigned 1000 a. to Gervase Dodson; wits. Gervase x Bell, John x Williams (Westm rec 1653-57, p. 21; Fleet 1:653
<u>16 May 1654</u>	Gervase Dodson of WEstm Co sold 200 a. in Upper Machaticke to John Jenkins (Westm Rec 1653-57, p. 23; Fleet 1:653)
<u>7 Jul 1654</u>	Capt Thos Davis of Warwick Co gave his "Lre of Attu" to his "loving friend" Gervase Dodson to sell land for him (Westm Rec 1653-57, p.22; Fleet 1:653)
<u>20 Jul 1654</u>	"The Court doth order that Mr Dodson shall goe downe and see what the difference is between them [Thos Gaskins v. David Spiller] and that he take with him John Gresham, Rich Budd, Thos Hopkins, John Waddy, and report the difference to the next Court" (VCA(1) 2:61; Northumb OB 2:27)
<u>Aug 1654</u>	Gervase Dodson assigned 1300 a. in Stafford Co, Upper Machodoc Neck adj the Townshend patent to Maj John Smith (W&M(1) 12:247-48; GVF 2:99-101)
<u>22 Aug 1654</u>	Gervase Dodson, Surveyor, sold 1000 a. Westm Co to John Dodman (Ibid.)
<u>22 Aug 1654</u>	Gervase Dodson, Surveyor, sold 300 a. on Mackaticke R adj Gervase Bell and also adj himself [Dodson], "running Westerly a mile into the woods" (Westm Rec 1653-57, p.23; Fleet 1:653)
<u>25 Feb 1655</u>	Ger. Dodson gave a "sworn statement re his survey of Indian lands," showing boundaries, etc. (Northumb Bk 16.72 Fleet 1:521)
<u>20 Aug 1655</u>	On this date "Mr Gervase Dodson" gave a deposition, swearing that his age was " 34 years or thereabouts" (Northumb Rec 1652-55, 14:52; Fleet 1:399,521)

3 Mar 1657 Gervas Dodson received a patent near Corotoman Ck and Haddaways Ck "near the glade above Wicc ___ Indian Town" (Lancaster Co Rec 1637-40, Bk 2:318; Fleet 1:153)

16 Sep 1657 Mr Gervayse Godson [sic] was granted 600 a. by Sam Matthews, Esq in Lanc Co, S side Corotoman Ck, bounded by land "by some called Mr Wetherlyes land," adj John Taylor, dcd, for tr of 12 persons (lanc Rec 1637-40, Bk 2:190; Fleet 1:130)

27 Apr 1658 Mr Gervise Dodson was granted 750 a. in G.W. Parish, which later devolved to his wid Isabel, his heir (Northumb Bk 16:223; Fleet 1:591)

17 Aug 1658 Gervas Dodson sold to John Smith a tract in Upper Machodick Neck "which deed had been acknowledged by Dodson's atty in Northumb Co" (VMH 20:326)

27 Aug 1658 A grant of 2000 a. was made to Gervase Dodson during "the usurpation of Cromwell," by the Governor of VA; later, this land was assigned to Henry Corbin (VMH 5:222)

27 Aug 1658 Sam Mathews, Esq granted to Gervayse Dodson 2000 a. "in Potomac ffreshes, above Capt Brent's, adj land of Mr Burbage and that of Mr Henry Vincent, for tr of 40 persons"(Lanc Re 1637-40, Bk 2:368; Fleet 1:161)

13 Oct 1658 Gervas Dodson patented 600 a., 231 a., and 100. Lying in St Paul's Parish, Staf Co, VA (Staf DB 2:429; GVF 1:266)

29 Nov 1658 Gervase Dodson was granted 500 a. on the Potomac near Corotoman Ck (later sold to Mr Geo Wale) (Lanc Rec 1637-40, Bk 2:318; Fleet 1:153)

29 Nov 1658 Col John Trussell & Gervase Dodson patented 1000 a. Northumb, E of Chickacone R., adj Jacob Coutanceau, Col Mattrom, dcd, Mr Chandler; for tr of 20 persons (C&P 1:382)

20 Dec 1658 Gervayse Dodson of Northumb Co sold for £ 40 sterling to be pd in London by Mr Geo Wale to Col Wm Clayborne "according to tenor of three bills of Exchange" directed "to Mr Nich Trott at Vine Court in 'Bishops Gate St …'" (lanc Rec 1637-40, Bk 2:190; Fleet 1:130)

20 Dec 1658 Gervayse Dodson assigned to Mr Geo Wale "a survey of 500 a. … near Wiccocomoco Indian Town … enter in the office with Mr Tho Brereton"; wits. Will Strachey, will Spicer (Lanc Rec 1637-40, Bk 2:191; Fleet 1:131

20 May 1659 Gervase Dodson gave a calf to John, s/o John Hulett (Northumb Bk 15:21)

24 May 1659 Gervayse Dodson & wife Isbell appointed "our loving friend Thos Jones" their atty to acknowledge sale of 660 a. to Mr Geo Wale; wits. Rich Nealmes, Tho Shelton, signed by both Dodsons (Lanc Rec 1637-40, Bk 2:191; Fleet 1:131)

22 Oct 1659 Gervayse Dodson assigned 2000 a. in Potomac ffreshes, received from Saml Mathews, Esq, to Hen Corbyn, wit. Will Bayliffe, Tho Middleton (Fleet 1:161; Lanc Rec 1637-40, Bk 2:369)

9 Mar 1660 On this date, "acting under the Royal Proclamation of pardon, Gervas Dodson, who was a soldier several years in Ireland and England for the King and Parliament, 'till the death of King Charles I, when he left all and came into this country, petitions for the benefit of the proclamation. He ever loved the King's person and posterity, and only opposed that [which] the parliament said ruined him and the country – evil Counsel" (Northumb Co Rec, cited in VMH 10:318)

26 Jun 1660 — Gervase Dodson was given 20 lashes for being a Quaker, he having met at the home of David Dussin with Robt Lambdon, John Smith, Thos Shields "contrary to law" (Northumb Bk 2:122; in Fleet 1:521)

1 Aug 1660 — Jarvis Dodson sold to Nath Jones 460 a. in Staf Co (GVF 2:809; W&M(1) 12:269)

2 Oct 1660 — Thos Dodson "gave land to Jervas Dodson" (Northumb Rec 1645-1720, Bk 3:64)

7 Jan 1661 — Gervase Dodson's will of this date; Isabel was his relict and extr (Northumb Bk 15:58; Fleet 1:521)

4 Feb 1662 — Robt King's patent on Great Wiccocomoco R. referred to land of Gervase Dodson, dcd (C&P 1:488)

10 Mar 1662 — John Haynie's 350 a. at the head of Wiccocomico R. "bounded S and E upon land of Gervase Dodson, dcd" (C&P 1:462)

29 Apr 1662 — Jas Pope & wife Dorcas sold to Wm and Peter Presley 1000 a. upon the head of Chingohem Creek adj Mottran, the sd Presleys, Trussell, and Gervace Dodson (W&M(1) 22:210)

23 Aug 1669 — "Abra Joyce ran a chain for him [Jervise Dodson] 14 or 15 years ago for surveying land for the Glebe" (Northumb Bk 16:93; Fleet 1:521)

30 Jul 1746 — The will of Henry Lee, Gent conveyed to son Henry land in Prince Wm Co at "Free Stone pt, Neapsco, and Powels Ck which was granted by patent to Gervase Dodson [see 27 Aug 1658, above] for 2000 a." (Westm D&W 10:364, as cited in T 4:215) [This became the site of "Leesylvania," the historic plantation.]

Dodson's Legacy

Although the relationship (if any) of Thomas Dodson to Gervais Dodson has not been established, they were the only two men of that name in this community. Thomas Dodson had several patents recorded (other than any mention of him above). The entries that follow appear to be the last mention of Thomas Dodson in the Northern Neck.

22 Mar 1666 — Rich Lynny's patent described 1200 a. Northumb Co, "upon the high lands above the head of Deviding Ck, etc," granted unto Thos Dodson 29 Nov 1658, by him deserted (C&P 1:556)

17 Oct 1668 — Thos Dodson willed his estate to wife Frances and son Thomas "who is under 21 yrs of age" (Westm WB 1; Crozier, Wills, p. 5)

Later, other Dodsons lived in the Northern Neck, but they do not claim descent from Thomas. It is as if Mr Gervais Dodson, of the many land holdings, had never been there.

APPENDIX B
OTHER COLONIAL WOOLLARDS: IN VIRGINIA
OTHER THAN RICHMOND COUNTY

In the history of Virginia, the very earliest appearance of the name (allowing for spelling/transcription errors) occurred in 1610/11 when John Wooller/Wooler was a subscriber of the Virginia Company Of London. Wooler's share in the amount of £37.10.0 was the equivalent of nearly $1000 American in 1978. No effort made to identify this John Wooller.

As already demonstrated in this research [see Part II], the colonial records for the 17th century provide evidence that a family of the surname "Woollard: came in 1650 to the Northern Neck where they were communicants of North Farnham Parish. There is only one other person of that name elsewhere in the colonies during that period of time, which naturally leads to the assumption that they may have been related to each other. However, the other Woollard – William by name – was living in isle of Wight County on the James River; this in itself does not preclude a family connection, but on the other hand there is no evidence that they were related. Nevertheless, William Woollard's presence in the colony needs to be documented as part of the total picture.

Most of the references to William Woollard are in respect to his legal attempts as an heir of Justinian Cooper, dcd to collect his due; however, Colonel Nathaniel Bacon, Jr was also a claimant. And their suits were in the courts for almost a quarter of a century; the final settlement – not until 1672 – was an equal division in terms of monetary value.

Justinian Cooper, Gentleman was prominent in the James River area, and his name appears frequently in the records of the time. Apparently, he was not survived by children of his own. The claims of Woollard and Bacon may derive from debts, loans, or mutual business ventures. Selected excerpts, as given in the chronology below, provide glimpses of these men.

From these scant glimpses, only a few personal details can be derived. It is know that Captain William Woollard, referred to as a merchant and also a mariner, was from Harwitch in Essex, before residing in Isle of Wight County, 1626-1672.

Chronology

<u>1610 – 1611</u>	John Wooller/Wooler was a subscriber to the VA Company of London, pledging £ 37.10.0; his name appears on the Huntington List (VCA (2) 3:7, 19)
<u>20 Sep 1629</u>	Justinian Cooper, Gent & wife Anne (wid/o Jas Harrison) bought land on Warrisquick bay from Giles Jones (Boddie-1938, 530)
<u>13 Sep 1636</u>	Just Cooper was granted a patent for 1050 a. In Warris Co, NW upon headwaters of Lawnes Ck, SE upon the Back CK, "NE upon his dwelling howse & into the woods" for trnsp of 20 persons (C&P 1:47)
<u>26 Mar 1650</u>	Just Cooper's will mentioned "godchildren," his bro Rich Cossey, and Edw Pyland; friend Capt Wm

Barnard to be overseer (Boddie-1938, 531-2)

20 Feb 1666   Capt Wm Woolard gave letter of atty to Mr John Cary to make "public clayme" to the estate of Just Cooper, dcd as "lawful heir" (IofW Co Rec, 167; W&M(1)7:224-25, 228)

1671   Wm Woolard of the IofW, merchant [No other commentary but it does identify him as a merchant] (VLR, 170)

1671   Deed of Wm Woolard, "late of Harwich in Essex, England, mariner, but nor resident in IofW Co, VA, heir of Just. Cooper since deceased, to Coll. Nath Bacon, Esq" (VLR, 170; W&M (1) 7:224-25 VMH 21:63

9 Feb 1671   Wm Woolard appointed Thos Moore his atty (Boddie-1938, 563)

26 Mar 1672   "Indenture made 26 March 1672 between Wm Woolard, late of Hartwich in Essex, mariner but now resident of Isle of Wight. The said Woolard is the next heir of Justinian Cooper long since dead of one part, and the Hon Col Nathaniel Bacon of the other part. Whereas there have been divers suits at James City between said Woolard and sd Nathaniel Bacon…." [Final resolution: Bacon took the land and reimbursed Woolard 40,000 lbs tbco; wits. Wm Cole Jas Powell] (Boddie-1938, 563-4)

NOTE: If this was the same man who led "Bacon's Rebellion," then he had only a few years to enjoy the lands acquired from Just Cooper, for that Nathaniel Bacon died in 1676. However, one source says that the rebel Bacon (born in Suffolk) did not emigrate to Virginia until 1673 in which case he probably could not have been pressing his legal suits for some twenty years. According to one source, Col Nath Bacon of IofW was uncle to the rebel.

7 Jul 1688   An interesting follow-up to the above is an estate settlement in Saffron Walden in Essex, England that mentioned John Woollard, chandler, and John Cooper. The links to Capt Wm Woollard of IofW in Virginia are the maritime occupations of ship captain and chandler, and also association of the names Woollard and Cooper (Currer-Briggs, 547).

An Incident in Loudoun County, Virginia

A number of religious groups were present in colonial Loudoun County, Virginia. Most of their written records no longer exist, but those that are available contain interesting glimpses of local events and customers, in addition to reporting the usual business activities of the church.

The Religious Society of Friends (Quakers) was in the vicinity as early as 1745, as part of the Fairfax Monthly Meeting. Entries for 1772 refer to a serious transgression of one of their members, Abraham Todhunter, who was reported as having "behaved badly toward a young woman, daughter of Wm. Woolard." Two months later it was reported that Todhunter had submitted a paper in which he "condemned his scandalous conduct toward a young woman." However, his confession was not sufficient to redeem his "act so highly immodest scarce to be paralleled." The Meeting expelled him for "the general looseness of his conduct and neglect of duty."

The father of this unfortunate young woman may have been William[4] Woollard (died 1785, Loudoun County) who is known to have had four daughters. Three of them would have been appropriate age to be referred to a "a young woman."

(From *Early Church Records of Loudoun County, Virginia*, compiled by Marty Hiatt. D.G.R.S.)

Other Colonial Woollards: In North Carolina

It is believed that emigrants from Nansemond and Ile of Wight Counties in Virginia established North Carolina's first permanent settlement (Boddie-1938, 493). At any rate, by the 1690s, many Virginians had moved across the Carolina dividing line into the Albemarle region that was established in 1663; other early counties included Perquimans in 1668 and Chowan in 1671 where Woollard families are to be found. Later, Beaufort and Craven Counties (1712), Bertie Countie (1722), Edgecombe County (1741), and Martin County (1774) were established to accommodate the Albemarle overflow as its residents – including Woollards – pushed westward to acquire new living space.

Generally, it is conceded that the earliest North Carolina Woollards were members of the Virginia nuclear family in Richmond County. Certainly, Richard [son of John 2 Woollard] was one of the earliest, and the name "Richard Woolard" was present there in North Carolina for many generations to come.

Two other given names that help establish the link with Richmond County are "Jesper" and "Willoughby." Samuel[4] Woollard married Mary Anne Jesper, c1750; one of their sons was William Jesper Woollard. About the same time, a list of Richmond County voters for 1758 included John and Thomas Jesper. Later, the North Carolina censuses listed Jesper Woollard (written sometimes as "Jasper") in Beaufort, Craven, Cumberland, and Edgecombe Counties between 1790 and 1828.

The Willoughby family was prominent in the Northern Neck counties from very early times. The earliest Woollard of record to bear that name was Willoughby Woolard, son of John (1758-1833) in Bath County. The North Carolina census for 1800 shows Willibough Woollard as a resident of Beaufort County; in 1810 he was listed as "Wiley." Still later, some of the sons had moved into Tennessee, notably Maury County, and in 1820 the census listed Williiba Wollard in that county. The use of this name continued – it may still be found.

The North Carolina branch has been extensively documented and is characterized by its spelling form (one I rather than two I's). The purpose of this summary is the distinguish among the three basic groups: in Richmond County, Virginia; in North Carolina since the 1690s; and the small line which went to Loudoun County, Virginia and from there to Kentucky, Indi-and, Illinois, Ohio, and Tennessee.

Other Colonial Wollards: In West Virginia

There is another colonial group of the same name but not related to those who originated in Richmond County, Virginia. They were immigrants to the Port of Philadelphia out of that came to be called "Pennsylvania Dutch." The name "Wullart" underwent Americanization, appearing usually as "Wollard" or "Wollart."

An example is John Wollerd of Hardy County, West Virginia, whose will was dated 15 August 1809; his daughters were named Christina, Catharina, and Magdalena, typical Swiss and German custom of that era (R.B. Johnston, 142).

Another example of the Germanic Woolard families in West Virginia is Ludwig Wollard. He made his will on 26 February 1821 in Harrison County, West Virginia (Johnston, 125).

John Woollard, Soldier of Revolutionary War

Of the several Woollards who saw service during the Revolutionary War, one has been identified as a native of Loudoun County, Virginia. Surely, this John must be a brother of Isaac Woollard of Green and Hardin Counties, Kentucky, but has not yet been fully researched. The information given below is abstracted from a letter (dated 5 March 1937) from A.D. Hiller, Executive Assistant to the Administrator [address in Ohio not identified].

"John Woollard was born 1744, Loudoun County, Virginia. On 1 September 1780 he volunteered to the 'westward destines' to fight against the Indians. He was in the Company of Capt Jas Radican, under Lt Thomas Cravens and Ens Hutchinson and went to Fort Pitt [Pittsburg]. He was discharged 1 March 1781.

"About May 1781 John Woollard was drafted into the service of the United States for 3 months, in the

Company of Capt Hugh Douglass, Lt Thomas King, and Ens Abraham Mason in Col Merriewether's Virginia Regiment, attached to the Battallion of Maj Thomas Risby.

"He returned to Loudoun County where he remained until 1817, when he moved to Ohio. He was about 88 years of age in 1832, residing in Richland Township, Clinton County, Ohio."

From Official Records and the National Archives, Washington, DC

The official records of military service during the Revolution contain several entries for "John Woollard." The following references are thought to refer to the John Woollard of Loudoun who "moved to Ohio."

- Woollard, John – Clinton, Ohio Militia Pension List; approx age in 1833 – 90 yrs. From John H. Gwathmey's Historical register of *Virginians in the Revolution, 1775 to 1783*

- Woollard, Jno – Age 90; Clinton Co, Ohio. From Joseph Thompson McAllister's *Virginia Militia in the Revolutionary War* (in a section titled "List of Pensioners Residing Outside of Virginia in 1835, whose Pensions were Granted for Services as Virginia Militiamen")

- # 2434 John Wollard (Thos Warren, Assignee), Pvt., Cont Line, 3 yrs, 9 Feb 1784. From Samuel Mackay Wilson's *Catalogue of Revolutionary Soldiers and Sailors of Commonwealth of Virginia, Land Bounty Warrants*

APPENDIX C
ALLIED FAMILIES

To this point, the chief objective of this compilation has been the tracing of Isaac Woollard's line through his grandson William S. Woollard of Hickman County, Tennessee. All statements were supported by chronologies of events. In this section, however, the focus will be on the collateral lines of the Woollards through their spouses (if known), beginning with Mary Laxton, wife of Samuel Woollard, and continuing with Harriett Lancaster and her line, Mary Alston Jones, Luther Everett Mathis, and John Cyril Malloy (all on the right side of the tree in Chart 1) and their respective lines.

Descendants of Isaac Woollard of Virginia & Kentucky
Through his grandson William S. Woollard of Hickman County, Tennessee

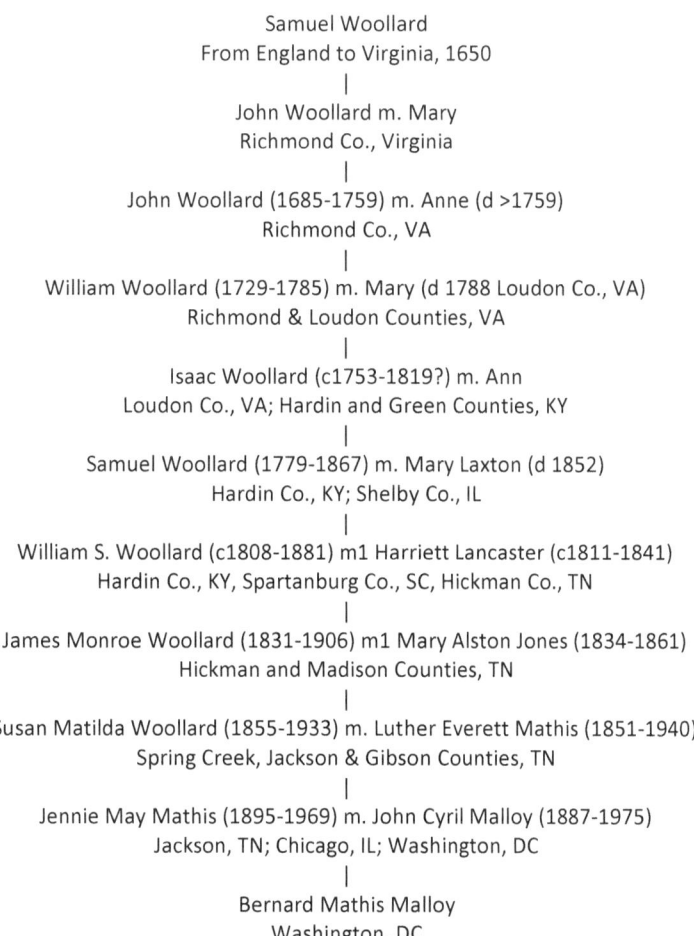

Samuel Woollard
From England to Virginia, 1650
|
John Woollard m. Mary
Richmond Co., Virginia
|
John Woollard (1685-1759) m. Anne (d >1759)
Richmond Co., VA
|
William Woollard (1729-1785) m. Mary (d 1788 Loudon Co., VA)
Richmond & Loudon Counties, VA
|
Isaac Woollard (c1753-1819?) m. Ann
Loudon Co., VA; Hardin and Green Counties, KY
|
Samuel Woollard (1779-1867) m. Mary Laxton (d 1852)
Hardin Co., KY; Shelby Co., IL
|
William S. Woollard (c1808-1881) m1 Harriett Lancaster (c1811-1841)
Hardin Co., KY, Spartanburg Co., SC, Hickman Co., TN
|
James Monroe Woollard (1831-1906) m1 Mary Alston Jones (1834-1861)
Hickman and Madison Counties, TN
|
Susan Matilda Woollard (1855-1933) m. Luther Everett Mathis (1851-1940)
Spring Creek, Jackson & Gibson Counties, TN
|
Jennie May Mathis (1895-1969) m. John Cyril Malloy (1887-1975)
Jackson, TN; Chicago, IL; Washington, DC
|
Bernard Mathis Malloy
Washington, DC

In Appendix C, the treatment of each distaff pedigree consists of *belief* narrative descriptions, *general* in nature rather than particular, intended to present an overview of what is known at this time about each family branch. Some of this material was drawn from the published genealogies of other compilers; some of it is based on family collections handed down to Bernard Mathis Malloy, not necessarily proven by new research (hence, no chronologies are given as documentation – except for the Lancaster line, which does break new ground for inclusion in this work). In other words, Appendix C presents the findings up this point in time [as available to the compilers] without verification.

Research of the Mathis-Carlton-Shelley line is in progress by the authors, and publication is planned. Also, new research on the Cooke-Rucker-McGehee line has not been completed and may yield further information. Likewise, research of the Ashtons is ongoing.

Laxton

Among American surnames, "Laxton" is one of the most unusual; even today, occurrences of this name are quite rare. Searching for Laxtons in the record books of Colonial America is further complicated by a change which has taken place in cursive writing styles: namely, the uppercase L and S were almost identical throughout most of the nineteenth century, resembling very closely the "S" as it is capitalized by contemporary writers. As a result, transcribers of early records tend to interpret "Laxton" as "Saxton." Ideally, in order to resolve this ambiguity, a researcher should seek out the original copies of all Saxtons to determine if any of them were actually Laxtons; unfortunately, this is not always feasible. Fortunately, for a period of thirty years following the Revolutionary War, the Laxtons of Green County can be clearly identified, as presented below. Dubious instances of "Saxtons" have been omitted from the description that follows.

Laxtons in Virginia

The majority of Kentucky's earliest settlers came from Virginia; it is possible that the Laxtons of Jefferson County, Kentucky may also have lived first in Virginia. For examples, in 1752, one Thomas Laxton was listed as a tithable of Lunenburg County, Virginia.

The French & Indian Wars. In 1758 the campaign known as the French & Indian Wars was being waged by militia units drawn from many Virginia counties. Among these men were Thomas Sexton of Bedford County and Samuel Sexton of Brunswick County. [Note that Brunswick was the parent county of Lunenburg, mentioned above, as home of Thomas Laxton.]

In Loudoun County. At Least one family named "Laxton" lived in Loudoun County during the period that William Woollard and his sons were residing there. In 1769 the names of Charles Laxton, Charles Laxton Junr, and Nathaniel Laxton appeared on a list of tithables taken by Craven Peyton; also on that list were William Woollard and his son Isaac.

Lord Dunmore's War. By 1774 Fincastle County was the frontier of Virginia and, incidentally, the administrative center for the Kentucky Territory. The settlers were harassed by an uprising of the Shawnee Indians, which prompted the governor, Lord Dunmore, to raise troops from all the Southwestern counties to meet the enemy at Point Pleasant. Few details are available, but a list of payees show that James Laxtent served 103 days in Bledsoe's Company and Samuel Paxton was stationed at Maiden Springs Station.

Laxtons in Kentucky

In 1782, William Lagston was among those early Kentuckians in Jefferson County who qualified for a grant of 400 acres by Act of the Virginia Assembly. This is the earliest appearance of this surname in the western part of Virginia which would become Kentucky.

Although the Kentucky census of 1790 was destroyed in the War of 1812, Thomas Lagston's name appears in the Nelson County Circuit Court Minutes for that year as the defendant in a complaint brought by Robert Elder.

In 1795, the Green County tax records showed three adults of that name: Thomas Laxton, James Laxon, and James Laxon, Jr. Clearly, two generations were represented here. The following year, Joseph Saxton was living in Jefferson County, probably a descendant of the original William. It is reasonable to assume that all were related.

Thereafter (1798 to 1810), a very small group of adult Laxtons was represented on the tax and marriage records of Green County. There were three men – George, James, and Thomas – and two women, Hannah and Mary. As already shown, Mary married Samuel Woollard, and about 1820 they moved to Hickman County, Tennessee. After 1810, no Laxtons appear in the record books of Green and Hardin Counties, Kentucky.

Laxtons in Tennessee

There are no Laxtons on the 1820 census for Green County, Kentucky. What could have happened to them? Perhaps they moved to Tennessee along with the Woollards, for the 1820 census shows James Laxton ("over 45 years of age"), Thomas Laxton (26 to 45 years), and Jesse Laxton (16 to 26 years) were in Hickman County. This appears to be a three-generational span -- two generations, certainly. The name "Jesse" can be interpreted as a link to the Green County Laxtons, deriving most probably from Thomas Laxton's marriage in 1799 to Hannah Elkin, daughter of Jesse Elkin. In 1830 James, Thomas, and John Laxton were listed on the Hickman County census.

This is all that is known of the Laxtons of Green County. Where they came from before 1782 has not been established, although the presence of a Laxton family in Loudoun County, Virginia at the same time as the Woollards is strong evidence. Other speculation is possible, of course, but these are few clues; the most logical supposition – based on the history of the region – is that they came from Virginia.

Chronology

1752	Thos Laxton was listed as 1 tithe on a list taken by John Phelps, Lunenburg Co, VA (Bell, Sunlight, 209)
Sep 1758	Thos Sexton was listed on militia roster of Bedford Co, VA for French & Indian War (Hening 7:206)
Sep 1758	Saml Sexton on militia roster of Brunswick Co, VA for F&I War (Hening 7:212)
1769	Chas Laxton, Chas Laxton Junr, and Nath Laxton, as well as Wm Woollard and son Isaac, were included on a "List of Tithables taken by Craven Peyton," Loud Co, VA (Loose papers, Loud CO Ct Hse)
1774	Military and public service accts of Lord Dunmore's War show Saml Paxton in Smith's Company and Jas Laxtent in Bledsoe's Company (Kegley, 19, 20)
3 Dec 1782	Wm Lagston was among those who were entitled to a grant of 400 a. by an Act of Assembly in May 1782. (Jeff Co Ct Min, 14; eff Co Rec 1:12-13)
KY Cns 1790	These records were destroyed by the British during the War of 1812
13 Aug 1790	Docketed: Robt Elder, pltf vs Thos Lagston, deft (Nels Co circ Ct MinBk, 1790-1791:273,279; LDS # 009637)
15 Dec 1790	Disposition of Robt Elder's complaint agst Thos Lagston in Nels Co: "Ordered that this Petition be Abated (?) by the return thereof" (LDS # 009637:331)
30 May 1795	Tax List for Green Co, Ky included Thos Laxton, Jas Laxson, and Jas Laxson Jr, all listed as "over 21" (LDS # 8004)
11 Oct 1796	Jos Saxton was wit. When Thos Norris m. Honor Andrews (see Alex Andrew), Jeff Co (Thurston, 26)
5 Jul 1798	Geo Saxton m. Sally Burks, consent by Isham Burks, Green Co, #367 (LDS Film # 592673)

<u>3 Jan 1799</u>	Jas Laxtin m. Zelpha Merideth d/o Wm L. Merideth/Mereda, Green Co, Bond #285 (Scott, 30)
<u>1799</u>	Hannah Laxton m. Jesse Elkin, sec Saml Willard
<u>7 Dec 1799</u>	In Green Co, Thos Laxtin m. Hannah Elkin d/o Jesse Elkin, sec Saml Woollard, # 284 (Scott, 30) [Later, Jesse Laxton lived in Hickman Co, TN]
<u>12 Dec 1799</u>	Saml Woolard m. Mary Laxton/Saxton; sec Thos Laxton, min. John Mulky, Bond #265 (Scott, 59); also reported as being on "the report of "Benj Lynn, Min. (Green MB A: 41)
<u>US Cns 1800</u>	Records of KY were destroyed by the British during the War of 1812
<u>1800</u>	Jas Saxon was on the Green Co, KY Tax List (Jackson, Early KY 1:15)
<u>1800</u>	Thos Laxton was on the list of the Sheriff of Green Co who collected "fees" for the year; on same list was Saml Woolard (GCR 2:3)
<u>12 Aug 1803</u>	Thos Sexton (Saxton?) was on Tax List for Madison Co, KY (Riedel)
<u>1805</u>	Geo Laxton purchased 2 barrels of corn at the estate sale of Wm Gee (LDS # 594-634, Green Will Ndx, 1794-1830)
<u>KY Cns 1810</u>	Geo Laxton (45 or older) was in Green Co, 4000-03001 (p.265)
<u>KY Cns 1820</u>	No Laxtons were listed in this census
<u>TN Cns 1820</u>	Jas Laxton (45+), Jesse Laxton (16-26 yrs), and Thos Laxton (26-45 yrs) were in Hick Co, TN
<u>TN Cns 1830</u>	Thos (50-60 yrs) and John Laxton (age not shown) were in Hick Co (p. 271), as was Jas Laxton (age 40-50) (p. 294)

The following chart is a back construction of three *hypothetical* generations of Laxtons based on the chronology above. It is believed that the father of Mary Laxton was either James or Thomas, but there is no proof other than the fact that Thomas Laxton was security when Mary married Samuel Woollard (1799).

Chart 2: *Hypothetical* Ancestry of Mary Laxton of Green & Hardin Co, KY

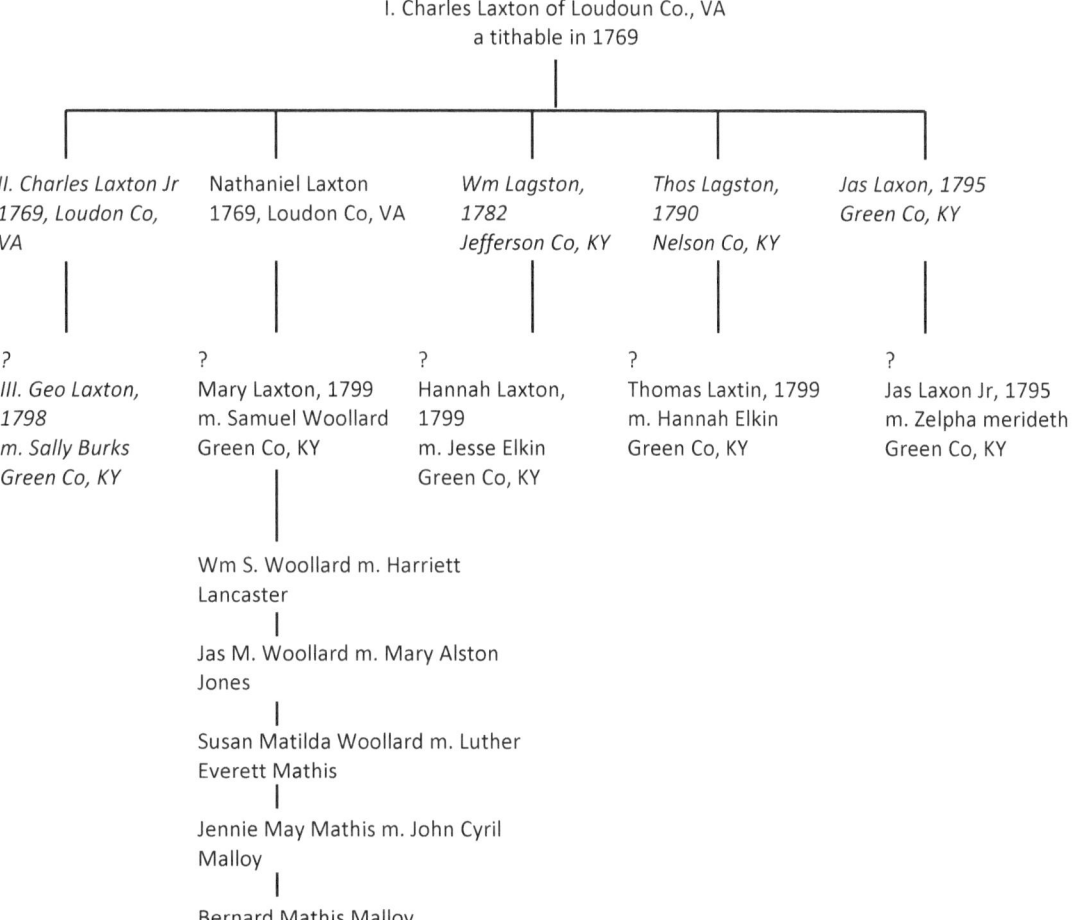

I. Charles Laxton of Loudoun Co., VA
a tithable in 1769

II. Charles Laxton Jr	Nathaniel Laxton	*Wm Lagston,*	*Thos Lagston,*	*Jas Laxon, 1795*
1769, Loudon Co,	*1769, Loudon Co, VA*	*1782*	*1790*	*Green Co, KY*
VA		*Jefferson Co, KY*	*Nelson Co, KY*	

? ? ? ? ?

III. Geo Laxton,	Mary Laxton, 1799	Hannah Laxton,	Thomas Laxtin, 1799	Jas Laxon Jr, 1795
1798	m. Samuel Woollard	1799	m. Hannah Elkin	m. Zelpha merideth
m. Sally Burks	Green Co, KY	m. Jesse Elkin	Green Co, KY	Green Co, KY
Green Co, KY		Green Co, KY		

Wm S. Woollard m. Harriett Lancaster

Jas M. Woollard m. Mary Alston Jones

Susan Matilda Woollard m. Luther Everett Mathis

Jennie May Mathis m. John Cyril Malloy

Bernard Mathis Malloy

- All *known* Laxtons in Loudoun Co, VA and the Green / Hardin Co, KY region, 1769-1799, have been incorporated into this chart.
- Generations I and II are partially hypothetical, as indicated by *italics* and question marks
- Assuming that I-Charles Laxton of Loudoun Co, VA is the grandfather of Mary Laxton, her father might be his son or nephew (as shown in Generation II).
- Mary, Hannah and Thomas Laxton of Generation III all married in 17999, an indication that they were of the same generation.

Laxton or Saxton? Samples of 18th Century Script

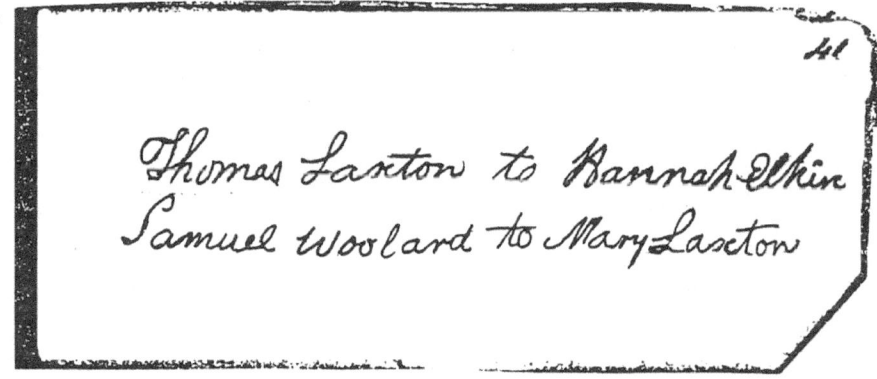

The entry above from the Green County "Little Book" of marriage records (page 41) shows the marriages of Thomas Laxton to Hannah Elkin and Samuel Woolard to Mary Laxton. "Laxton" has been interpreted as "Saxton" by several transcribers. At first glance, it could be mistaken for Saxton, but a closer look shows that this clerk's style of handwriting does distinguish between the two – compare the S of Samuel with the L's shown.

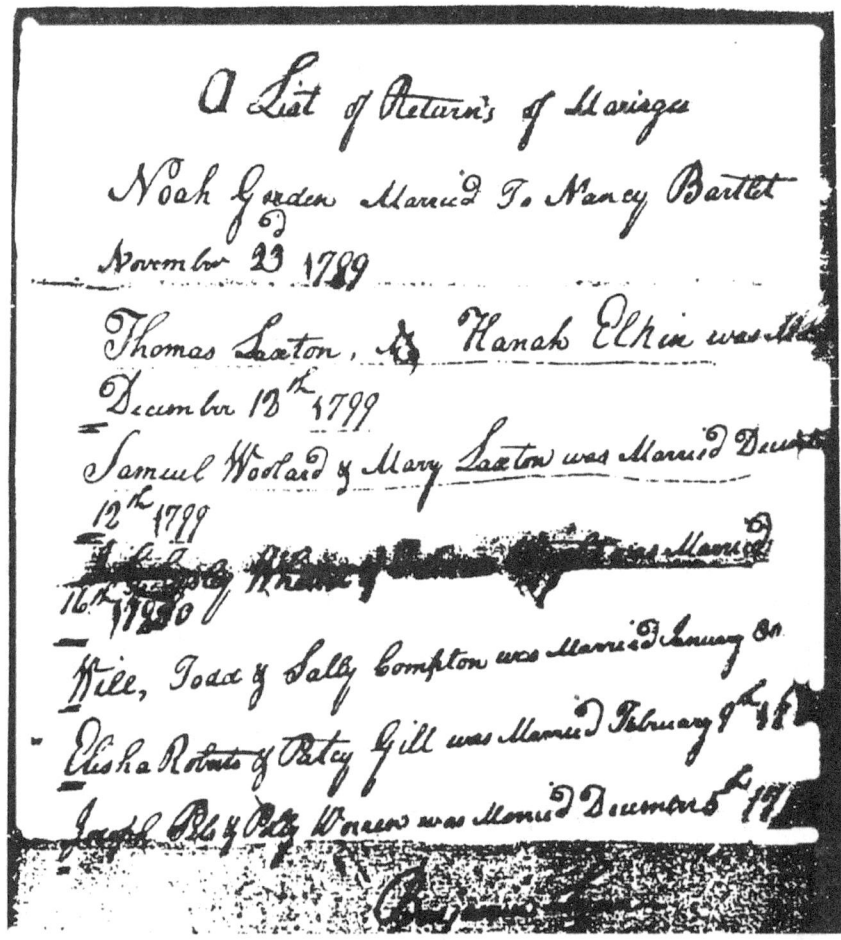

In "A List of Return's of Mariages" submitted by Benjamin Lynn, several publications have rendered "Laxton" as "Saxton;" however, close inspection of this copy shows the difference of S as written in "Samuel" and the L's of "List," "Laxton" (twice), and the signature "Lynn." Adding to the confusion, the S of "Sally Compton" differs rom that of "Samuel," demonstrating two forms of uppercase S in use at that time.

Lancaster

Numerous searches have investigated the American origins of the Lancasters of colonial Virginia; each genealogy varies at some point from the others. Two books that represent good research are *Lancaster Ancestors* by Ruth Fay Wright Kilgore and *The Lancasters: 300 years in America* by Bayard L. Teigan. Both are pertinent to the Surry County family, and both coincide, to varying extent, with our own findings, which are concerned with the line that descends from Lawrence to Harriett Lancaster, who married William S. Woollard. Anyone who may be interested in the other Lancaster lines should refer to the books by Kilgore and Teigan.

Robert[1] Lancaster of Surry County
Planter, Surveyor, and Juror

Robert[1] Lancaster came to Virginia by the year 1652, when he signed a petition which is to be found as an entry in the first "great Book of Surry County." In 1677 he served on a jury and the following year appeared on the tax records. In 1679, he was listed as a headright of William Powell, and in that same year he bought land on Blackwater Swamp, his earliest deed of record. Blackwater Creek and the Swamp of that name formed the boundary between Surry and Isle of Wight Counties; thereafter for four generations the Lancasters were prominent in the community of the Blackwater region.

Robert Lancaster served in the militia, served as juryman, served as surveyor, and was appointed guardian of Thomas and Mary White. His name appeared regularly on tax lists of Lawnes Creek Parish; after 1691 and 1694 respectively, his sons Robert Jr and Samuel were also listed.

There were three known children; a daughter Elizabeth married Thomas Pitman. The name of their mother is not known. His second wife was Mrs Sarah Bennett, widow of Richard; she survived him by two years, leaving a will which did not name any Lancaster as an heir.

Robert's will was dated 28 April 1720 and presented in court on 23 May 1720. He named his "loving wife" and son Robert as executors. The document was initialed and sealed by Robert "Lanquishear." His burial place is not known, nor those of his children. From his will, it appears that he prospered and left his sons property, for they in turn also prospered.

Issue: Elizabeth, c1670 - >1730; **Robert[2],** c1675-1738; Samuel, c1678-1761

Robert[2] Lancaster of Blackwater Swamp
Planter and Appraiser

Robert[2] and Samuel Lancaster, sons of Robert[1] Lancaster, appeared on the tax rolls of Surry County in 1691 and 1694 for the first time; if these are indeed their first times, their age at each instance would have been 16, thus indicating birth years of 1675 and 1678. They remained in the Blackwater region, and the record books over the years mentioned them as tax payers and landowners. Some of their associates were John and Unity Harris, Joseph and Arthur Holloman and Nathan Williford who may have been related to them, for the association lasted through successive generations, in North Carolina and Tennessee a century later.

Before 1707, Robert Lancaster, Jr had married **Judith Clary,** daughter of Thomas. They had six children: sons Samuel, **William[3]**, and Joseph, and daughters Elizabeth, Ann, and Mary. The family lived on Robert's plantation in Lawnes Creek Parish, and he owned another plantation that was occupied by his son Samuel.

Although he grew tobacco, Robert was patently a business man; for one thing, his will listed money scales. In addition, however, Robert left 4,000 cypress boards, 3,000 garden pails, and fifty gallons of brandy, "all which I have now ready for a market." All six children were named but not his wife, who must have predeceased him; he left his youngest son "Joseph Landcaster in the care of William Androes and his estate till he come to the age of twenty one years old." He was ill when he made the will in November, yet able to think prudently about the marketable inventory; the unusually large numbers of that inventory suggest an export business since a comparably large market demand did not exist in the colony.

Issue: Samuel, c1691-1745; **William³**, c1696-1740; c1723; Elizabeth; Ann; Mary

William³ Lancaster of Blackwater Swamp

Very little is known about this second son of Robert Lancaster and Judith his wife. He was willed the plantation of his grandfather Lancaster on Blackwater Swamp, and by the will of his own father he received 20 shillings and "a razor and none"; this bequest indicates that William was already provided for [in respect to land, by his grandfather's legacy].

William's wife may have been a daughter of the Lawrences, a family that had been prominent in Isle of Wight since very early times -- at least by 1642 when Robert Lancaster held land on Lawnes Creek next to Alice Bennett. Thought to be a younger son of Sir John Lawrence, Baronet, of London who had mercantile connections with the Bennetts in trading with Isle of Wight County, Virginia, Robert was a Justice for Nansemond County in 1659-60. His son George received a patent of 830 acres on the Blackwater. Between 1664 and 1677, Mr Richard Lawrence had dealings with Thomas Pitman, Roger Williams, and Robert Lancaster; after a break in the records, Charles Lawrence and John Laurance again appeared in association with Lancasters – this a century later, demonstrating that they certainly had known each other for a very long time so that marriage was indeed possible. [See box on the Lawrences, page c-10.]

William's wife was named **Mary [LAWRENCE?].** She was given administration of his estate in January of 1740/1 when he died without a will; his age was about 44. The court ordered an inventory and his estate was appraised by WM Rose, Bartho. Figurs, and Samuel Maget.

Issue: Lawrence⁴, c1720 – Robert⁴ Lancaster, d. <1738 – William⁴ Lancaster, d.1740

Chronology: Lancasters of Blackwater Swamp, Virginia

Robert¹ Lancaster, d. 1720
Robert² Lancaster, d. <1738
William³ Lancaster, d.1740

1634	James City Co and Isle of Wight Co were established
1635	Robt1 Lancaster b. in England
1637	Formation of Upper Norfolk County which was renamed Nansemond County in 1646
1640-42	Lawnes Ck Parish was created in Surry Co
1647	Southwark Parish was created in James City Co
1652	Surry Co, VA was formed from James City Co
7 Nov 1652	Robt Lancaster signed a petition which was entered in "the First Great Book of Surry Co" (Bk 1:4; Davis, 1) [Only 4 of 74 signers were named in the Rec Bk]
25 Apr 1667	Wm Lancaster was listed as a head right of Nich Meriwether, Surry Co, on Black-water Swamp and Blackwater creek (C&P 1:213)
c1670	Saml² Lancaster was b. in Surry Co [Birthyear derived from first known taxation at age 21]
10 Jun 1670	Surr co tithable lists included Capt Pitman, Xper Holliman, Robt Lancaster for Par of Lawnes Ck; on Jun 7, Roger Williams was listed in Southwark par (Ct Rec Bk 2:372-3; Haun, 44-45)

1677	Robt Lancaster of Lawnes Ck served on a jury in Surry Co which convicted local men involved in Bacon's Rebellion, including Rich Lawrence (Boddie-1948, 143)
1678	Robt Lancaster appeared on tax records (Boddie-1948, 189)
29Nov 1679	Robt Lancaster, a headright of Wm Powell, IofW Co, on Nansemond R (C&P 1:205)
2 mar 1679	Robt Lancaster bought 150 a. from Wm Lyle on Blackwater Swamp [which separates Surry and IofW Co's] (Surr D&W Bk 1:135; LDS Film # 034100, p.135)
1683	Robt Lancaster on tax list, Lawnes Ck Parish (Boddie-1948, 193)
May 1686	Robt Lancaster surveyed land in the Parish
1687	Robt Lancaster served in a militia Troop of Horse, Surry Co (Boddle-1948, 211)
1688 – 1702	Robt Lancaster was on the tax lists of the Parish
4 Jul 1689	Robt Lancaster paid 2400 lbs tobacco for 150 a. in Lawnes Ck Parish (DB 3:134)
1691	Robt Lancaster Jr appeared on the tax list, being tithable age, 16 yrs (LDS Film#034100)
1694	Saml[2] Lancaster's first appearance on the tax list (Boddie-1948)
May 1694	Robt Lancaster was appointed guardian of Thos and Mary White (Surr W&A Bk 5:25)
Jun 1694	Surr Tax List named Robt, Robt Jr, and Saml Lancaster (Teigan, 1)
1698	All three appeared on the tax list of Lawnes Ck Parish (MVG, Aug 86:76-83)
1701 – 1703	All three appeared on the tax list for these 3 years (lbid)
1704	Robt Lancaster was on the Quit Rent Rolls, paying for 100 a. (Des Cognets, 212)
< 1707	Robt Lancaster, Jr m. Judith CLARY, niece of Thos (Davis, 31)
9 Nov 1708	Saml Lancaster was appointed to administer the estate of John Harris; Saml also gave security to adm estate of Unity Harris, dcd [Unity Harris may be Unity Lancaster who was dau or niece of Robt[2] and Saml[2] Lancaster] (Surr OB, 1691-1713:3)
19 Aug 1712	Robt Lancaster, Jr, Planter of Surr Co bought from John Allen, Gent for 6000 lbs tobacco "300 a. on the mouth of a branch on S side of the main Blackwater Swamp" which divided the land from Saml Lancaster (DB 6:108)
<1720	Robt[1] Lancaster m. (2) Mrs Sarah _____Bennett, wid/o Rich (Boddie-1938, 295)
Unrated	Thos Pitman, IofW, m. Eliz Lancaster, d/o Robt (Bk 2:28; Boddie-1938, 242)
28 Apr 1720	Robt[1] Lancaster's will named sons Robt and Saml; dau Eliz Pitman (w/o Thos); g-children Saml, Wm, and Unity (f) Lancaster; g-children Saml, Lettis, and Ann Pitman; extrs were his wid Sarah and son Robt; will was initialed and sealed (IofW Great Bk, 28)
20 Aug 1720	Deeds were recorded for Saml Lancaster and Thos Pittman (Surr D&WB 7:297)

31 Oct 1722   Date of Sarah Bennett Lancaster's will; it was pr 29 Jan 1723, Surr Co; it contained no bequests to Lancasters (Boddie-1938, 296)

14 Jan 1730   Eliz Pitman wid/o Thos appointed her "loving brother Robert Lancaster to be my lawfull Attorney" at the next Surry Court; wit. By Jos Holloman and Saml Lancaster (Boddie-1938)

20 Oct 1736   Saml² Lancaster appraised the estate of John Holloman (Surr W&D Bk 8:654)

1738   Albemarle Parish was created, serving Surry and Sussex Co's

12 Nov 1738   Robt² Lancaster had sons Saml, **Wm³,** and Jos, 3 daus Eliz, Anne and Mary according to his will of this date which had been "sealed with a wafer" (Surr W&DB 9:53)

21 Jan 1740   Wm Lancaster d. without a will; wid Mary was given admin. (Surr W&A 9:264)

2Feb 1740   Death of Ethelred Lancaster was reported by John Andrews Sr "and was entered …" (Boddie – 1964, 85) [This entry appears to have been bracketed with the preceding entry, a member of the family apparently]

34 Mar 1741   Wm Lancaster's death was reported to the Parish by John Andrews Sr, also. Were these deaths so close together caused by an epidemic? [Mary COX & Jos Lancaster, br/o Wm³, had a son named Ethelred; this Ethelred was thought to be s/o Wm thereby bro/o Lawr] (See Richards, 307)

1749   IofW was divided, creating Southampton Co out of its southern portion

7 Nov 1749   On this date, Cath Williams of Surry made her will, naming extrs son Thos Williams and [s-in-l] Lawr Lancaster; Legatees were daus Eliz Na(e)rns [sic] and Mary Lancaster; she named 4 minor g-children [presumably the children of her dcd children, none of them Lancaster]; will not recorded until 16 Jun 1752 (D&W 1738-54:799)

1751   Nathan Williford Sr moved to Warr Co, NC; his daus Susannah and Sarah were married to Lancasters (Warr WB 1790-1825, v.5)

1751   Lawr Lancaster sold his land in Southamp Co, VA and left for NC [See c-13 ff]

13 Dec 1760   The will of Jos Crocker of IofW Co left his son Robt to his f-in-l Robt Lancaster, son Saml to Wm Williford, and dau Mary to Martha Lancaster Jr (Adams-Chapman-1938, 35)

28 Dec 1760   Saml² Lancaster's will named his wife Eliz as extr with Arthur and Jos Holleman as co-extrs; wits. John White, Nathan Williford; daus Silvia and Fliz were named but "other children" were not named; pr 1761 (Teigan, 8a)

The Lawrence Family in the Blackwater Region

1642   Robt Lawrence, s/o Sir John Lawrence(?) of London, pat. Land on Lawnes Ck adj Alice Bennett (Boddie-1938, 489-98)

1659 – 1660   Robt Lawrence was Justice for Nansemond Co (Ibid)

Apr/May 1664   "Thos Pittman appoints John Rawlings to confess judgment …"; on the next page, an indenture described a "plantation on SW Swamp" adj Mr Wm Lawrence (RB 2:234-5)

7 Jul 1668   Roger Williams this date recorded a note [loan]; at the same Surry Ct Wm Dowling, deponent, testified about Mr Rich Lawrence (CR 1664-71, Bk 2:304-06)

15 Sep 1668   Mr Rich Lawrence was atty of John Barber to collect "a debt by bill" from Thos Pitman (Surr RB 2:307-9; Haun, 48)

1676   Mr Rich Lawrence, Esq was Burgess from James City and Jamestown (Boddie- 1948, 167)

8 Mar 1676   "rich Lawrence is proclaimed a "Rebell & Traytor"; he was fined 2130 lbs tobacco (Surr RB 2:121; Davis-1956, 140) [For his part in Bacon's Rebellion]

May Ct 1677   Robt Lancaster of Lawnes Ck was on the jury for trial of "the depredations of the Baconians," among them Mr Rich Lawrence (OB 1671-99:139; Boddie-1948, 143)

4 Jul 1677   Wm Kitto's deposition on "Bacon's Rebellion" stated that "they had all the Governor's Goods at Lawrences (i.e., Rich Lawrence of Jamestown, one of Bacon's chief men)" (Boddie-1948, 126)

Bacon's rebellion was an uprising against Governor Berkeley, growing out of Nathaniel Bacon's attempt to organize the colonists to punish the Indians for their incursions. At first, Berkeley gave permission but when he rescinded it and declared the Baconians to be rebels, they retaliated by attacking him. Loyalties were divided – few people believed the Baconians to be in revolt against the Crown and many of the gentry had supported the action. Bacon's untimely death settled the issue, and survivors accepted their punishment and took the Oath of Allegiance.

8 Apr 1762   In separate actions, Chas Lawrence and Jos Lancaster appeared at the Southampton Ct Hse on this date (Adams-Chapman-1947, 43-44)

19 Apr 1767   On this date, the nuncupative will of Silviah Lancaster was recorded; also on that date the inventory of John Mead, appraised by John Laurence, was recorded (Surr D&W 1754-68:494-5; Hart, 85)

**Southside Counties of Virginia
1634 to 1739**

and

The Parishes of Lawnes Creek, Southwark, and Albemarle

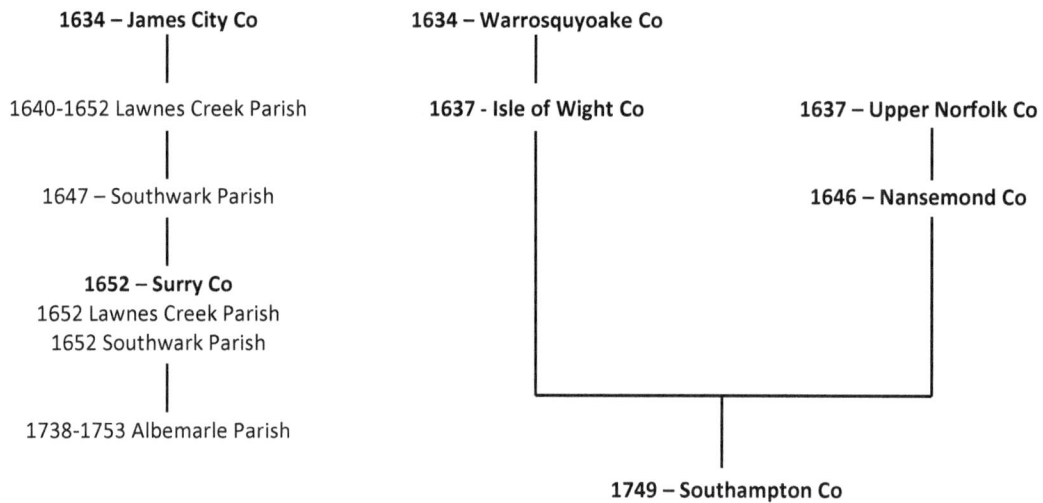

- James City County and Warrosquyoake County were two of the original eight shires created in 1634. The name of Warrosquyoake was changed in 1637 to Isle of Wight County.
- In 1637 Upper Norfolk County was established, its name changed in 1646 to Nansemond.
- Blackwater River was the dividing line between Surry and Isle of Wight Counties.
- Surry County was formed from James City County in 1652.
- Southampton County was formed in 1637 from Isle of Wight County; part of Nansemond County was added to it later.

Robert Lancaster was born in England, probably about 1635. At that time across the Atlantic Ocean in the Colony of Virginia, the James River was the site of new settlements, with new shires (counties) lined up along both sides of the river. James City County was north of the river; below the James was Surry County. Next to Surry was Isle of Wight County, and below that was Nansemond County, each with its own system of county court sessions.

In addition to the county courts which administered legal business, the parishes of the Church of England kept the records of social and family matters (marriages, christenings, burials); hence, a dual system of public administration existed. In 1640 Lawne Creek Parish was created in James City County and in 1652 included newly created Surry County – this was the "southside" where in time Robert Lancaster would come to reside. Southwark Parish dates from 1647 in James City County until 1652 when it was in Surry County. As populations increased, so also did the parochial jurisdictions, and in 1738 Albemarle parish was formed in Surry. The early Lancasters of Virginia lived here, clustered along the Blackwater Creek and Blackwater Swamp. To trace them, one must search throughout this county-parish system.

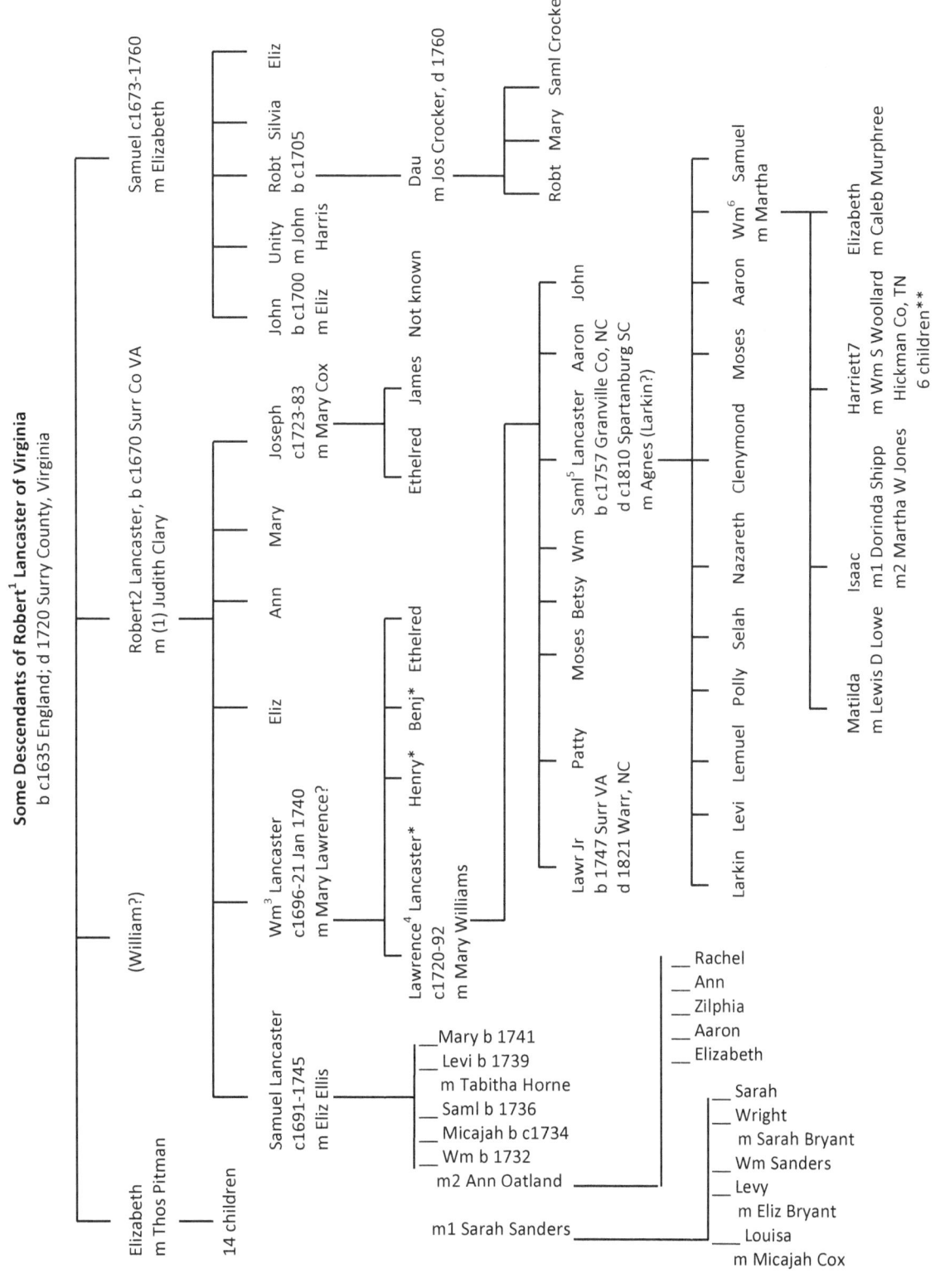

Some Descendants of Robert[1] Lancaster of Virginia
b c1635 England; d 1720 Surry County, Virginia

* Parentage not documented

** See Woollard tree (p. 58)

The Lancasters Move to The Carolinas

Lawrence[4] Lancaster
b. Isle of Wight County, Virginia – d. Warren County, North Carolina

The birthplace of **Lawrence[4] Lancaster** in about 1720 was Isle of Wight County, which became Southampton County in 1749. His supposed parents were William and Mary LAWRENCE? Lancaster; William died interstate in his early forties, so that no existing document names his heirs. However, Lawrence held land in the heart of "Lancaster country," and since there are no deeds to show his purchase it can be assumed that he inherited it; in his will, Robert 1 did "give to my Grandson William Lanquishear ye plantation at Blackwater after my wive's Decease to him and his heirs lawfully Begotten of his own body," but that William failed to make a will. Others of that era who bore the named William. Lawrence's wife was **Mary WILLIAMS**, one of three daughters of **Rogers Williams** and his wife **Catherine GREEN,** so identified by the will of Roger Williams dated 1744 and Catherine's will dated 1749.

In 1747, the birth of their son Lawrence (Jr) was recorded in Albemarle Parish, the only one of their children to appear in the christening records. In that same year, Lawrence Lancaster was godparent to Elizabeth Holleman, daughter of John and Martha Halleman, who was christened in Albemarle Parish. Although it appears that Lawrence, Jr was the oldest child of Mary and Lawrence Lancaster, it is possible that their daughter Patty was their first-born. In all, the couple had eight children.

As for community activities, Lawrence belonged to a close social group that had interacted and intermarried for a century. In 1748, he witnessed Samuel Lancaster's deed for land that adjoined Thomas Pitman; Joseph and Robert Lancaster and John Stephenson. When in 1747 Mary and Lawrence's son Lawrence was christened, the sponsors were Martha and John Holloman and Arthur Williams. In 1750 Lawrence Lancaster was a witness to Reuben Cook's will. These activities are evidence of a well integrated group of people, bonded to their special part of the earth; however, the picture was about to change.

In 1751, Lawrence Lancaster sold land in Southampton County, Virginia, and the next information relates that Henry Laughter of Granville County, North Carolina had sold land to "Lawrence Lancaster of Southampton County, Virginia." By 1754, Lawrence was a sergeant in Captain Daniel Harris's militia company in Granville. Also moving to North Caroline were his Kinsmen William, Micajah, Levi, and Samuel Lancaster, appearing there at least by 1758 (according to records in Northampton, Dobbs, Wayne, and Bute Counties). In 1764, Lawrence Lancaster sold land in Warren County to Len H. Bullock, witnessed by Samuel and John Lancaster. Nathan Williford began selling his lands on Blackwater in 1765 and 1766 and subsequently moved to Granville County also. In 1770, Lawrence and Samuel Lancaster were mentioned in the estate sale of Jane Harris. IN 1778 Lawrence bought 640 acres adjoining the lands of Matthew, Charles, and Joseph Harris, William Person, and John Lancaster in Bute County. Others came too -- the Haslewood, Holloman, Shand and Golightly families of Blackwater origin appeared about this time in the Granville County area of North Carolina.

The North Carolina State Census of 1786 showed Lawrence as the head of household in the District of Captain Jordon Harris, the census taken by Nathaniel Harris; there were four females and seventeen Negroes. Nearby lived sons Lawrence and Moses, as well as two John Lancasters. [In his will Lawrence mentioned son John Lancaster and son-in-law John Lancaster.]

Lawrence named twelve children in his will; his daughter Celah having died, he left her portion to Celah's daughter Betsy. His wife received no bequest, but one of the buyers at the estate sale was "Mrs Lancaster, Widow." Other buyers were Brittain Williford and Moses Bennett. Items at the sale included a hymn book and a Bible, a powdering tub, one Rifle gun and a "smothe" [bore] gun, some books, a sundial, and a pair of spectacles, these being only a few of a long list.

The sizeable estate included eight negroes. To son Lawrence he gave "a negro woman Agy to him during his natural life. Afterwards I give her freedom"; in addition, he said "I leave Old Faithy at her liberty to live where she pleases amongst my children during her natural life."

Like most Virginians of their time, the Lancasters practiced the religion of the Church of England. Their child was baptized in Albemarle Parish; Lawrence was the godfather of Elizabeth Holleman. At the time, christening was a most important ritual of communal life, a tradition of centuries. By the early 1700s, a Quaker community existed in the region, and subsequently some descendants became Quakers. After the Revolutionary War, the Anglican "establishment" church was no more, and Lawrence's children who had left Virginia adopted other forms of worship. As for Lawrence himself, his inventory mentioned firearms and a sword. He was a member of the militia, which rules out his being of the Quaker persuasion; nor was his son **Samuel[5]** who saw active service in the Revolutionary War.

The estate of Lawrence Lancaster was settled in August of 1792, but in 1802 several of the heirs who had moved to Spartanburg District of South Carolina sued the executors of the estate for their "equal parts" and appointed Thomas C. Williams as their attorney. This doc-ment was signed and sealed by A. Lancaster, Samuel[5] Lancaster, Brittain Willigord, Mary x Haselwood, and Samuel Williams and witnessed by John Golightly and Willis Williford.

Issue: Lawrence Jr, Patty, Moses, Celah,* William, **Samuel[5]**, c1757-c1810, Aaron, and John Lancaster; and Lucy Williford, Mary Haselwood, Nancy Williams, and Absolem

* One Interpretation of Lawrence Lancaster's will shows Celah (Celia) as his deceased first wife rather than his deceased daughter.

Chronology: Lawrence[4] Lancaster
From Southampton, VA to Warren Co, NC

c1720	Lawr[4] Lancaster b. in Isle of Wight Co, VA
21 Jan 1740	Wm Lancaster, f/o Lawr, died interstate (Surr W&A 9:53)
c1741	Lawr Lancaster m. Mary Williams, d/o Cath & Roger Williams (Surr W&A 1671-1750:43)
c1743	Birth of dau Patty [conjecture]
7 Aug 1744	Roger Williams made his will, mentioning his three daughters, one of them being Mary Lancaster, wife of Lawr (Surr W&A 1671-1750L110)
23 Aug 1745	Lawr Lancaster witnessed a deed of Saml Lancaster to Wm Drake, IofW, adj lands of Thos Pitman; wits: Arthur Crocker, Jos and Robt Lancaster
12 Feb 1746	Lawrence was appointed to appraise the estate of John Williford, other appraisers being Jos Lancaster and John Stephenson (IofW WB 2:335)
22 Jul 1747	Son Lawrence was christened in Albemarle Par; godparents Arthur Williams, Jos Holloman, Martha Halliman (Richards, 34; Boddie-1958)
2 Oct 1747	Lawr Lancaster was godfather for Eliz Halleman, d/o Martha & John Halleman, who was christened in Albemarle Par; Unity Williams also a sponsor Richards, 94)
1749	Southampton Co was formed from southern portion of Surr Co
24 Feb 1749	Laur Lancaster wit. Will of Cath Doles, IofW (Surr W&AB 9:683; David, 43)
7 Nov 1749	Lawr Lancaster was extr of Cath Williams' will, his m-in-l (Surr D&W 1738-54:79)
19 Nov 1750	Lawr Lancaster witnessed Reuben Cook's will (IofW DB 2:335)
25 May 1751	Lawr Lancaster sold 82 a. in Southam Co, VA on Terrapin Swamp to John Williford; wits. Wm Williford, Thos Williford (Southamp DB 1:250,252)
5 Jun 1751	Lawr Lancaster bought land, Granville Co, NC, from Henry laughter (Gran DB B: 50)

15 Mar 1753	"Law" Lancaster wit. Francis Pattason's will (Gran Unrecorded Wills, p. 45)
8 Oct 1754	Lawr Lancaster was a "serjeant" in Capt Danl Harris' militia company under the command of Col Wm Eaton (NC Arch, Gran Mil T.R. 1-37, p. 5)
1 Mar 1757	Thos Hill sued Lawr Lancaster, prob in Warr Co, NC (Gran Ct Min 1754-70:43)
15 Nov 1760	John Williford's will mentioned land bought from Lawr Lancaster (Southamp W&A Bk 1:367; Adams-Chapman-1947. 35)
12 Feb 1761	Saml Lancaster wit. The will of his uncle Thos Williams, his mother's brother (Gran Co)
1764	Bute Co was formed from Gran Co
11 Jul 1764	Lawr Lancaster sold land [later in Warren Co] to Len H. Bullock; wits. Saml and John Lancaster (Bute DB A: 77)
11 Mar 1778	Laur Lancaster bought 640 a. on line of Matt Harris to lines of Chas and Jos Harris, John Lancaster, and Wm Person (Holc-1974, 91)
1779	Warren Co and Franklin Co were formed from Bute Co
14 Jul 1781	Lawr was on Warr Co tax list, along with sons John, Moses, Lawr Jr, and John Lancaster (Wellman, 221-2) [By this time, sons Saml, Absalom, and Aaron, and daus Mary Haslewood and Lucy Williford had moved to South Carolina]
1786	NC State Cns listed Lawr Lancaster in Warr Co in Capt Jordon Harris' Sit, taken by Nath Harris, with 4 females and 17 Negroes in household; sons Lawr Jr, Moses, and John lived nearby, as also did another John Lancaster, possibly Lawr's s-in-l (p. 159)
NC Cns 1790	Lawr Lancaster's valuation was £2598; sons Lawr Jr, Joel, John, Moses; another John [s-in-l of Lawr]
SC Cns 1790	Saml Lancaster was listed in Spartanburg Co
27 Jun 1792	Lawr Lancaster executed a will, making bequests to sons Lawr, John, Moses, Aaron, Wm, and Saml 5; daus Patty and Betsy; Lucy Williford, Mary Haselwood, Absolam Lancaster, and Nancy Williams; extrs sons Lawr and Wm, s-in-l John Lancaster; signed and sealed in the presence of Jas and Morris Harris, and Danl Pegram (Warr Co unbound Wills, 1780-1907)
11 Jul 1792	Inventory of Lawr Lancaster, dcd was filed by Wm, Saml, and John Lancaster (Kerr, 40)
Aug Ct 1792	Will was proved by Jas and Morris Harris
Nov Ct 1792	Account of estate sale listed "Mrs Lancaster, Widow" as a buyer; she was not referred to in the will (Warr Co OB, 1792:140-1)
NC Cns 1800	No listing found for wid/o Lawr Lancaster
SC Cns 1800	Saml Lancaster (yrs) & wife with 9 younger persons, Spartanburg Dist (p. 89)
24 Apr 1802	Absalom, Saml, and Aaron Lancaster, Brittain Williford, Mary Haslewood, and Saml Williams of Spart Dist, SC filed to obtain their "equal parts of the said deceased Estate" and appointed Thos C. Williams of Warr Co s their atty; John Golightly, Willis Williford were wits. (Warr Co Bk 4:120)

Samuel⁵ Lancaster, Esquire
Justice, Planter, revolutionary War Cavalryman
b. c1757, Southampton County, Virginia
d. c1810, Spartanburg County, South Carolina

Samuel⁵ Lancaster was born about 1750, probably in Southampton County, Virginia. He was the son of Mary WILLIAMS and Lawrence Lancaster, who sold their land in Virginia and moved to Granville County, North Carolina in 1751. The first adult mention of Samuel Lancaster was when he witnessed a Granville County deed in 1764; from this it appears that his birthdate may have been earlier than 1750. He grew up in Granville County and married there. Samuel's wife was named **Agnes;** their marriage date has not been established. It is speculated that she may have been a Golightly or Williford, the names of longtime friends of the Lancasters from Virginia days – or perhaps a Larkin since their eldest son was given that name.

By 1780 Samuel Lancaster had moved to Spartanburg District, South Carolina with family members: his brothers Absolom and Aaron, sisters Mary Haslewood (wife of Samuel) and Lucy Williford (wife of Brittain). They traveled by oxcart. The Revolutionary War was being fought, and Samuel signed up for six months' duty as a horseman in Captain James Elder's Company of Colonel Benjamin Roebuck's Regiment. Six months after his first enlistment, Samuel Joined up a second time with Smith's Troop in Thomas' Regiment of Sumter's Brigade; terminal date of this service has not been determined.

Samuel had acquired land and become an active member of the community. In 1785 he served on a jury and the following year on the Grand Jury. He was elected a Justice and was one of four justices whose names appeared on a contract to build the first courthouse in 1787.

Agnes and Samuel Lancaster had eleven children, born between about 1770 and 1790. The only verified birthdate is that their youngest child, Samuel, who was born on 19 February 1790. From that information, other tentative birthdates can be assigned to the rest of their ten children.

The 1790 census listed Samuel Lancaster with four males of age 16 and above, four males under 16, and five females. At that time, his brothers Aaron and Absolem Lancaster were nearby, as were Williford Britton, and David and John Golightly.

Two years later, Samuel's father Lawrence Lancaster died; his will included those of his children who had moved to South Carolina (three sons and three daughters). However, as happened in those days, the out-of-state legatees eventually had to go to court to obtain "their equal parts of the said deceased Estate.' The plaintiffs were Aaron, Absalom, and Samuel Lancaster, and their sister Mary Haslewood and brothers-in-law- Brittain Williford and Samuel Williams [on behalf of wives Lucy and Nancy, who may have been deceased], all of them of Spartanburg, South Carolina.

Samuel did not long survive his father; his will was dated 29 August 1797. He named his wife Agnes and eleven children –"eldest sons" Larkin, Levi, and Lemuel; four daughters Polly, Selah, Nazareth, and Clenymond; and "my four sons" Moses, Aaron, **William⁶,** and Samuel Lancaster. IT appears that none of the daughters had married; eldest sons Larkin, Levi, and Lemuel were named as executors. The will enjoined his loving wife to reserve a part of her income "to school my youngest children"; regrettably, those youngest children were not identified, but it appears that William may have belonged to that group. The will was witnessed by Willis Williford, Willie (Wylie) Williford, and Joseph Smith.

After Samuel's death, some of the family packed up their belongings and traveled by oxcart to Tennessee. The party included Agnes and her sons Levi, Aaron, William, and Samuel, as well as in-laws among the Golightly and Williford families. They went first to Giles as well as in-laws among the Golightly and Williford families. They went first to Giles County and were enumerated in the 1820 Giles County census, but the next census year found the brothers Williams and Samuel Lancaster in Hickman County.

Agnes Lancaster may have resided with her son William, for in 1830 his household included "1 female aged 80 to 90 years." Her son William died in 1844, but Samuel, who named a daughter for his mother, lived to 1882, "lacking 3 days of his 93ʳᵈ birthday.' Samuel was prominent and colorful; after the Civil War he never took the oath of loyalty to the Union.

Issue: Sons Larkin, Levi, Lemuel, Moses, Aaron, **William**[6], and Samuel (b.19 Feb 1790, m. (1) Mary Cooper, (2) Martha Fowlkes, d.16 Feb 1882); daughters Polly, Selah, Nazareth and Clenymond)

Chronology: Samuel[5] Lancaster, Esquire
b. c1750, Southampton Co, VA – d.c1810, Spartanburg Co, SC

c1750	Birth date of Saml[5] Lancaster in Southampton CO, VA (year not confirmed)
1751	Saml's father Lawr Lancaster sold land in Southampton Co, VA and bought land in Gran Co, NC
11 Jul 1764	Saml Lancaster wit. A deed, Gran CO, NC (Bute DB A: 77)
1764	Bute Co was formed from Gran Co

Saml Lancaster. Agnes (Williford? Golightly? Larkin?)

8 Jun 1770	Estate sale of Jane Harris, dcd mentioned Lawr and Saml Lancaster
1771	Saml Lancaster was on the Bute CO tax list
1779	Warren CO was formed from Bute Co
c1780	Saml Lancaster moved to Spartanburg Dist, SC with family members: brothers Absolom and Aaron, sisters Mary Haslewood, Nancy Williams (w/o Saml), and Lucy Williford (w/o Brittain); traveled by oxcart (Spence, 280-81)
15 Dec 1780	Saml Lancaster was a horseman in the Rev War, Capt Jas Elder's Company in Col Benj Roebuck's Regt (SC Arch AA 4414-A)
14 Jul 1781	Warr Co tax list did not include Saml, Aaron, and Absalom Lancaster; named on the list were Lawr and sons John, Moses, Lawr Jr, and John Lancaster [thought to be a cousin] (Wellman, 221-2)
Sep 1781	Saml Lancaster's 6-month service ended (SC Arch AA 4414-A)
1 Apr 1782	Saml Lancaster served with Smith's Troop in Thomas' Regt of Sumter's Brigade (Salley, 197)
21 Jan 1784	Moses Lancaster conveyed a tract of 100 a. "beginning at Dutchmans CK" to his bro Levi, "a Tract originally granted to Saml Lancaster, Esq" who deeded and willed it to Moses Lancaster (Spart DB Q:334)
1785	Saml Lancaster served on a jury (Landrum, 26) and was Tax Collector of Upper Dist between Broad and Saluda Rivers (Ruth Watson, 30 Aug 1981, letter to BMM)
1786	Saml Lancaster served on the Grand Jury (Landrum, 27)
1787	Saml Lancaster was one of 4 Justices whose names appeared on a contract to build the county's first courthouse (Laudrum, 31)
1788	Birthdate of **Wm**[6] **Lancaster** (conjecture based on birthdate of bro Saml jr)
19 Feb 1790	Birthdate of Saml Lancaster [the younger], known to be Saml's youngest child; this is the only authenticated birthdate for a child of Agnes & Saml [From paper inside a daguerreotype of Saml Jr & wife Polly COOPER] (Kilgore, 12)

SC Cns 1790   Saml Lancaster of Spart Dist headed a household of 4 males over 16 yrs [Larkin Levi. Leml, Moses]; 4 males under 17 [Aaron, Wm, Saml]; 5 females (p. 87); his bros Aaron and Absolem lived nearby (p. 89); John Lancaster in Union Co (p. 93); four Golightly families were living nearby (pp. 86, 89)

27 Jun 1792   Saml's father Lawr Lancaster executed a will which included Aaron, Absolom, and Saml Lancaster, and also daus Lucy Williford, Mary Haselwood, and Nancy Williams, all of them having moved to SC (Warr Co Unbound Wills, 1780-1907)

11 Jul 1792   Saml, Wm, and John Lancaster filed the inventory of Lawr Lancaster, dcd

29 Aug 1797   Saml Lancaster made his will; he named his wife Agnes and 11 children: "eldest sons" Larkin, Levi, Leml; 4 daus Polly, Selah, Nazareth, Clenymond; "youngest sons" Moses, Aaron, Wm, and Saml; wits. Were Willis Williford, Willie Williford, Jos Smith; the oldest and any other land to divide among them; daus received horse and saddle as well as feather beds and "furniture," which was traditional (WB 1-A:5-7)

SC Cns 1800   Saml Lancaster and wife were listed with 9 younger persons (p. 89); nearby were Aaron, Absolem, John, Larkin, and Wm Lancaster, and also Brittain and Wylie; Agnes Lancaster was not listed as a widow, hence Saml had not executed a "death bed" will

24 Apr 1802   Aaron, Absalom, and Samuel Lancaster, Brittain Williford, Mary Haslewood, and Samuel Williams, all of Spart Dist, filed against their father Lawrence Lancaster's executors for their "equal parts of the said deceased Estate" (Spart Bk 4:120)

9 Feb 1810   Saml Lancaster's will was not proven until this date (Spart WB 1-A-:7-5)

SC Cns 1810   Agnes Lancaster was listed as H/H in Spart Co (p. 195)

18 Aug 1817   Deed: Levi Lancaster of Spart Dist to Isaiah Rhen, "all that plantation … originally granted to Saml Lancaster …."; recorded 10 Nov 1819 (Spart DB Q: 334)

C1818   The wid Agnes Lancaster, with sons Levi, Saml, Aaron, and Wm, moved to Giles Co, TN; also in the travel party were members of the Golightly, Williford, and Brittain families (Fullerton's letter to BMM, 8 Jun 1979)

TN Cns 1820   Agnes Lancaster (age 45+) was listed in the Giles Co, TN cns (p. 19); neighbors were Aaron Lancaster (p. 16); Wm Lancaster; Henry Golightly [Absolom Lancaster's wife was a Golightly], four Willifords, and Willie Britton (p. 19)

16 Oct 1820   Deed: Levi Lancaster "of the State of Tennessee, Hickman County" sold land on Dry Fork of Sugar Creek, "being part of a tract of land originally granted to Saml Lancaster, Esq bearing date 29th May 1807"; recorded 8 Dec 1821 (Spart DB Q:405)

8 Dec 1821   Levi Lancaster of Hickman Co, TN filed in settlement of his father's estate (Spart DB Q: 405)

C1823   The Lancasters had moved on to Hickman Co, TN

TN Cns 1830   Agnes Lancaster may have been residing in Hick Co with son Wm whose household included "1 female 70-80 yrs" (p. 279) However, there is also evidence that this "older woman" was not Agnes but someone who had been living with them all along. Date of Agnes Lancaster's death not known

William[6] Lancaster
Landowner, Magistrate
b. c1780, Spartanburg County, South Carolina
d. 1844, Hickman County, Tennessee

William[6] Lancaster was the son of Agnes and Samuel Lancaster, born in Spartanburg County, South Carolina about 1780. William's wife was named **Martha** (born 1789), and by census time in 1800 they were the parents of a son and daughter, both under ten years of age. Also in their household was an older female (age given as 26 to 45 years), who was probably the mother of Martha.

William's father died about 1809 or 1810; although Samuel's will was dated 26 August 1797, he lived until 1810, attested to by his listing in the 1800 census and at least one land transaction showing him still living in 1802. Samuel's will was not proven until 9 February 1810, and in the 1810 census his wife Agnes was listed as the head of household. Agnes and several of her children sold their land in preparation for a move to Tennessee. William was one of those who joined her in the journey by ox cart; their travel party included his brothers Levi, Aaron, and Samuel and various members of the Golightly, Williford, and Brittain families. They went first to Giles County, probably in the year 1818, and were listed in that county in the census of 1820.

The 1820 census showed that William and Martha Lancaster (in the age bracket of 226 to 45 years) had four children – a son (10 to 16) and three daughters under 10; their family group still contained an older woman (age given as "over 45"). [NOTE: In the 1830 census the older woman's age was given as 70 to 80.] Nearby was Agnes, mother of William, and brother Samuel, but brother Levi had already moved on from Giles County.

It wasn't long, however, until William and Samuel Lancaster had both moved from Giles to Hickman County where they settled permanently on Beaverdam Creek in the 9th District. In 1822 William Lancaster was a magistrate.

William Lancaster began acquiring land. Deeds and grants for this survey totaled 431 acres; there may have been more. The Lancaster's land on Blue Water Stream was near the home of William S. Woollard and his wife **Harriett[7],** who was the daughter of Agnes and William LANCASTER. Woollard died of blood poisoning in 1838, leaving six children.

In 1844 William Lancaster died interstate; his son Isaac administered his estate for the heirs, who included William's wife Martha, daughters Matilda Lowe and Elizabeth Murphree, and the six children of his deceased daughter Harriett Woollard. Settlement of this estate stretched out over the years; the lands were divided, the dower was set aside for Martha, the slaves were distributed, tracts were sold off – and the last mention found was in 1861.

Isaac Lancaster's marriage woes occurred during this period. He and his first wife Dorinda Shipp were divorced, after which he married Martha M. Jones, the widow of Dennis G. Jones. They also were divorced, after acrimonious testimony, Martha Lancaster gave a deposition in 1855, which established her birth year as 1789. [NOTE: This evidence conflicts with the 1800 census; her husband's birth year has also been difficult to establish.]

The date and circumstances of Martha Lancaster's death (after 1855) are not known.

Issue: All born Spartanburg Co, SC:[3] **Harriett[7]** (b. c1810; m. James M. Woollard); Matilda (b. 1812; m. Lewis D. Lowe [her age from 1860 cns]); Isaac (b. 1822 [from 1850 cns]; m. (1) Dorinda Shipp, (2) Martha M. Jones Elizabeth (m. Caleb Murphree)

---

[3] Conflicting evidence about birth years; the 1800 census (which may be faulty in its transcription) does not agree with 1850 and 1860 censuses

Chronology: William[6] Lancaster, Magistrate
c1780, Spartanburg Co, SC – 1844, Hickman Co, TN

c1780   Wm[6] Lancaster was born in Spartanburg Co, SC, son of Agnes & Samuel Lancaster, Esquire [NOTE: Not an established date because of conflicting evidence]

SC cns 1800   Wm Lancaster of Spart CO & wife (ages 16-26) had 1 son and 1 dau under 10, and an older female (26-45) in the household (p. 201)

SC Cns 1810   In Spart Co, two Wm Lancasters listed, family tally not given (pp. 188, 195)

c1818   Wm Lancaster moved to Giles Co, TN with his widowed mother Agnes and brothers Levi, Aaron, and Saml; also, members of Golightly, Williford, and Brittain families moved with them (Fullerton's letter to BMM, 8 Jun 1979)

3 Jun 1822   Deed: Wm Lancaster bought 118 a. on S side Duck R., E side Beaverdam Ck in Hick Co from David Russell, adj John C. McLemore, John David, Levi Lancaster (Hick Roll 24, Bk D-G:206)

25 Jul 1822   Deed: Wm Lancaster bought from Danl Perrett 3 tracts on Duck R. in Hick Co, a total of 76 a., adj Hughlett and Asa Shutes (Hick Roll 24-G:38)

9 Feb 1826   Wm Lancaster acquired a grant from the State on TN of 50 a. at one cent per acre, on Beaverdam Ck of Duck R., adj McLemore and Davis (Grant #5978, MidTn Roll 104/7:449)

27 Jan 1829   Wm Lancaster acquired another State grant of 100 a., same terms and location, adj John Berryman and John Ragsdale (Grant #12329, Mid TN Roll 116,Bk 16:97)

TN Cns 1830   Wm Lanc & Wife (40-50 yrs) of Hick Co had 1 male (5-10), 1 female (10-15), and 1 female (80-90); nearby lived dau **Harriet 7** with husb Wm Woollard (20-30) and their infant dau; also, [Wm Lancaster's] dau Matilda, w/o Lewis Lowe (15-20), all listed on p. 279

22 Dec 1835   Deed: Wm M. Lancaster bought from Stiles Bugg, 52 a. adj. Chas Yates, Chas Cagle, and Dixon Walker; wits. Wm Lancaster and Wm Woollard (Bk L: 96)

10 Dec 1836   Deed: Wm Lancaster received a grant of 35 a. on N side Duck R., adj lands of Yates and Ragsdale (Grant #14229, Mid TN Toll 118, Bk 17:209)

1836 & 1837   In Dist #9 for both years, Wm Lanc was listed with 118 a.; also listed in same dist was s-in-l Wm Woollard, with 200 a. (Hick Tax Rec, 1836-37) [Poll tax was required by law for white males 21-50 yrs; tax levied on black males 21+yrs]

C1838   Death of Wm Lancaster's dau Harriett Woollard, who left 6 children; a thorn in her heel had led to blood poisoning (TN Arch Roll 1a, Hick Min Bk: 331-35)

TN Cns 1840   Wm Lancaster & wife (50-60 and 40-50 yrs) of Hick Co and 1 male (15-20) and 1 female (10-15) (p. 177)

21 Apr 1844   Death of Wm Lancaster; heirs included wife Martha and surviving children Matilda Lowe; Isaac Lancaster; Harriett's children: Matilda J., Jas M., Mary A., Eliz A., Rachel C., and Saml J., represented by their widowed father Wm S. Woollard; and Eliz Murphree (TN Arch, Roll 1a, Hick Min Bk:331-5)

Aug 1844   The heirs petitioned to lay off lands of Wm Lancaster, dcd (Ibid)

Jul 1846 — Lewis D. Lowe, et al petitioned to sell five slaves of Wm Lancaster (TN Arch Roll 1a, Hick Min Bk:436-7)

Aug 1846 — Isaac, son of Wm Lancaster, dcd was his adm (WPA #164-44-6999, p. 45)

May 1848 — Guardian report of Wm Woolard for Wm Lancaster's g-children (WPA #165-44-6999, Vol D, 1847-52, p. 16)

Oct 1849 — In a Guardian Report, Wm Woolard, "Father of Said Matilda," gave notice of the death of Matilda J. (WPA #165-44-6999, Vol D:65)

16 Jun 1855 — Martha Lancaster (age 66) gave a deposition in the divorce proceedings of her son Isaac and Martha M. (Jones) Lancaster (Hick Co Chanery Ct Loose Papers, 6 pp)

4 Dec 1856 — "Lot # 3 of the lands belonging to the estate of Wm Lancaster, Dcd" on Beaverdam Ck was transferred to Jas M. Woolard by other heirs; also, they conveyed their interest in the dower lands of Martha Lancaster, "widow of Wm Lancaster, Dcd" to Jas M. Woolard (TN Arch Roll 26, Hick Bk P: 344-5)

3 Oct 1857 — Heirs sold to Jas M. Woollard for $25 each their interest in Lot#3 of the estate of Wm Lancaster, dcd, and also their "interest in & to the dower of Martha Lancaster, widow of Wm Lancaster, Dcd" (Ibid)

TN Cns 1870 — M. Lancaster, age 70, b. NC, was listed in Hick Co's 9th Dist as "seamstress," living alone (p. 11)

Chart 3: Ancestry of Harriett Lancaster
of Hickman Co., Tennessee

Robert Lancaster m. (1) Not Known
by 1652 in Surry Co, VA   (2) Sarah ___ Bennett,
d 28 April 1720   (widow of Richard)

Robert Lancaster m. Judith Clary (dau of Thos Clary)
b. c1675, Surrey Co, VA | d. < 1738
d. c1738, Surrey Co, VA |

William Lancaster m. Mary Lawrence?
b. c1696, Surrey Co, VA | b. c1698
d. Jan 1740, Surrey Co, VA | d. > 1741, Surrey Co, VA

Lawrence Lancaster m. Mary Williams
b. 1720, Surrey Co, VA | b. c1722 (dau of Roger Williams & Catherine Greene)
d. 27 June 1792, Warren Co, NC | d. > 1792

Samuel Lancaster m Agnes
* b. c1757, Granville Co, NC | b. c1759 (NC?)
d. c1810, Spartanburg, SC | d. >1820, Hickman Co, TN

William Lancaster m. Martha
b. c1780, Spartanburg, SC | b. 1782 or 1789
d. 1844, Hickman Co, TN | d. > 1857, Hickman Co, TN

Harriet Lancaster m. William Samuel Woollard
b. c1810, Spartanburg, SC | b. c1808, Hardin Co, KY
d. c1838, Hickman Co, TN | d. 1881, ,Hickman Co, TN

James Monroe Woollard m. Mary Alston Jones
|
Susan Matilda Woollard m. Luther Everett Mathis
|
Jennie May Mathis m. John Cyril Malloy
|
Bernard Mathis Malloy

* If this birth date is accurate, Samuel's birthplace was Southampton Co., Virginia.

Harriet[7] Lancaster, Wife of William S. Woollard
b. c1810, Spartanburg County, South Carolina
d. c1838, Hickman County, Tennessee

Harriett[7] Lancaster[4] was born in Spartanburg County, South Carolina about 1810. Her parents were William Lancaster (son of Agnes and Samuel) and his wife Martha. She had a brother, Isaac, and two sisters, Matilda and Elizabeth.

By 1818 the family had moved from South Carolina to Giles County, Tennessee. They traveled by ox cart, accompanied by Harriett's widowed grandmother Agnes Lancaster and uncles – Levi, Aaron, and Samuel – as well as other relatives among the Golightly, Williford, and Brittain families. According to the 1820 census, Harriett was then under ten years of age.

The Lancasters and their relatives did not stay long in Giles County but moved on to Hickman County, settling on the Beaverdam Creek of the Duck River in the 9th District. Her father acquired land (at least 500 acres, according to known deeds) and was a magistrate of his community. Others in the vicinity were the Jones, Yates, McNeilly, and Woollard families who, in years to come, would intermarry.

Their neighbors on Beaverdam Creek were the Woollard family. Except for nineteen-year-old William, the Woollards decided to move northward into newly opened lands in Indiana and eventually Illinois. The day they left was his birthday, and on that day **William S. Woollard** married young Harriett Lancaster; the year must have been 1827, but the records have not been found.

Harriett and Williams S. Woollard had six children, two sons and four daughters. They prospered as a family; William became a magistrate and was active in various community activities, including those of the Liberty Baptist Church. IN about 1838, young Harriett died of an infection in her heel – while walking in the orchard she stepped on a thorn. William selected a lot of the hillside, "north from the spring and east from the garden," for a cemetery for the family.

Her father did not long survive Harriett; he died in 1844, and Harriett's children received their mother's paternal legacy, under the guardianship of their father W.S. Woollard.

Issue: Matilda J. (1830-1850); **James Monroe** (1831-1906); Mary Agnes (b.1833, m. Will Edwards); Elizabeth A. (b.1835, m. Green Leeper); Rachel Carolina (b.1836, m. J.S.J "Rocky" Lancaster, d. Chickamauga in Civil War); Samuel J. (1837-1865, d. in Civil War, bur Union City, TN)

Chronology: Harriett[7] Lancaster

c1811   Harriett Lancaster b. Spartanburg Co, SC, d/o <Martha & Wm (W.L. Pinkerton, in a letter dated 3 Mar 1948, identified her as first w/o Wm S. Woollard)

c1818   Harriett's family moved to Giles Co, TN

c1820   Harriett's family moved to Hick Co, TN

c1827   Harriett m. Wm S. Woollard, s/o Saml Woollard (d. Shelby Co, IL)

1830 – 1837   Six children were born to Harriett & Wm S. Woollard in Hick Co, TN

c1838   Harriett LANCASTER Woollard d. of tetanus; bur in family cemetery

---

[4] Although referred to as "Harriett," there is uncertainty as to the actual name of this daughter of Martha and William Lancaster. So far, no contemporary records referring to her by her given name have been found. First reference to her as "Harriett" is in a letter writing by W.L. Pickerton (3 March 1948); also, she was identified by that name in "recollections of JMM." However, a letter from John T. Walker (10 June 1929) said that her name was Matilda.

The Lancasters of Surry County, Virginia:

A Summary

The Lancaster of Hickman County, Tennessee (who were neighbors of the Woollards in the vicinity of Beaverdam Creek in the 1820s) descended from the earliest of the American Lancasters. In the seventeenth century they lived in Southside Virginia – in the vicinity of Surry, Isle of Wight, and Southampton Counties. From there they moved westward to the region formed by a cluster of counties – Bute, Warren, Franklin, and Granville – situated in the northeastern part of North Carolina, just across the line from Virginia. From Warren County, several members of the family moved farther south to the Spartanburg District of South Carolina just below the state line that separated it from North Carolina; from there, one group of the Lancaster family migrated to Hickman County, Tennessee. This was a typical migratory pattern of that era.

Having traced these American Lancasters from 1652 to the 1990s, the several genealogists who were involved in the search have not yet determined the specific English roots from which they sprang. The Lancaster name (spelled variantly in colonial records as Lanchester, Lancashear, Landcaster, and Lanquisher) was undeniably English, thought to have derived originally from the English county of that name. In one of the American lines, tradition holds that originally seven brothers came to the colony of Virginia and that our Lancaster descends from one of the original brothers. It is a not unreasonable assumption, as our data has shown; certainly, many sons were born and in several generations they were seven or more in number, thus correlating with the family legend as it was handed down to successive generations.

The name is certainly of pre-Conquest origin, by virtue of the fact that "-caster," the final part of the word, clearly derives from Latin castra (camp), which survived in Old English as –caster, -chester, and –cester, suffixes which indicate places: Doncaster, Winchester, Leicester. It has been suggested that governor of Castle Lancaster was William, son of Gilbert, and he took Lancaster as his surname. In 1267, Henry III gave the title of Earl of Lancaster to his son Edmund. In 1299, John de Lancaster was a Member of Parliament for the Barony of Kendall. By 1362, there were no male heirs to carry on the name. At that time, John of Gaunt, fourth son of Edward III, took the title Duke of Lancaster after marrying Blanche of Lancaster. From 1399 to 1461, the ruling family of England was Lancaster, who contended against the Yorks in the Wars of the Roses.

Jones

Mary Alston[7] Jones (b. 17 October 1834, Hickman County, Tennessee), wife of James M.[8] Woollard (m. 4 March 1852), was a seventh-generation American, descended from colonists who emigrated to Virginia from England in 1653. After a hundred years in Virginia, Mary Jones' great-great-grandfather had moved to North Carolina "where he became a prominent and influential citizen" (*Hickman County Times*, 24 Oct 1957). In 1807 Mary's grandfather left North Carolina for Hickman County, where he is recognized as one of its "pioneers" (Spence, 273).

Mary and James M. Woollard had four children, of whom only two daughters survived. Mary and her infant son died of typhoid fever during the Civil War, at which time her husband was a prisoner of war, wounded and captured at the Battle of Shiloh. Mary died o 11 August 1861 in Madison County, Tennessee at their home in Spring Creek.

Brief Descriptions of her ancestry will follow, starting with her earliest ancestor and bringing the lineage up to her father. A more complete history of this Jones family in America is the book *Descendants of Captain James Jones* by James Jones Banks (Rome, Georgia, 1971).

Edward[1] Jones was a resident of Isle of Wight County, Virginia in 1653. An old record names him as an "overseer" of a will dated 22 February 1661. He was survived by his son, also named Edward.

Edward[2] Jones married **Jane Harris** daughter of **Thomas** and **Ann.** He died 15 January 1722 leaving his son, the third Edward born in America.

Judge Edward[3] Jones (b. 1701) moved his family to North Carolina, where he helped shape the growth in that expanding area, settling at Shocco Springs. In 1739 the Justices of newly created Granville County held the first meeting in his home. His wife was the remarkable **Abigail Sugan.** Their Children were Sugan, Priscilla (w/o Gideon Macon), Sarah, Obedience, **James,** Edward, Rebecca, Daniel, and Robert (posthumous). Judge Jones died in 1751 while attending the General Assembly New Bern.

Captain James[4] Jones, b. 1730 in Isle of Wight County, Virginia, was married to **Charity Alston** on 12 August 1761. A captain in the North Carolina Militia, he was also a Member for Wake County at the Provincial Constitutional Congress; during the Revolution he served in the North Carolina Light Horse Cavalry with rank of captain. In 1777 he was the first senator elected to represent Wake County in the General Assembly, dying in office. The children named in his will were Mary, Priscilla, Willis, Rachel, Thomas, and James; his son **Solomon** was born posthumously.

After the death of her husband, Charity ALSTON Jones married (2) Major Pollard (4 April 1778). They had three daughters: Elizabeth Pollard who married Thomas A. Steele of Orange County, Charity Pollard (m. William Loftus), and Nancy Pollard (m.___Smith).

Captain Solomon[5] Jones was born in Wake County, North Carolina about 1777. The will of his father named six children but did not include Solomon who was born after the will was written; he was named for his maternal grandfather Solomon Alston. Solomon Jones married **Christian Charity Alston**, his second cousin. Their children were Absalom, John, Thomas, Priscilla, and Dennis G., all born in North Carolina. In 1807 Solomon Jones moved his family to Hickman County, Tennessee where three more children were born: **William Alston[6] Jones,** Martha, and Mary.

In Hickman County, Solomon Jones was a pioneer of the Beaverdam Creek region. "Later he returned home to North Carolina and induced hi [half] sister [Elizabeth Steele] to come to Tennessee. Several of his brothers-in-law, the Alstons, came in 1810, and settled on Beaver Creek" (Spence, 191). Spence also wrote that "some of those who came to Tennessee through the influence of Jones were Andrew Clark, Jesse Fuqua, James Alston, and Mrs Steel" (p. 196). Spence also wrote that "some of those who came to Tennessee through the influence of Jones were Andrew Clark, Jesse Fuqua, James Alston, and Mrs Steel" (p. 196). After the death of Major Pollard, Solomon's mother Charity ALSTON Jones Pollard also moved to Tennessee, to be near her children Solomon Jones and Betsy Green (Banks, 113).

After the death of his wife Chrissie, Solomon Jones married secondly Elizabeth BROWN Murphree (wid/o Daniel, d/o Col James Brown)); they had a son named James George Jones (m. Elizabeth Griner). His will was written 4 December 1840 and probated 3 November 1841; he is buried in the Jones and Sparks Graveyard, sharing a double headstone with his first wife (Chrissie).

William Alston[6] Jones (b.23 September 1812) was born in Hickman County, Tennessee, where his parents Chrissie and Solomon Jones had moved from North Carolina. On 24 December 1833 he married **Susan McNeilly** (b.16 September 1816, d/o **Mary Yates** and **James A. McNeilly, Jr)**. Their seven children were: Solomon, Dennis, **Mary Alston[7],** Martha, Nancy Sophia, and Priscilla. Son Solomon died during the Civil War; son Dennis became a prominent Baptist minister.

Will Alston Jones died very young (age 33), leaving an estate of considerable size, and was buried at his home Duck River below the mouth of Beaverdam Creek. His widow married (2) William Phillips.

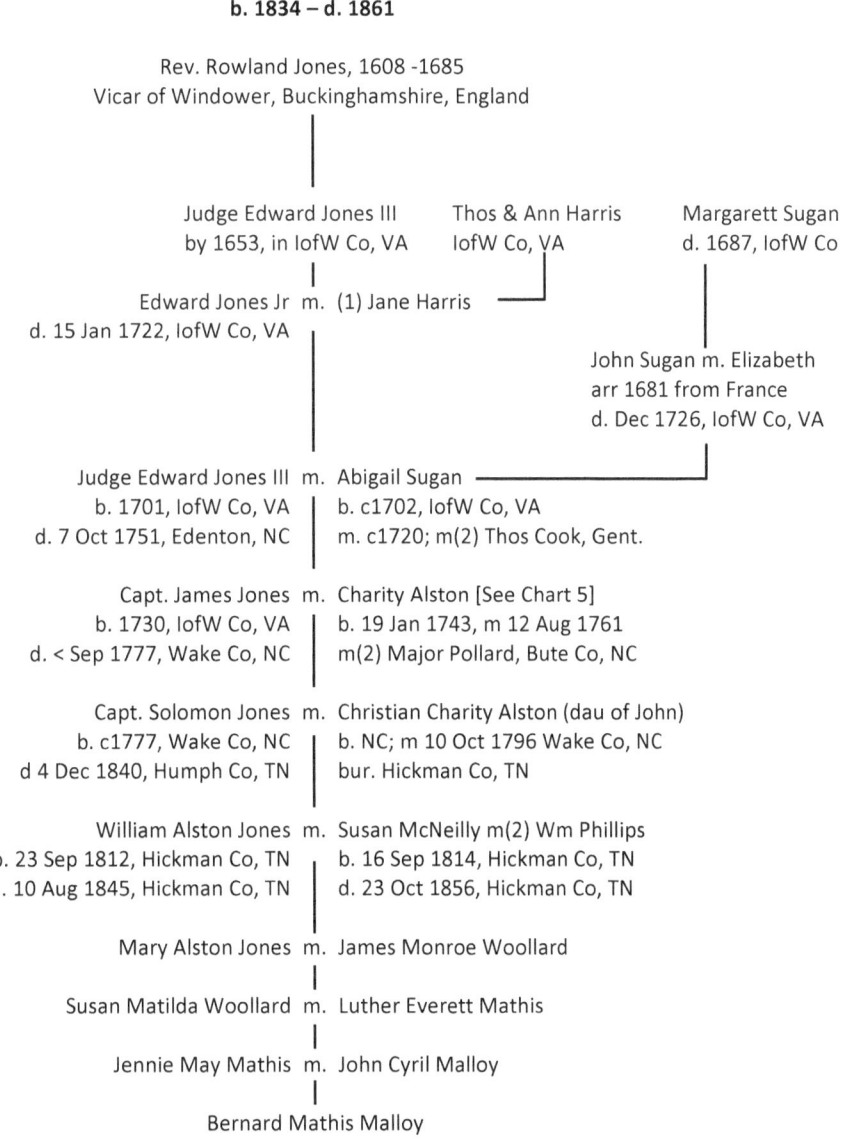

Chart 4: Ancestry of Mary Alston Jones of Tennessee
b. 1834 – d. 1861

Rev. Rowland Jones, 1608 -1685
Vicar of Windower, Buckinghamshire, England

Judge Edward Jones III — Thos & Ann Harris — Margarett Sugan
by 1653, in IofW Co, VA — IofW Co, VA — d. 1687, IofW Co

Edward Jones Jr m. (1) Jane Harris
d. 15 Jan 1722, IofW Co, VA

John Sugan m. Elizabeth
arr 1681 from France
d. Dec 1726, IofW Co, VA

Judge Edward Jones III m. Abigail Sugan
b. 1701, IofW Co, VA — b. c1702, IofW Co, VA
d. 7 Oct 1751, Edenton, NC — m. c1720; m(2) Thos Cook, Gent.

Capt. James Jones m. Charity Alston [See Chart 5]
b. 1730, IofW Co, VA — b. 19 Jan 1743, m 12 Aug 1761
d. < Sep 1777, Wake Co, NC — m(2) Major Pollard, Bute Co, NC

Capt. Solomon Jones m. Christian Charity Alston (dau of John)
b. c1777, Wake Co, NC — b. NC; m 10 Oct 1796 Wake Co, NC
d 4 Dec 1840, Humph Co, TN — bur. Hickman Co, TN

William Alston Jones m. Susan McNeilly m(2) Wm Phillips
b. 23 Sep 1812, Hickman Co, TN — b. 16 Sep 1814, Hickman Co, TN
d. 10 Aug 1845, Hickman Co, TN — d. 23 Oct 1856, Hickman Co, TN

Mary Alston Jones m. James Monroe Woollard

Susan Matilda Woollard m. Luther Everett Mathis

Jennie May Mathis m. John Cyril Malloy

Bernard Mathis Malloy

Sugan / Sucre

Abigail Sugan (b.c1702) was the daughter of Huguenot parents who came to Virginia – Isle of Wight County, or perhaps King & Queen County. Abigail married **Edward³ Jones** and in 1726 inherited land from her father **John Sugan** on the Malvern River. By 1736 Abigail and Edward Jones had moved to North Carolina, settling at Shocco Springs in Edgecombe Precinct (which became Granville County). Edward prospered and became a distinguished member of the colony.

It was said of Abigail that she was "one of the most remarkable women of the last or any preceding century …. A woman of marked traits of character who left her impress upon succeeding generations of her posterity, and a more distinguished progeny than any [other]." This praise was attributed to Colonel Wharton Jackson Green. According to Dr Solomon Green Ward, she was said to have been "a remarkable woman for the strength of her intellect, and for the firmness and energy of her character ….[and] indomitable energy" who, left a widow very young, raised "a house full of children … to become the leading and most useful citizens of the country – five of whom were at one and the same time members of our legislature, and two of them in Congress" (Banks, 7).

After the death of her husband in 1751, she remained a widow until 1765 when she married Thomas Cook, Gentleman.

John Sugan, father of Abigail, may have been the son of **Margarett Sugan** who made her will in Isle of Wight County on 9 June 1687. The original Frech form of his name may have been Jean Sucre; translated, <u>sucre</u> means "sugar," and "Sugar" became one of the ways the name eventually was spelled, with Sugan/Shugan variations becoming the mixed-up consequence of linguistic confusion. His wife was named **Elizabeth**, and their children were Elizabeth, **Abigail**, and Priscilla, according to his will dated 21 December 1726 (proved 25 September 1727). He left his family with considerable worldly goods, including land for Abigail. His name lives on in North Carolina and Tennessee where the name "Sugar Creek" still remains, found in several counties. [See Chart 4]

Alston

Charity Alston, the wife of **Captain James Jones**, was born 19 January 1743 in Chowan County, North Carolina. She was the daughter of **Anne Hinton** (d/o **Mary HARDY** and **Colonel John Hinton**) and **Solomon Alston** (s/o **Mary CLARKE** and **Colonel John Alston**). Her mother had a sister named "Charity" (Charity HINTON, married name not known), as did her father (his sister was Charity ALSTON Dawson), and the name would be handed down through numerous generations to come.

Theirs was not the only marriage between the Alston and Jones families, for her sister Rachel Alston married Edmund Jones, the nephew of her brother-in-law James Jones. Ann Hunt Jones, daughter of his sister Priscilla JONES Macon (wife of Gideon) married Captain John Alston. Furthermore, Charity and James' son Solomon married her niece, Christian Charity Alston [Chart 5].

The marriage of Charity ALSTON and James Jones produced seven children, between about 1762 and 1777, the year of his death; the seventh children, Solomon, was born after his father's demise. The young widow Charity (probably in her early thirties) married Major Pollard on 4 April 1778. Their three daughters were Elizabeth, Charity, and Nancy Pollard. Charity Jones was a widow once more, by 1810 when her daughter Elizabeth POLLARD Steel moved to Hickman County, Tennessee to relocate near her half0brother Solomon Jones; Charity Pollard also moved there at about the same time. Her date of death is not known, but an old gave at the Baptist Church House at Mount Zion is thought to be her. [See Charts 4 and 5.]

Charity's grandfather John Alston was the first American colonist of this family line through his sons Solomon and James (father and uncle respectively to Charity). Beginning with the first American Alston, descriptions of these three men follow at this point. [Chart 5 for <u>partial</u> information about the English ancestry of the Alstons.]

Judge John Alston of Bedfordshire, England was the earliest emigrant of this Alston line to Colonial America. He was the son of **Anne Wallis** (d/o **John**) and **John Alston**, (d.1704, s/o **Dorothy TEMPLE** and **John Alston**, d. 1687). He was christened 5 December 1673 in Bedfordshire at Felmersham.

Although it is believed that John Alston came first to Virginia (Isle of Wight and Nansemond area), his earliest record is a grant in 1711 to 270 acres on Bennett's Creek in Albemarle, North Carolina – just across the Virginia line from Nansemond County. By 1732 he owned at least 1421 acres in Bertie Precinct and 684 acres in Chowan Precinct.

Active in public life,, he served as juror (1715, 1721, 1722), grand juror 91724), Justice of the Peace (1724 to 1729 continuously), vestryman of St Paul's Parish (1738 to 1747), and Sheriff of Chowan County (1746). After 1729 his title was "Colonel."

Colonel John Alston married **Mary CLARKE** (d/o **John Clarke** and his wife **Mary Palin;** her father became Chief Justice of North Carolina). In 1728 the Alston were visited by William Byrd of Virginia, whose written commentary on that occasion alluded to the "beauty … [of] Alston's daughter" (*Society and Family Book* 1:32).

John Alston died in 1758, survived by his wife; his will was dated 20 Feb 1755 and probated 2 December 1758. The ten children of Mary CLARKE and John Alston were: Joseph John (m.(1) Elizabeth Chancy, (2) Euphan Wilson); Mary (m.(1) Henry Guston, (2) William Seward); **Solomon** (m. Anne Hinton); Martha (m. Lemuel Wilson); William (m. Ann Kimbrough); Philip (m. Winifred Whitmel); James (m. Christian Lillington); Elizabeth (m. Samuel Williams0; Sarah (m.Thomas Kearney); and Charity (m.(1) Robert Hilliard, (2) Col John Dawson).

Colonel Solomon Alston, father of Charity, was born about 1708 in Isle of Wight, Virginia. His father, **Judge John Alston,** came from Bedfordshire, England to America, first to Virginia and then to Chowan County, North Carolina by 1695, marrying **Mary Clarke.**

Solomon Alston's wife was **Ann Hinton,** probably born in England before her father immigrated to North Carolina. The Hinton lineage is very distinguished and has been documented for many generations. [See Charts 6 and 6a.]

At some point, Solomon moved to the Granville area that included Bute and Warren Counties. The eleven children of Anne and Solomon included Mary (m. Nathaniel Kimbrough), Solomon (m. Sarah), John (m. Elizabeth Hines), William (m. Charity Alston, d/o James and Christian LILLINGTON Alston), Ann (m. Jesse Hunter), Phillip (moved to Natchez District), **Charity** (who married James Jones), Martha (m. Isaac Hinter), Rachel (m. Edmund Jones), Sarah (m. ____ Morgan), and James (m. Sarah Kearney).

All children were identified in his will dated 4 September 1780; there was no mention of his wife, indicating that he was widowed. A codicil to the will was dated 18 April 1781, and the will was probated at the January Court of 1785 at Warren County.

James Alston, brother of Solomon, lived in Craven County near New Berne; there he married **Christian LILLINGTON,** daughter of **Hannah** and **George Lillington.** He moved to Chowan County in 1745 where he purchased Troy Island on Bennett's Creek near his father. His wife Christian inherited 640 acres from her father; this land was near New Berne, and in 1745 James sold it.

James Alston was a Justice for Chowan County, and on 5 December 1757 he was appointed to the Commission of Peace and Dedimus. In 1758 his father died, naming him sole executor. After his father's death, James Alston moved to Orange County, where he lived on Elebye Creek and died there in 1761.

The children of Christian and James Alston were **John**, Mary (d. prior to 1764), James (m. Grizel Yancey); Charity (m. Lieut-Col William Alston, w/o Anne and Solomon); and Sarah (m. (1) Sir Thomas Dudley, (2) William Cain). Christian survived her husband.

John Alston was the eldest child of his parents. His father left a considerable estate in cash and land. From his father, John received land in Orange County (more than 200 acres); his father's land on Neuse River; "two Lotts in Newbern Town"; the land and plantation in Chowan County on Bints Creeks "whereon my Father formerly lived"; and after the death of his mother John was to have the plantation on which she lived.

The wife of John Alston has not been identified; there were eleven children, so John may have married more than once. In 1774 John lived in Wake County, North Carolina, but he died in Orange County in 1814.

His children were: John, George L., Philip, Lemuel (d. 1818), Alfred, Mary K., Martha, Sarah, James, Absolom, and **Christian Charity** (m. Capt Solomon Jones).

Christian Charity Alston, youngest daughter of John Alston, was born in Wake County, North Carolina.

Called "Chrissie," she was named for her grandmother Christian LILLINGTON Alston, and on her father's side she was the eighth [known] generation to have the name "Charity," including her mother-in-law Charity ALSTON Jones [who was also Chrissie's first cousin once-removed].

On 10 October 1796, Chrissie and **Solomon Jones** were married in Wake County. Five of their children were born in North Carolina: Absalom, John, Thomas, Priscilla, and Dennis G.

In 1807 Chrissie and Solomon Jones moved to Hickman County, Tennessee, thus becoming pioneers along Beaverdam Creek. Three more children were born in Hickman County – **William Alston,** Martha, and Mary. Others of their family joined them there in Tennessee – several of her brothers (Alstons) and her husband's mother, his brother James, and two half-sisters (of the Jones side). All became prominent members of their new community.

The date of her death is uncertain, but Christian Charity ALSTON Jones' burial place is known – she shares a headstone with her husband in the Jones and Sparks Graveyard in Hickman County, Tennessee.

For the further genealogical information on the Alston family, refer to *The Alstons and Alllstons of North and South Carolina* by Joseph A. Groves, M.D. (Atlanta, 1961) and *Society and Family Book*, Volume 1, a publication by the Alston-Williams-Boddie-Hilliard Society (Winston-Salem, North Carolina, 1961). Both are excellent.

CHART 5: Ancestry of Charity Alston (1743- aft 1810)

Thomas Browne, Royal Standard Bearer,
m. Lucy Neville, d/o John, Marquis of Montagu

Sir Anthony Brown KG
m Alice Cage, d/o Sir John Cage KG

Sir Anthony Brown KG, Viscount Montagu
m Jane Radcliffe, d/o Robt, Earl of Sussex

Anthony Browne
m. Mary Dormer d/o Sir Wm Dormer

Dorothy Browne
m Edward Lee of Stanton Barry, Bucks

John Palin, Chief Justice NC 1731 (d Feb 1737)
m Sarah

Mary Palin
m John Clarke (d 30 May 1689)

Edward Lillington d 1736 Craven Co NC

Justice Geo Lillington m2 <1714 Hannah
Resided Craven Co NC

Justice James Alston m Christine Lillington b1725 Craven Co NC

John Alston b Chowan Co NC; d 1814 Oran Co NC
m. Wife's name not known – 11 children

Christian Charity Alston

Miles Sandys, Esq

Hester Sandys
m Sir Thos Temple (d 1637 Stowe)

Sir John Temple m. Dorothy Lee

Rev John Wallis of Emanuel, Camb & Queens,
Oxford; Royal Society (Charter Member)

William Alston d 1307 Stisted, Essex, England

John Alston of Newton, Suffolk

William Alston m Ann Symonds
d 1564 Newton   d/o Thomas

Edward Alston m Elizabeth Coleman
of Saxham Hall, Newton   d/o J Coleman

William Alston m Elizabeth Hampstead
Saxham Hall | Halstead, Essex

Thomas Alston m Frances Bloomfield
Suffolk   d/o Simon of Coddenham

John Alston m Dorothy Temple
(1610-1687) Bedfordshire; m 4 Jan 1634
at Odell Castle

John Alston m Anne Wallis   d/o
d 1704 Bedfordshire |

Judge John Alston m Mary Clark
b 5 Dec 1673 Bedfs | b <1687
d 20 Feb 1755 Chowan Co NC   d >1758

Col Solomon Alston m Anne "Nancy" Hinton
b c1708 IofW Co VA | b c1710 Eng?
d 1780-1784 Warr Co NC   m c1729 NC

Charity Alston m. Capt James Jones
(see Chart 4)

Capt Solomon Jones

m

William Alston Jones m Susan McNeilly

Mary Alston Jones m James Monroe Woollard

Susan Matilda Woollard m Luther Everett Mathis

Jennie May Mathis m John Cyril Malloy

Bernard Mathis Malloy

Hinton

Ann Hinton, also called "Nancy," may have been born in England but she married Solomon Jones in North Carolina. Both her parents were of royal descent and their several proven lines are extensive. Her father, Colonel John Hinton, was the son of a London barrister of Lincoln's Inn whose three sons all went to America.

The earliest English ancestor of the Hintons was **Eruald de Hynton** who came to England with William the Conqueror and is listed in the Domesday Book. His descendant, **Sir Richard de Hynton,** was the first member of the family to receive knighthood, conferred by Henry III in 1250. Understandably, a full treatment of the entire Hinton line is beyond the scope of this account; however, brief descriptions of the generations immediately preceding Ann's generation (1532-1732) in the Colonies will provide a background of this notable family.

Anthony Hinton, Esquire was born in 1532. His wife was **Martha WARNFORD,** of Sevenhampton, Wiltshire. In May 1598 Anthony Hinton died at the age of 66 and was interred in the south aisle of St John's Church, Wanborough, Wiltshire.

Sir Thomas Hinton, son of Martha and Anthony, was born in 1574. He received the Bachelor of Arts from Queen's College, Oxford. His first wife was **Catherine PALMER,** mother of five children; she was of Royal and Margna Charta surety descent. The family seats were "Earlscott," Wiltshire and "Chilton Foliot."

Sir Thomas was Member of Parliament for Bournton, Berkshire (1621-1622) and for Ludershall, Wiltshire (1625-26). He was a large stockholder in the London Company for settlement of Virginia and it is thought that he may have visited Virginia. He was "one of the wealthiest commoners of his day" (Banks, 117). He died 1 February 1635.

Sir John Hinton, son of Catherine PALMER and Sir Thomas Hinton, was born in 1603. He received the Bachelor of Arts from Queen's College in 1625; thereafter he served as a Field Surgeon in the Royal Army, as Fleet Surgeon on Drake's flagship "Mayflower," and as Physician in-Ordinary to Queen Henrietta Maria and the Prince of Wales, and also to the Royal Couple after Charles II assumed the throne. Sir John Hinton married **Elizabeth DILKE.** He died on 10 October 1682.

James Hinton, son of Sir John and Elizabeth DILKE Hinton, was born in 1642. He also was a graduate of Queen's College on 10 March 1659; admitted to Lincoln's Inn in March 1659, he was called to the bar in 1666. The name of his wife is not known; three sons – James, **John,** and William – settled in Chowan Precinct of the Province of North Carolina.

Colonel John Hinton, son of James, came to North Carolina about 1720, as indicated by a grant dated 4 April 1722 for 350 acres of land on Bennett's Creek in Chowan Precinct. It appears that he had come first to Virginia, for some of his descendants settled there in Isle of Wight County.

His wife was **Mary HARDY,** descendant of **Sir Robert Hardy,** a royal lineage. John and Mary Hinton had eleven children: Colonel John (m. Grizzella Kimbrough d/o Buckley), Hardy, William, Malachi, Rachel, Mary (m. Wiley Jones?), Sara (m. Benjamin Blanchard), **Ann,** Charity, Rose, and Judith.

John Hinton was "a man of prominence wealth, and widely spread connections," as was evidenced by his title of "colonel" (Banks, 118). He died in 1732, survived by his wife.

CHART 5: Ancestry of Anne Hinton Alston (b c1710 England – d Granville Co, North Carolina)

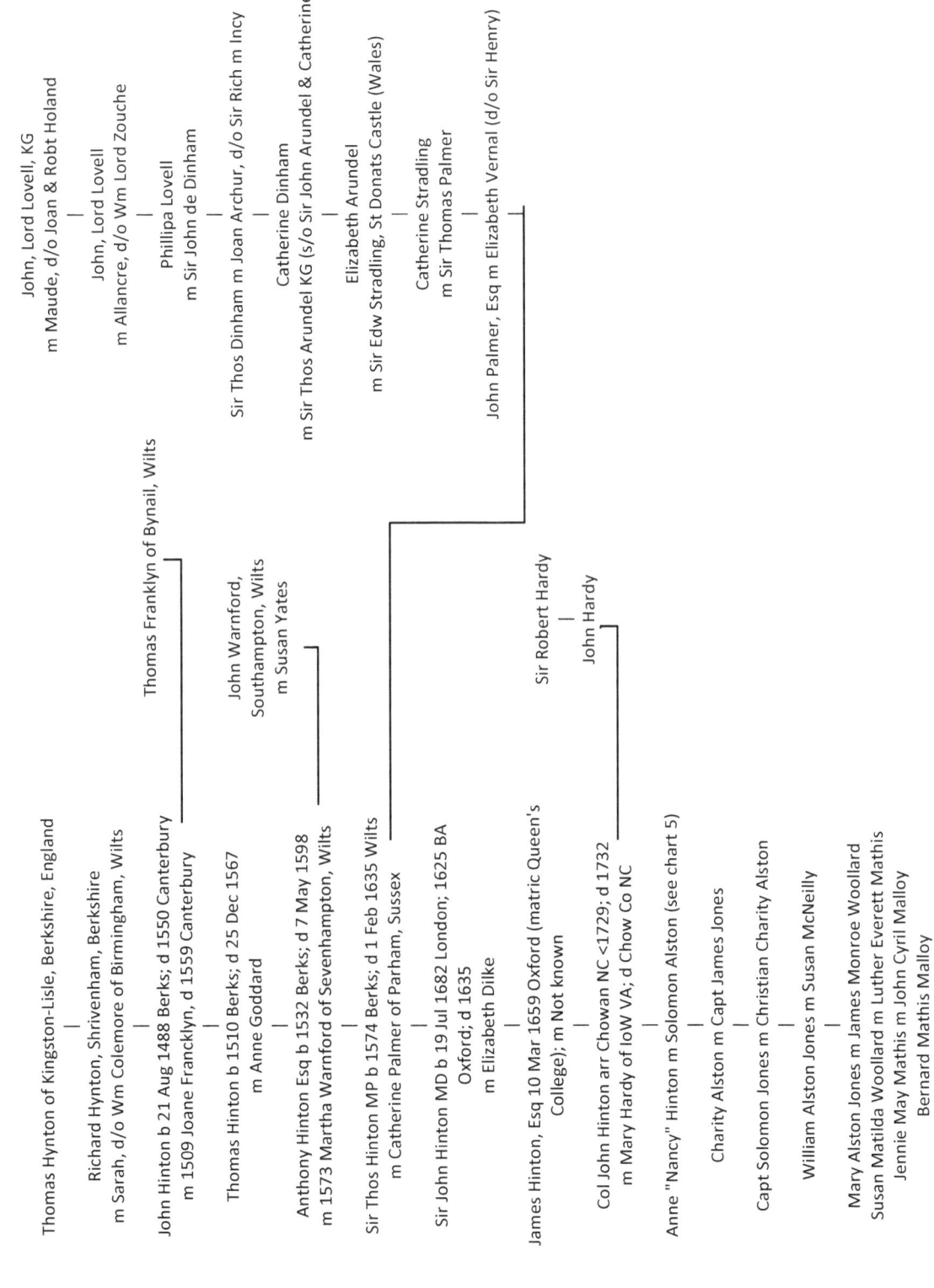

Chart 6a: Possible Ancient Ancestry of Anne Hinton

Eruald de Hynton, 1070

|

Elias de Hynton, 1167 (great-grandson of Eruald)

|

Robert de Hynton of Hynton-Brackley

|

Richard de Hynton m. Aceline

|

Hugh de Hynton of Hynton-Woodford m Maude (Matilda) Foliot

|

Sir Richard de Hynton of Wiltshire, c 1250

|

Capt Hugh de Hynton of Hynton-Woodford, c 1265
m Matilda de Eyden, d/o Geoffrey of Eyden, Northamptonshire

|

John de Hynton the Elder of Hynton-Woodford; m Agnes

|

Sir John de Hynton the Younger of Hynton-Woodford, c1310
m Petronilla de Massingham, d/o Laurance, High Sheriff of Huntington

|

Sir John de Hynton III of Huntingdon, d 1350
m Margaret de Coteford, d/o Henry de Coteford

|

Geoffrey de Hynton, Comptroller of Customs, Lincolnshire

|

Henry de Hynton of Hynton, Warwickshire

|

Philip de Hynton of Hynton, Warwickshire

|

Thomas de Hynton of Coventry, Warwickshire

|

Thomas de Hynton, Manor of Southall, Parish of Dunmore

|

John de Hynton, Kingston-Lisle, Berkshire
at Siege of Hartieur (1414) and Battle of Agincourt (1415)

|

John de Hynton of Kingston-Lisle, Berkshire

|

Thomas Hynton of Kingston-Lisle, c1511-1540
his cleric son was associate of Bishops Cranmer, Latimer, Ridley

|

See chart 6 for remainder of line forward to
Ann Hinton and then to
Bernard Mathis Malloy

Lillington

Christian Lillington of Craven County, North Carolina was the daughter of **Hannah** and **George Lillington;** she was born no later that 1725. In 1741 she inherited from her father his "dwelling plantation" (after the death of his widow) as well as household goods, livestock, and Negroes. Special bequests were a large gold ring, four silver teaspoons and tongs, and his "Church Bible."

Christian married James Alston of Chowan County, North Carolina and moved with him to that county. In 1745 Christian's husband sold her inherited land in New Berne, which probably indicates the death of her mother Hannah, thereby releasing the land of Christian.

Her husband was a Justice for Chowan County and was appointed to the Commission of Peace and Dedimus in 1757. Their five children – **John**, Mary, James, Charity, Sarah – were born in Chowan County. After 1758 they moved to Orange County where her husband died in 1761; Christian Alston survived James.

It appears that Christian's grandfather was the first generation to America, in the company of his two brothers.[5] According to one version, they came first to Massachusetts but also to Barbados and Philadelphia before settling in North Carolina. Information about her grandfather and father is given below. [Refer also to Chart 5]

Edward Lillington was a member of the Warwickshire family of that name (which also appeared as Linnington and Lunnington). Several generations had been clergymen, out of Oxford, and when Edward and his brothers [Alexander, George?*] came to the colonies they had money to invest. At any rate, by 1724 Edward Lillington and his son **George** were in Craven County on the Neuse River.

Edward died in 1736, leaving a will that named his children: **George,** Christian (who m. _____ Malone), Mary (m. Dennis Sherlock), and Edward.

George Lillington, like his father Edward (above) lived on the Neuse River. In 1739 he was appointed Justice of the Peace but died two years later (24 January 1741). He had married twice and left two daughters by each wife. The first wife's name is not known, and his widow was referred to in his will as **Hannah.**

His older daughters, Ann Hutchinson and Elisabeth, received £50 each. The two younger daughters of Hannah, **Christian** and Mary Elisabeth, were given his land and possessions, to be divided to them at the age of seventeen or at marriage.[6]

McNeilly

Susan McNeilly of Hickman County, Tennessee was married on Christmas Eve in 1833 to William Alston Jones (s/o Christian Charity ALSTON and Captain Solomon Jones). She was the daughter of **Mary "POLLY" Yates** and **James Arnold McNeilly, Sr,** born 16 September 1814.

Susan and William A. Jones had seven children: **Mary Alston** (m. James Monroe Woollard), Martha, Amanda (Nancy), Sophia, Solomon, Dennis, and Priscilla. William A. Jones died young (age 33, 10 Aug 1845) and was buried at their home on Duck River.

After the death of her husband, Susan McNEILLY Jones married (2) William H. Phillips. He was elected Sheriff of Hickman County (for three terms) and served one term as State Representative. They had three children: William H., Jacob, Nellie Phillips (m. W.S. Nunnelly).

Susan Phillips died 26 October 1856. Susan, described in the Spencer book on Hickman County pioneers as "good wife" and "universally beloved daughter of James McNeilly" (p.250), was buried beside husband William

---

[5] As for the two supposed brother, George Lillington, Esq was thought to have been a colonel in the British army. Known to have been in Barbados in 1685, he was President of the Council in 1709 "as governor and commander in chief of the Barbadoes. He subsequently returned to England" (Groves, 248).

[6] Alexander Lillington, presumably brother to George and Edward, was in 1675 a resident of Albemarle County, married to Sara James, daughter of Thomas of that county. In 1679 he was appointed an associate justice, judge of Precinct Court in 1690, and in 1693 was deputy governor of North Carolina. He died in Perquimans County in 1697, naming children John George, Anne, Elizabeth, Mary, and Sarah in his will.

Phillips in the Millington Easley Cemetery in Pinewood, Hickman County, Tennessee.

Her full American lineage is not known – just her father's line, which is discussed briefly below. For additional information on the McNeilly/McNeeley/McNeely family, see James Kenneth Tyler's <u>McNeely Family Genealogy</u> (Mountain View, CA, 1986).

James Arnold McNeilly, Sr, father of Susan Jones, was born 20 March 1787, probably in Caswell County, North Carolina. He was orphaned when quite small and was bound out, as was customary, to someone in the community. The man to whom James was bound was so cruel that another man – Charles McKinley – took the lad and gave him a good foster home where he remained until he reached adulthood (Tyler, §16:1).

James McNeely's name was on the 1803 Caswell County Tax Lists, the only person of that surname. The following year he married **Mary "Polly" Yates,** on 6 September 1804, Caswell County; Robert Samuel was bondsman. Between 1808 and 1811, James McNeely's name appeared in the public records of Halifax County, Virginia (including 164 acres on the Dan River) which was just across the state line from Caswell County, North Carolina. It has been suggested that McKinley died in 1807. In 1811 Polly and James McNeely sold this 164-acre farm, having left the region to live in another state.

With their son William they moved in 1807 to Hickman County, Tennessee and settled on Sugar Creek near Duck River, where in time they acquired large holdings – including a profitable grist mill, a sawmill, and a distillery. In They operated a very popular inn for years from their home on Reynoldsville Road. It was the custom then to sell ginger cakes on Election Day and Muster Day; those sold "at McNeely Mill were the best ever eaten" (Tyler, §16:2). On those occasions, every male in the 8th District would gather at the mill.

James McNeilly was Magistrate in the 8th District. He also was one of the Commissioners who laid out the township of Centerville, the county seat of Hickman County; this is evidence of the prestige and wealth he had attained. James and wife Polly had nine children: William Yates, Thomas, **Susan,** James Jr (moved to Kentucky), John, Matthew P., Nancy, Ann, and Mary McNeilly.

James McNeilly died 3 February 1839 (or 1840), at age 52. He is buried with his wife in a small local burying ground, their graves marked by plain sandstones; down the road a short distance lies a millwheel – still unrusted – fashioned by James from native ore and used in his grist mill for many years.

Chart 7: Ancestry of Susan McNeilly
  b. 1814, d. >1856, Hickman Co., Tennessee

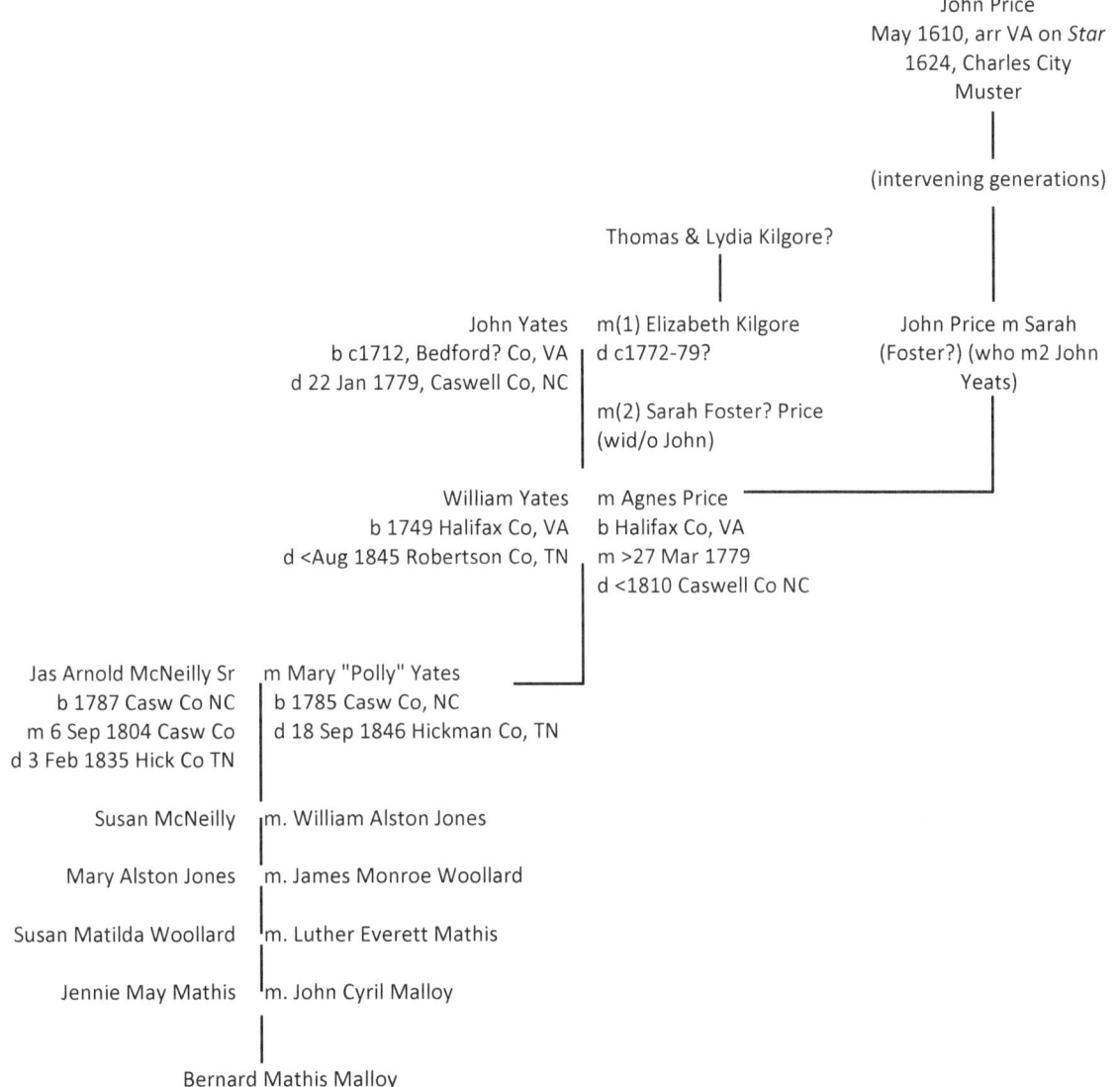

Yates / Yeates

<u>Mary "Polly" Yates</u> married James Arnold McNeilly and was the mother of Susan McNeilly. Polly Yates was born in 1786, Caswell County, North Caroline; her parents were **Agnes PRICE** and **William Yates**. Polly Yates grew up in Caswell County; after their marriage, Polly and James **McNeilly** moved to Hickman County, Tennessee.

Of Polly's nine children, only Mary – the youngest – did not survive to adulthood. After her husband's death in 1839 (1840?), she was listed in the census as a widow. In 1846 Polly transferred ownership of property to her son James Jr. Polly died 18 September 1846 at age 40 and was buried with her husband in a family burial ground near Sugar Creek.

Of her antecedents, only two generations of this Yates family are definitely identified – her grandfather and her parents. Brief discussions of each appear below. For further reading on this family, consult *John Yates, 1712-1779 and His Descendants to 1989* by Evelyn Yates Carpenter (Clarksville, TN, 1989).

John Yeats, grandfather of Mary YATES McNeilly, was a Virginian who migrated to North Carolina. He may have been born about 1712 in what is today Bedford County (formerly Halifax, Lunenberg, Brunswick counties). Halifax County was created in 1752, and on 20 November 1755 the name of John Yeates appeared in the Antrim Parish vestry records on a list of processioners. In 1766 Halifax was once again partitioned, the western edge of the county falling thereafter in newly created Pittsylvania. From 1768 to 1777 John Yeats and his family lived near the boundary line – "on the waters of Winn Creek," partly in Virginia (Pittsylvania and Halifax Counties) and partly in North Carolina (Orange County which became Caswell County in 1777).

John must have married about 1748, but there is no reference to it; his wife's name is not known, but tradition says that she was **Elizabeth Kilgore**. They had eight children: **William**; Thomas (m. Rebecca Ragsdale); John Jr (m. Jemima Roper); James (m. Lydia Ann Kilgore, 21 July 1784); Joyce (m. Edward Swann); Keziah (m. William Roper); Elizabeth; and Mildred (m. John Swann). John's wife died before 1779 and may have been buried in Edmondson Square in Old Halifax County Cemetery.

John and Williams [a brother?] Yates from Bedford County, Virginia served in the French and Indian War. The name of John Years appeared on deeds from 1755 to 1778; in 1777 he signed a petition to divide Orange County. He was living in Orange County by 1771; he married (2) **Sarah Price** (widow of John Price) after 1772 and before 1 May 1779, the date of his will which named Sarah as his wife. It appears that earliest spellings of the name were as "Yeats" which eventually gave way to "Yates," that usage having prevailed by mid-nineteenth century.

William Yates, son of Elizabeth KILGORE (?) and John Yeats, was born in Bedford County, Virginia in the year 1749. His age was given as 22 on the 1771 Tax List of Halifax County; his father and brother Thomas were listed, too. Their names appeared also on the 1777 Tax List. William served three enlistments, from Hillsborough District, North Carolina, during the Revolutionary War, one of them on the Continental Line, together with his brother Thomas. Various deeds of William Yates were recorded between 1782 and 1810.

In 1779 (between March and June) William Yates married **Agnes Price** (d/o **Sarah** and **John Price** of Halifax County, Virginia). Their twelve children were: John Price 9m.Jane Yates); Sara (m. Blueford Warren); William Jr (m. Chloe Walton); **Mary "Polly"**; Mildred (m.George Randolph); Agnes (m. William Tillman); James (m. Mary Jane Brooks); Elizabeth (m. Jas Brooks); Laurah [Idah?] (m. Thos Potts); Nellie (m. William Holman); Susannah (m. Sterling Harwell); and Martha (m. Valentine Winston Bernard). Wife Agnes died in Caswell County, North Carolina before 1810.

In 1810 William Yates was appointed Inspector of Tobacco and Flour at Milton, North Carolina. That same year he sold his land in Caswell County and went to Robertson County, Tennessee where two of his brothers had preceded him. Deeds and other court records are on file. He soon married (2) Rachel Childress, but according to his will dated 30 January 1838 they had separated by that time. His death occurred by 1844, and he is buried in Carr Cemetery, Cross Plains (Robertson County), Tennessee; his grave has a DAR marker.

Grant #1650 to William Yeates, surveyed 13 December 1782, Surry County, North Carolina
(Surry Co WB 77:35-36)

Kilgore

Elizabeth Kilgore may have been the wife of John Yates. Her parents were **Lydia** and **Thomas Kilgore.** They had a daughter named Betsy who married some one named Farmer. It is possible that after his death Betsy married (2) John Yates. Nothing else is known about Betsy KILGORE Farmer, but tradition has it that she became John Yates' second wife.

Thomas Kilgore was born about 1715. His wife was named **Lydia,** and they lived in the Caswell-Orange Counties area of North Carolina. He was there as early as 1752 and in 1769 and 1770 acquired some 510 acres of land on the Kilgore Branch of the North Hico Creek. He served in the Revolutionary War.

Only three of the children of Lydia and Thomas Kilgore are definitely known. Their son Thomas married Pheby Lea, and daughter Lydia married James Yates. The other daughter was Betsy who married _____ Farmer and possibly (2) John Yates; nothing else is known about her.

Thomas Kilgore died in 1823 in Robertson County, Tennessee near Cross Plains, having moved there at some unspecified time.

Price

Agnes Price, mother of Mary YATES McNeilly, was the daughter of **John Price** of Halifax County and his wife **Sarah** (thought to be a daughter of **Ambrose Foster).** Agnes was born in Halifax County, Virginia, probably about 1755. Her father John Price died in 1772, and by 1779 (a seven-year period), her mother Sarah Price had taken as a second husband John Yates. In 1779, very soon after her stepfather's death, Agnes married his son William Yates.

Agnes and John were the parents of twelve children, all of whom lived to adulthood. Agnes PRICE Yates died in Caswell County, North Carolina about – probably before – 1810. Her father's lineage is described below.

John Price, born in England or Wales about 1584, arrived in Virginia in May, 1610, aboard the "Star." He was listed in the Charles City Muster of 24 January 1624/5 as one of the survivors of the Indian Massacre of 1624. [NOTE: He is not listed in *C7P* as an Ancient Planter, nor does *C&P* list any arrivals of the "Star" during the year 1610.] He settled in Henrico County, Virginia and is considered to be the founder of this family (Carpenter, 12). Obviously, several generations following this original John Price are lacking at this time.

John Price, father of Agnes PRICE Yates, was probably born in Lunenberg County, Virginia. While still living there in 1765, he bought land in Halifax County; William Price as a witness. There he and John Yates were neighbors among the Winn Creek settlers.

His wife was **Sarah** (perhaps the daughter of Ambrose Foster). They had eleven children: Hannah (m. Josiah Farley), Matthew, William, John, Elizabeth (m. ___ Blackwell), Mary (M. ___ Brooks), Sarah, Marcilua, Sookey, **Agga**, and Ann.

John Price, "being in a low state of health," made his will on 28 July 1771. He gave land to his three sons and made cash bequests to his eight daughters. His widow Sarah and son William were exeutors; they proved the will on 19 March 1772. (See Chart 7.)

Mathis

Luther Everett[5] Mathis was born 8 February 1861 in Gibson County, Tennessee; he was the son of **Martha Jane Rust** and **Alexander Littlejohn Mathis.** On 12 January 1888, he married **Susan Matilda Woollard** of Jackson in Madison County. After his marriage, Luther Mathis moved to Jackson where he owned a grocery store. Squire Mathis was a magistrate for 22 years; he was active in the Sons of Confederate Veterans, serving as Division Commander for eight years and as Assistant Inspector –in-Chief. For this discussion, he has been assigned to the fifth <u>known</u> generation of his Mathis line in America, although it is assumed that almost certainly there had been earlier antecedents among English colonists of that surname to America.

Susan Matilda and Luther Everett Mathis had two children: Paul Jones Mathis (1890-1946) and **Jennie May[7] Mathis** (1895-1967). Luther's wife died 19 June 1930, and he died 6 January 1940; both were buried in Hollywood Cemetery, Jackson, Tennessee.

Full treatment of the Mathis lineage will not be given here because *Mathis-Carlton-Shelley of Virginia, North Carolina, &Tennessee* proves this line of descent of the Mathis, Carlton, and Shelley families. Likewise, another book now in preparation (*Rust of North Carolina*) will prove the descent of Martha Jane Rust who married Alexander Littlejohn Mathis. Brief descriptions of Luther Mathis' ancestors follow, in chronological order from the earliest.

Jacob[1] Mathis' earliest grant of land in Duplin County, North Carolina, 100 acres on Rock Fish Creek , was dated 1770. He first appeared on the tax lists of Duplin County in 1783 and was listed continuously thereafter up to 1806 when he was listed as "Jacob Mathis, Sr." Earliest roots have not yet been verified (origins in Virginia and specific information during the Revolutionary War, for example) although there are certain references still to be pursued. The name was variously spelled as Mathis, Mathews, Mathies, and Mathers – with the letter "t" sometimes doubled

Mathis and others of his family (there were at least eight Mathis households in Duplin County from 1783 to

1806) were landowners; the plantation of James Mathis was a local landmark. They sat on juries and grand juries and served in various community positions as overseers of public road and constables, as well as in the militia. Jacob owned a grist mill on Stewart's Creek.

In 1786 Jacob Matthews received a warrant for 640 acres of land in Davidson County, Tennessee for service in the Continental Line. Jacob Mathis, Sr was listed in the 1820 census of Duplin County; from this it is assumed that his death occurred between that date and the 1830 census. John, Jacob Jr, and **William** have been identified as his sons.

William² Mathis was born about 1779, probably in the vicinity of Duplin County. He married **Lydia Carlton**, daughter of the **Reverend Thomas Carlton.** William Matthis appeared in the 1800 census and was on the Duplin County Tax List of 1806. He was appointed to be constable and gave bond in 1803, 1804, and 1805 to fill that office.

By 1807 William Mathews, "formerly of Duplin County, North Carolina," was in Rutherford County, Tennessee (formerly Davidson County), having acquired title to his father's bounty land. The Rutherford census lists him and his eldest son Elisha in 1810 and 1820, and the county records document their presence there in 1820, but by 1821 William Mathis had removed to Madison County, Tennessee.

William Mathis was listed in the 1830 census as residing in Gibson County. He died on 6 December 1846 in Gibson County, survived by his wife Lydia and nine children: seven sons included Elisha, Thomas, **Carlton,** William, Jacob, Edwin, Lebanon D., and their two daughters, Mahaly C. Weatherspoon and Angeline T. Sexton.

Carlton³ Mathis was born in Duplin County, North Carolina on 7 August 1801 and moved with his family Rutherford County**,** Tennessee and later Gibson County. His wife was **Mary SHELLEY.** Their children included Jacob, Alexandrer, Eli Mary, Elisha, Elizabeth, Lucinda, Nancy, Emma, and Lucretia (as listed in 1850 census).

The fourth of September 1828 was given as the date of Grant £4022 Issued to Carlton Mathis for 25 acres of land in Gibson County. He received another grant on 29 September 1847 for 48/34 = [sic] acres. His lands were "on the waters of Forked Deer River."

Carlton Mathis died in Gibson County 9 November 1888. He was buried in the Mathis Cemetery with his son **Alexander Littlejohn Mathis.**

Alexander Littlejohn⁴ Mathis was born in Gibson County, Tennessee on 9 September 1832. He was known to all as "Tall John." On 10 January 1855 he married **Martha Jane Rust** (b.1833) in Gibson County, daughter of **Nancy Rucker COOKE** and **John S. Rust).** A.L. Mathis was brockade runner during the Civil War; he was apprehended and condemned to hang, but was release because a Unionist friend interceded for him. On 2 August 1865, he signed the Amnesty oath. His underground activities weakened his health.

His somewhat early demise occurred on 8 October 1884 in Gibson County; Martha Jane, his wife, reached age 92, having lived out her widowhood in the home of her son Luther Everett Mathis. Their other children Edgar L., George Lee, Jennie, Atlas, Thomas Clinton, and James Mathis.

Chart 8: Ancestry of Luther Everett Mathis
of Jackson, Tennessee, 1861-1940

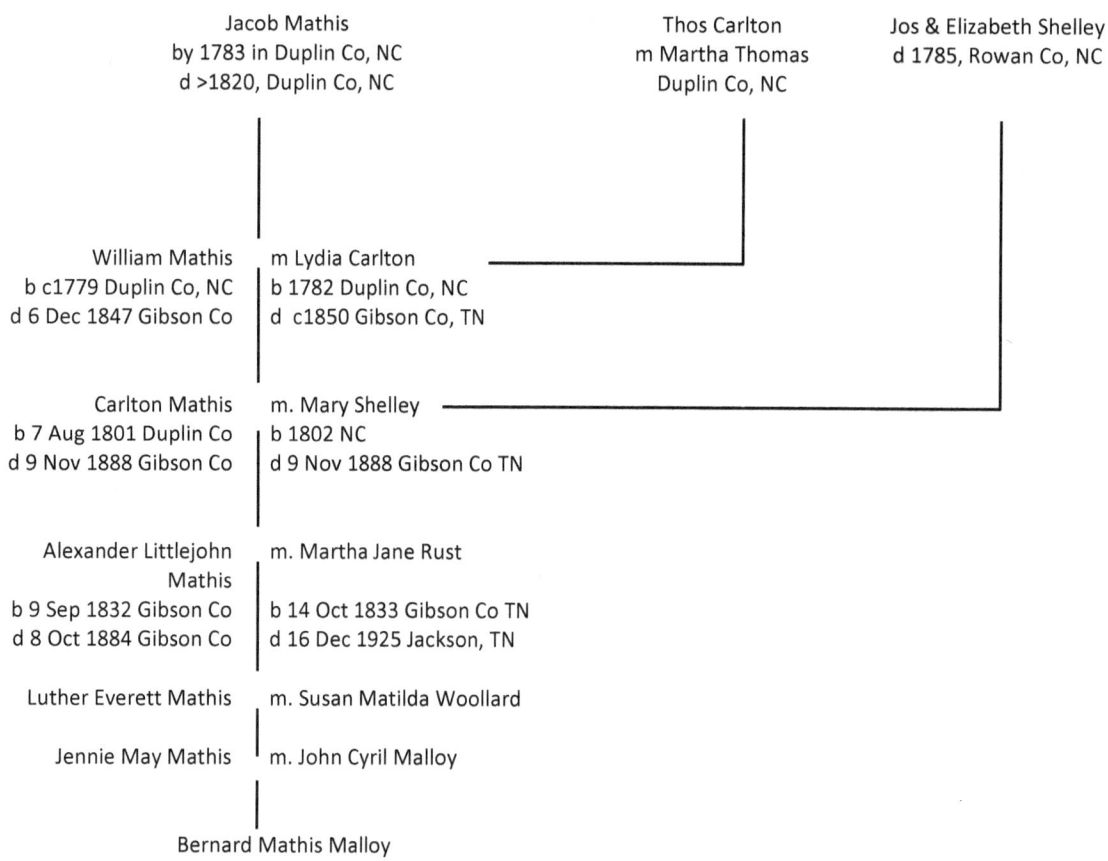

Jacob Mathis
by 1783 in Duplin Co, NC
d >1820, Duplin Co, NC

Thos Carlton
m Martha Thomas
Duplin Co, NC

Jos & Elizabeth Shelley
d 1785, Rowan Co, NC

William Mathis
b c1779 Duplin Co, NC
d 6 Dec 1847 Gibson Co

m Lydia Carlton
b 1782 Duplin Co, NC
d c1850 Gibson Co, TN

Carlton Mathis
b 7 Aug 1801 Duplin Co
d 9 Nov 1888 Gibson Co

m. Mary Shelley
b 1802 NC
d 9 Nov 1888 Gibson Co TN

Alexander Littlejohn
Mathis
b 9 Sep 1832 Gibson Co
d 8 Oct 1884 Gibson Co

m. Martha Jane Rust
b 14 Oct 1833 Gibson Co TN
d 16 Dec 1925 Jackson, TN

Luther Everett Mathis   m. Susan Matilda Woollard

Jennie May Mathis   m. John Cyril Malloy

Bernard Mathis Malloy

Carlton

Lydia Carlton was the daughter of the **Reverend Thomas Carlton** and his wife **Martha THOMAS** of Duplin County, North Carolina. She was born about 1780, and was named in the will of her father in 1795, still unmarried. She married William Mathis and moved with him to Tennessee.

In 1841 her brother –in-law, the Reverend Peter Carlton, died childless and distributed land to "the sons and daughters of Martha and Thomas Carlton, one of them being Lydia CARLTON Mathis.

Lydia was the mother of nine children. She survived her husband (died 1846 in Gibson County) and died prior to 1860. Lydia Mathis (age 68) was listed in the 1850 census as residing in Gibson County with eleven-year-old Phoebe J. Sentor (p.35, Hh249).

Thomas Carlton, father of Lydia, came to Craven County, North Carolina with his brother John before the Revolutionary War. Both Brothers served in the war and afterwards settled in Duplin County. They may have come to North Carolina from Chester County, Pennsylvania; according to that theory, their father was a native of England or Scotland by way of North Ireland and they were Quakers. Another version connects them with Richard Carlton who was in Craven County, North Carolina by 1747, having been exiled from Scotland after the uprising of 1745 and disastrous loss at the Battle of Culloden. The Carlton line has been researched by a number of independent inquiries, and the search continues.

Thomas and his wife Martha THOMAS setttled on Murrow's Branch, near the home of his brother John Carlton and also near Jacob Mathis; this vicinity was near the line where Sampson County was cut from Duplin. Thomas Carlton was a clergyman as was his nephew Peter. Today, the Carlton United Methodist Church of Magnolia (in Duplin County) stands on the site of the original Methodist Episcopal Church of 1790, some of the original timbers incorporated into its structure. [This negates the claim that they were Quakers, as does the military service.]

Shelley

Mary Shelley, wife of Carlton Mathis, was born in 1803, probably in Rutherford or Davidson County, Tennessee. Her parents were **Martha R.** and **Thomas Shelley**. The Shelley family had moved to Iredell County, North Carolina (probably from Virginia), and from there they had moved on to Tennessee.

The 1820 census for Overton County Tennessee listed Thomas Shelley whose household included a son and a daughter between 16 and 26 years, interpreted as Mary and her bother Joseph C. Shelley. Soon thereafter she married Carlton Mathis, and they settled in Gibson County. Mary SHELLEY Mathis died 9 November 1888.

The American origins of this English family undoubtedly are to be found in Virginia. There is abundant evidence of the Shelley family's presence in colonial Isle of Wight County; in addition, there are circumstantial indications that some of the family migrated to North Carolina as early as 1732. Several connections have not been documented, and continued research is underway; nevertheless, the Virginia origins of this family can be assumed. The reconstructed family line of the Shelleys (see Chart 9) as described below is tentative; most but not all links have been verified. For further information on the Shelleys of Virginia see Boddie's *Isle of Wight County, Virginia* and *Colonial Surry County.*

John Shelley, the earliest Shelley of record, was 23 years of age when he came to Virginia aboard the "Bona Nova." He lived at Jamestown at the time of the 1624 census; the following year's census showed him "living at Mr Blaney's plantation 'across the water,' which was in Surry County" (Boddie,v.4:65). Subsequently, Surry County records were destroyed in the Richmond fire of 1865.

Philip Shelley of Surry County, Virginia (d.1704) was descended from Phillip, son or grandson of John. Philip married **Ann CLAY Mason** (wid/o James, d/o Thomas) in 1660; she died in 1669. Their surviving children were Phillip Shelley, Jr and "youngest brother" John Shelley, Elizabeth Fones, **Thomas**, and "daughter Ann at John Sugars."

Thomas Shelley married **Mary** (d/o **Mary**, wid/o (1) Thos Hardy and (2) Chas Jarrett). His will, probated 2 May 1751, Isle of Wight County, named his wife Jane and five children: James, **Thomas**, Elizabeth, Martha, and

Ann.

Thomas Shelly, born c1720 in Isle of Wight County, Virginia, married **Elizabeth** (surnamed not known). They moved to Rowan County, North Carolina with sons John and **Joseph**.

Joseph Shelley, **Senr** of Rowan County executed a will 14 October 1786, naming his wife Elizabeth and five children; Benjamin, James, Richard, **Thomas**, Joseph, and Elizabeth. The following year, Elizabeth Shelly received a State Grant in trust for her children James, Richard, Thomas, Joseph, and Elizabeth Shelly, "orphans of Joseph Shelly, dcd."

Thomas Shelley was born in Virginia, probably in Isle of Wight County. His birth year (according to the census records of 1820, 1830, and 1840) was 1775. His father was **Joseph Shelley** who with other members of the Shelley family moved to Rowan County, North Carolina by 1786, and then to Tennessee. [The names Thomas and Joseph were used in each generation of his brother Joseph have a son named Joseph and likewise brother Benjamin name a son Joseph.] The brothers appeared in the Rowan Census of 1787 and in the 1800 census of Iredell County, which was formed from Rowan.

Thomas Shelley married **Martha R _____,** a native of Virginia. Their three known children were Joseph C. Shelley (b. 1801), daughter **Mary** (b.1803), and a son (b.1804-10). By 1821 his daughter Mary had married Carlton Mathis and lived on a farm adjoined the land of her gather Gibson County.

Thomas Shelley's death occurred by early months of 1848. Joseph C. Shelley administered his father's estate – later, Carlton Mathis administered the estate. Thomas Shelley was survived by wife Martha and their two children, Joseph Co. Shelley and Mary Mathis, wife of Carlton Mathis.

Chart 9: Possible Ancestry of Mary Shelley
Wife of Carlton Mathis

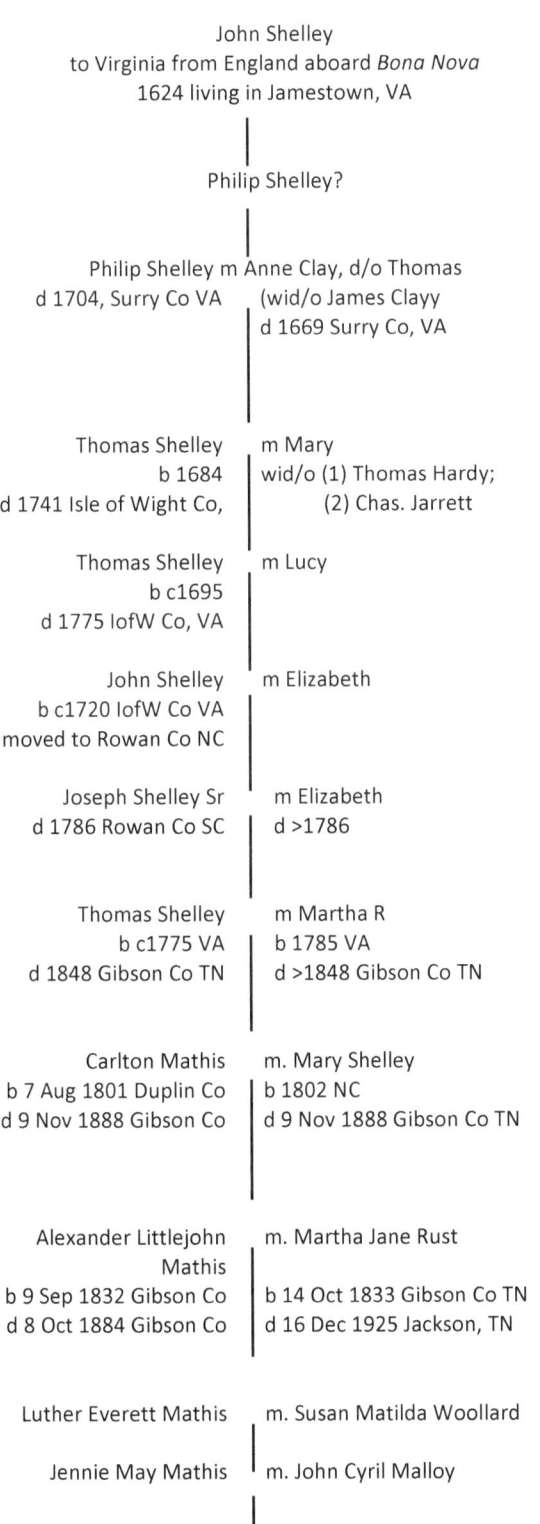

John Shelley
to Virginia from England aboard *Bona Nova*
1624 living in Jamestown, VA

Philip Shelley?

Philip Shelley m Anne Clay, d/o Thomas
d 1704, Surry Co VA   (wid/o James Clayy
                          d 1669 Surry Co, VA

Thomas Shelley   m Mary
b 1684   wid/o (1) Thomas Hardy;
d 1741 Isle of Wight Co,   (2) Chas. Jarrett

Thomas Shelley   m Lucy
b c1695
d 1775 IofW Co, VA

John Shelley   m Elizabeth
b c1720 IofW Co VA
moved to Rowan Co NC

Joseph Shelley Sr   m Elizabeth
d 1786 Rowan Co SC d >1786

Thomas Shelley   m Martha R
b c1775 VA   b 1785 VA
d 1848 Gibson Co TN d >1848 Gibson Co TN

Carlton Mathis   m. Mary Shelley
b 7 Aug 1801 Duplin Co   b 1802 NC
d 9 Nov 1888 Gibson Co   d 9 Nov 1888 Gibson Co TN

Alexander Littlejohn   m. Martha Jane Rust
Mathis
b 9 Sep 1832 Gibson Co   b 14 Oct 1833 Gibson Co TN
d 8 Oct 1884 Gibson Co   d 16 Dec 1925 Jackson, TN

Luther Everett Mathis   m. Susan Matilda Woollard

Jennie May Mathis   m. John Cyril Malloy

Bernard Mathis Malloy

This chart represents the generations of Shelleys
that, as of this writing, have been identified in
colonial Virginia between 1624 and 1720.
Their interrelatedness is not always clear. All of
them are thought to be related, but the first five
generations have not been documented as the
antecedents of John Shelley who moved to Rowan
County, North Carolina.

Rust

Martha Jane Rust was born 14 October 1833 in Gibson County, Tennessee. Her parents were **John S. Rust** and his wife **Nancy Rucker COOKE,** both of Granville County, North Carolina. She married Alexander Littlejohn Mathis of Jackson, Tennessee on 10 January 1855. Their children included Edgar L., **Luther Everett,** George Lee, Jennie, Atlas Oscar, Thomas Clinton, and James.

Martha RUST Mathis was widowed in 1884; during the rest of her life she lived with her son Luther and his family. She died in 1925 an age 92 and was buried at age 92 and was buried in Jackson, Tennessee.

The Rust family was from Westmoreland County, Virginia, having been there from 1650 to 1761, at which time Martha Jane's great-grandfather had established himself in Granville County. Several publications recount the history of the Rust family; the most complete is *Rust of Virginia, 1654-1940* by Elsworth Marshall Rust (Washington, DC, 1940). Now in preparation, *Rust of North Carolina* (by the authors) will continue the family history of those who moved to North Carolina in 1761. Hence, the family lineage of Martha Jane Rust will enumerate each generation with spouse and their dates; maternal lines, if known, will be listed in the same way. Note that the Rust numbering system of *Rust of Virginia* is used to identify the generations. [See Chart 10, following page.] Material lines, if known, will be listed in a section following the Rust family lineage. All summaries will be very brief.

William Rust came to Virginia in 1650 with a party of Royalists under the sponsorship of Sir Thomas Lunsford. He was unmarried and from all indications was a young man. He married **Ann Metcalfe,** daughter of **William Metcalfe** of Northumberland; Ann and William settled in Westmoreland County on Yeocomico River, just north of the Northumberland County line. Of five children, only **Samuel** left descendants (seven sons and two daughters), so that all Rusts of the Northern Neck descend from a common ancestor. As an educated member of the community, William Rust often served as a juror, a function which was performed by "the most able men of the county." He prospered as a planter and acquired considerable land.

Samuel Rust, Planter and **Martha** his wife had extensive land holdings – at least 1700 acres; in the 1704 Quit Rent Roll he was one of the largest landholders in all Virginia. He was a grand juror and estate appraiser; in addition to raising tobacco, he owned a mill. All their nine children married and left progeny; two grandsons of Martha and Samuel Russ – Jeremiah and Peter – signed the "Westmoreland Articles of Association" at Leedstown, the earliest formal declaration of colonial opposition to the policies of Great Britain. Samuel was a parishioner of Cople Parish, the church located very near the Rust plantation -- this was the childhood parish of Mary BALL Washington, who grew up on the neighboring plantation of George Eskridge, her godfather (and also an in-law of the Rusts).

John Rust (1695-1727) married **Agnes Clements** (d. <1727), daughter of **John Clements** (d. 1701) and **Jane** (d. <1717). The known children of Agnes and John Rust were **Samuel,** John, William, and Elizabeth. John died young, and his widow married (2) Roger Wigginton.

Samuel Rust (1715-1741) inherited land from his father; like his father, he too died young – Samuel was survived by two small children, **John** and Agnes. Samuel's wife was **Bridgett Turner,** daughter of **Phoebe SHIPPLEY** and **John Turner** of St Stephen's Parish, Northumberland County, Virginia. Bridgett Rust married (2) George Harrison, her husband's kinsman.

John Rust (c1736-1819) married **Sarah Cox,** daughter of **Eleanor LAMKIN** and **George Cox** (1700-1760) of Northumberland County. In 1761 the young couple sold their land on the county line and moved to Granville County, North Carolina; they were the first Rusts to move out of Virginia. John Rust was a captain of militia and served in the Revolutionary War; later, he was sheriff of Granville County. Sarah and John had nine children – two daughters and 7 sons: George, Samuel, John, Jeremiah, Sarah, **Matthew,** Mary "Polly"," Vincent, Lemuel.

Matthew Rust (c1770-1806) was a son of Sarah and John Rust of Granville County, North Carolina. He married **Priscilla Mills,** and his brother Jeremiah married Sarah Mills; they are thought to be daughters of **William Mills.** Matthew's death at age 36 left six orphans: William H., Mary Cox, Charnock Cox, John S., Joames, and George Boswell Rust. The children were bound out to their uncles and grew up in Granville County, Priscilla Rust married (2) Harlow Priddy; they moved to Gibson County, Tennessee.

John S. Rust, son of Priscilla and Matthew Rust, was born 11 October 1801 in Granville County, North Carolina. John married **Nancy Rucker COOKE** (1804-1877) who was the daughter of **William Cooke** and **Mary**

McGeehee (daughter of **Benjamin**) of Granville County. The children of Nancy and John S. Rust were William B., James, **Martha Jane**, Sarah, John W., George M., Atlas, and Nancy.

Like all his brothers and his sister Polly, John S. Rust moved to Tennessee; he and wife Nancy settled in Gibson County. Nancy died 7 August 1877, and John S. Rust died 9 March 1881; they were buried in the Rust Cemeter at Chapel Hill, Gibson County, Tennessee.

**Chart 10: A Line of Descent from William Rust
in Virginia, North Carolina and Tennessee**

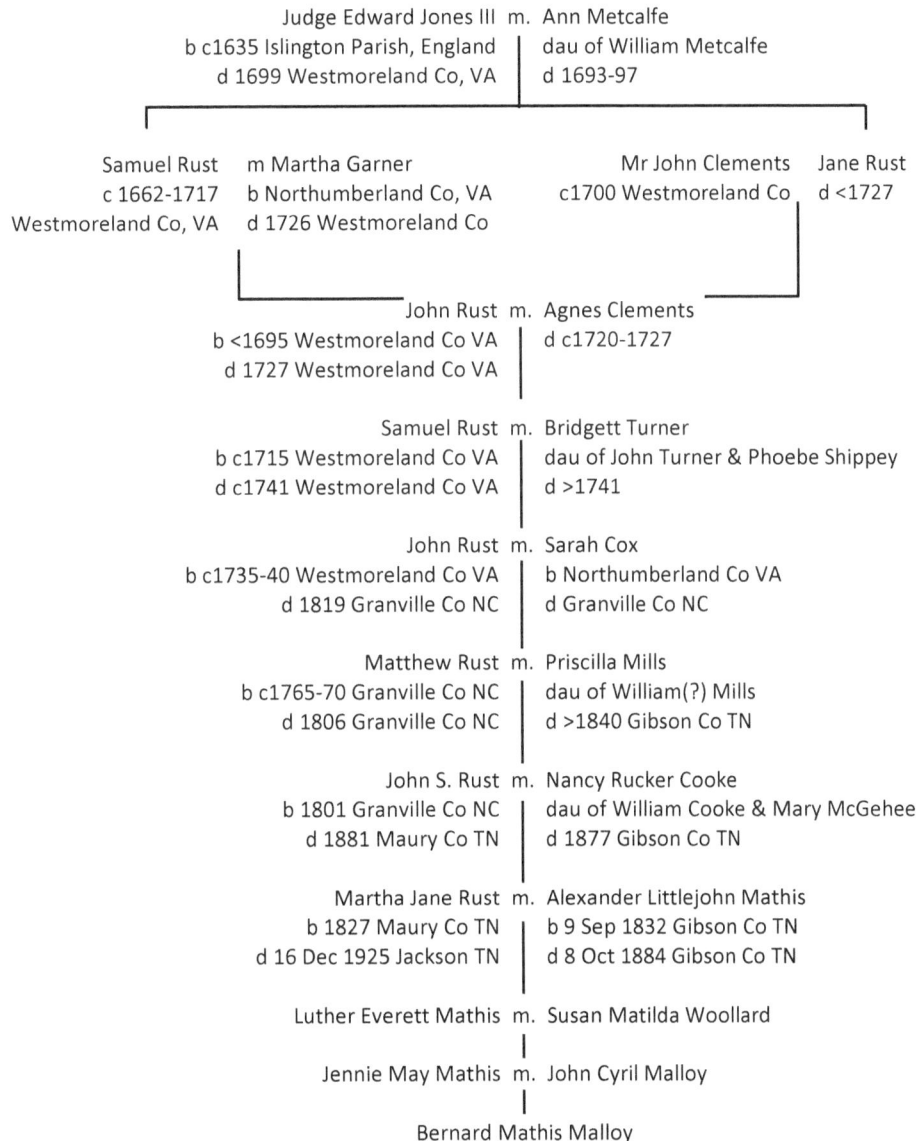

Metcalfe

<u>Ann Metcalfe</u> was the daughter of **William Metcalfe** (Medcalfe/Medraffe, with or without final <u>e</u>) of Northumberland County, Virginia just across the line from Westmoreland County on a neck of land called Cherry Point Neck. Ann's first husband, John Landman, was a landowner on the "S.E. side Yeocomoco Ricer." After his death (c1660), the young widow married (2) William Rust. Ann's name appeared with William's on deeds, and in 1662 she conveyed land in Northumberland County to William Landman, her brother-in-law, suggesting that she held property as the widow of John Landman. Ann and William Rust had four children; thereafter, all Rusts of Westmoreland descended from Ann METCALFE Rust and her husband William.

William Metcalfe was one of the earliest settlers in Northumberland County. His name appears on the earliest surviving record book of Northumberland County – an index of pages, now lost, which included "William Metceffe" and also Henry Fleet, both names found in earlier records of St Marys Parish, Maryland (just across the Potomac River). At that time, no one had settled officially in the Northern Neck, although refugees from Maryland had arrived as early as 1637, ousted by the dispute between William Claiborne and Leonard Calvert, the Lord Proprietor of Maryland.

In 1640 Claiborne had received a special grant of land on the Virginia side of the Potomac for "disaffected Protestants of Maryland"; in 1648 that strip of land was legally constituted as Northumberland County. It is possible that William Metcalf was formerly a Marylander, perhaps a descendant of John Medcalf, one of the "gentlemen adventurers" (lves, 109-10) who had come with the "Ark" and the "Dove" which in 1634 had brought the original settlers of Maryland. He may also have been the William Medcalfe who (with Abraham Moone) was transported to Virginia's "Middle Plantation" by Lieutenant Richard Popely in 1639.

William Medcalfe also signed the "Northumberland Oath of Loyalty to the Commonwealth, 1652." The 98 signers are Northumberland's earliest documented residents, among them several who were prominent in Virginia as well as some connected to the Medcalfes and the Rusts by marriage, as listed here: John Mottrom, Peter and William Pressley, Charles Ashton, Richard Clare, Thomas Coggin [Scoggin], Robert Newman, and Richard Walker, as well as Andrew Monroe, ancestor of the future President.

William Metcalfe died in 1655, leaving two sons, Henry and George, and five daughters including Ann, Katherine, Elizabeth, Jane, and Charity. William Metcalfe's seven orphans were minors, with the probable exception of Ann; at any rate her marriage to John Landman (though she was soon widowed) had conferred status as an adult. By 1661 she was married to William Rust and in July of that year he was appointed guardian of "minor orphan Jane Metcalfe, whose [elder] sister was wife of Wm Rust."

Ann METCALFE Rust was still living in 1693 but died before May 1697. [See Chart 11.]

Garner

<u>Martha Garner,</u> considered to be the wife of **Samuel Rust** (although proof is circumstantial) was the daughter of **Susannah KEENE** and **John Garner,** of Northumberland County, Virginia. All later Rusts of Westmoreland County trace their lineage back to William and Ann Rust through Samuel and Martha, who reared a family of nine children. Samuel, juror and estate appraiser, was one of the largest land owners in the Northern Neck at that time. Samuel Rust's will was dated 16 August 1717. His widow Martha GARNER Rust survived him by ten years; her will was dated 3 November 1726 (pr 25 February 1729). [Chart 11 describes her line.]

John Garner was born in 1633; he came to the colony from England in 1650, most likely as a Royalist refugee after the execution of Charles I. He married **Susannah Keene,** the daughter of **Mary** and **Thomas Keene,** also of Northumberland County. They lived near Cherry Point Neck, where neighbors included Joseph Fielding, William Metcalfe, and William Presley. Later, John and Susannah moved across the line to Westmoreland County. They had seven sons and three daughters – Martha being the youngest daughter, as named in john Garner's will, dated 22 January 1702.

Keene

Susannah Keene was the daughter of **Thomas Keene** and his wife **Mary Thorley?,** both from Suffolk, England; Susannah may have been born in Maryland before the Keene family moved to Northumberland County, Virginia. She married John Garner about 1660, and they had ten children. Susannah Garner died in 1716, having survived her husband by 14 years. For a complete description of these families, see *Garner-Keene Families of Northern Neck, Virginia* by Ruth Ritchie and Sudie Rucker Wood (Charlottesville, 1952). Her ancestry is described briefly.

Thomas Keene of County Suffolk, England, may have emigrated to the American colonies, but there is no direct evidence of it; however, his wife's family was prominent in the settling of Jamestown, so he also may have been one of the early comers. His wife was **Elizabeth Gosnold** of Otley, Earieshall, County Suffolk. Her kinsman was Bartholomew Gosnold, Vice Admiral of the fleet of three vessels which landed at Jamestown in 1607. [See Chart 11.]

Elizabeth Gosnold was the daughter of **Robert Gosnold, Esquire** of Otley, Earlshall in County Suffolk and his wife **Ursula Naunton** (d/o **William**). Robert Gosnold died in 1615. His will mentioned his daughter Elizabeth Keene ad his grandsons "now in Virginia," Thomas Keene and Anthony Gosnold. One of his executors was Mr Francis Cornwallis of Earleshall [Suffolk] – a significant indicator because the Cornwallis family was prominent in the settling of Maryland.

Thomas Keene, father of Susannah, was born in England, probably Suffolk, in 1593; his parents were **Elizabeth GOSNOLD** and **Thomas Keene.** He was living on Kent Island, Maryland in 1637 and about 1640 had married **Mary Thorley.** By 1650 they had removed to Cherry Point Neck, in Northumberland County, Virginia. In 1652 he was one of the signers of the Northumberland Oath of Allegiance. His will was dated 20 January 1652/3; it named their four children.

Mary THORLEY Keene, thought to be the daughter of **Edward Thorley** of Anne Arundel County, Maryland (circumstantial evidence), survived her husband and married (2) Henry Raynor and (3) Thomas Broughton. Her will, dated 2 January 1662, was recorded in Northumberland County.

Clements

Agnes Clements married her cousin 203-John Rust. Her parents were **Mr John Clements** and his wife **Jane Rust,** who was a sister of 102-Samuel Rust. Agnes Rust's sister Sarah was married to Nathaniel Garland, and all of them lived in Westmoreland County. [See Chart 11.]

Agnes and John Rust had four children: **Samuel,** John, William, and Elizabeth Rust. John's death in 1727 left his children orphans, for Agnes died before him. Their youngest child Elizabeth was the ward of Ann RUST and George Harrison (her aunt and uncle) and she resided with them.

Mr William Clements, grandfather of Agnes, was an early resident of Westmoreland County. In "the early 1660s" he married (1) **Elizabeth _____ Earl** (widow of (1) Causey; (2) John Howell, d. c1658; and of (3) John Earle, d. 1660), "who lived on the Yeocomico"; she may have been the mother of William's son **John Clements.** An early deed shows that in 1664 MR William Clemens acquired 300 a. from Samuel Earle, "son & heir of John Earle dcd."

In July of 1670, Mr William Clements and Mrs Frances Powell, widow, entered into a [pre-marital] covenant, "being about to enter into holy martymonie." It is not impossible that she, instead of Elizabeth, was the mother of John.

In addition to being a planter, William Clements engaged in a shipbuilding enterprise with Samuel Rust and his neighbor and business partner. The name was spelled variously as Clemens and Clement.

Mr John Clements inherited his father's share of the shipbuilding business on the Yeocomico River in partnership with Richard Tidwell. He was also active in court affairs of the county, appointed frequently as appraiser of landed estates. In 1698 he took Tidwell's son as apprentice.

He married **Jane RUST**, sister of Samuel Rust. Their known children were Agnes and Sarah (m. Nathaniel

Garland). In 1699 or 1700, Samuel Rust and John Clements bought land from Mrs Eunice Thistlewheat of St Sepulcher's, London. John Clements died very shortly following this transaction.

Jane administered her husband's estate. She married (2) Roger Wigginton and died before 1717, survived by Roger, who mishandled the inheritance of Jane's daughters, Agnes Rust and Sarah Garland, whose husbands, John Rust and Nathaniel Garland, sued on behalf of their wives. As yet, the disposition of this litigation over the Thistlewheat purchase is not known.

**CHART 11: Colonial Families of the Northern Neck of Virginia: Metcalfe, Rust, Garner-Keene, Clements
1648 – 1727 Northumberland & Westmoreland Counties**

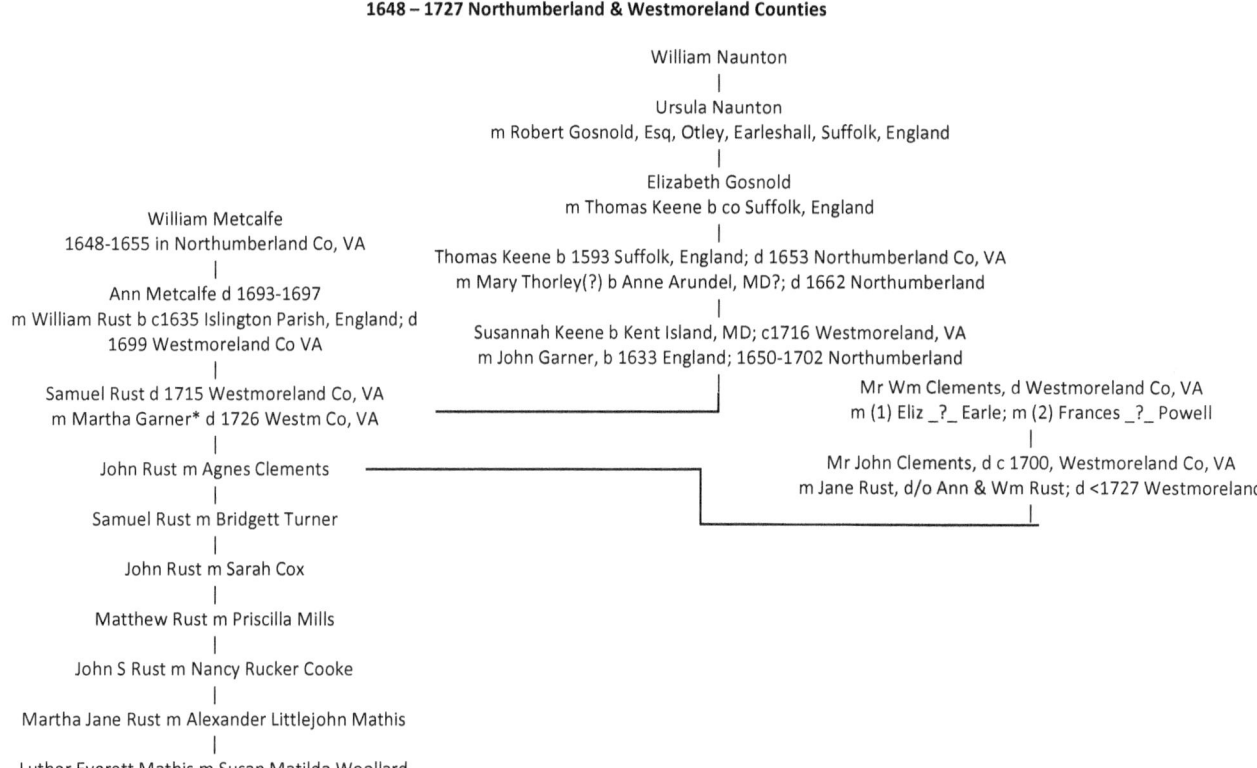

* The Garner-Keene connection has not been documented but has "always" been assumed to be a fact.

Turner

Bridgett Turner of St Stephen's Parish, Northumberland County, Virginia, was the wife of **Samuel Rust** of Couple Parish, Westmoreland County. Her parents were **Phoebe SHIPPEY** and **John Turner**. [See Chart 12.]

Bridgett and Samuel Rust lived on the plantation left him by his father; it lay along the border of the two counties. Bridgett's young husband died without leaving a will; her brother Henry Turner and her kinsman James Knott were guardians of her tow small children, **John** and Agnes. Bridgett TURNER Rust married (2) George Harrison, the cousin of her deceased husband; it is believed that they resided in Richmond County. Nothing more is known of Bridgett's life and death.

John Turner and his wife **Phoebe** were the parents of eight children: sons John, Henry, George, and Edward, and daughters Elizabeth (m.Richard Hayden), **Bridgett,** Monica, and Ann, as enumerated in John's will. John Turner died between 6 December 1741 and 12 April 1742, the date when the will was proved.

Shippey

Phoebe Shippey, mother of Bridgett TURNER Rust, was the daughter of **Richard Shippie** and his wife **Eleanor Mott.** The earliest form of this surname was "Shapleigh," also given sometimes as "Sheppy," "Shippey," and "Shippe." References to this branch of the family are found in the colonial court records of Richmond and Northumberland Counties. Phoebe married **John Turner** and her sister Priscilla married Henry Metcalfe; Phoebe and Priscilla were identified as legatees of James Jones (1715). Phoebe SHIPPY Turner was the mother of eight children. Earlier generations of Shippleys are given below. [See Chart 12.]

Captain Phillip Shapleigh of Northumberland County may have been the father of John Shapleigh (who was grandfather of Phoebe). His plantation and the Shapleigh Storehouse were on the Wiccomoco River; he also owned an Ordinary. He served as Justice in 1678 and 1687. Phillip Shjapleigh had at least five children – Thomas, **John,** Hannah, Judith, and Sara, four of them christened at St Stephens Parish (c1677 to c1695). His records date from 1675 to 1717, at which time his will was presented by his executors, Hannah and John Shapleigh.

John Shapleigh married **Mary English.** They were the parents of **Richard Shippie**. In 1714 John Shapleigh was guardian of his niece Elizabeth, only daughter of MR Thomas Shapleigh, dcd (brother of John).

Richard Shippey, father of Phoebe, married **Eleanor Mott** in 1691. In 1695 they lived in Richmond County. Richard's death occurred before 1714; in that year, his daughter Priscilla [being at least 14 years of age] chose William Metcalfe as her guardian. By 1715 Priscilla was married to Henry Metcalfe and her sister Phoebe was married to John Turner.

English

Mary English (grandmother of Phoebe SHIPPIE Turner) was the daughter of Abraham English of Rappahannock County. By 1669 Mary English was the wife of John Shippey; in that year she and her sister Sara Long recorded 350a. in Gloster Co which had been granted to their father in 1668.

Abraham English was the great-grandfather of Bridgett Turner and the father of Mary ENGLISH Shippy. Between 1638 and 1642 he patented 400 a. in Charles River County, renamed York and then Gloucester County. In 1649 he held land on the Rappahannock.

Mott

Eleanor Mott, who married Richard Shippey, was the daughter of **Mr George Mott** and his wife **Mary.** Eleanor was born in Rappahannock County. The will of Ellen Mott, dated 1741, was recorded in King George County but is now lost.

Mr George Mott and his wife **Ann** lived in Rappahannock County. In 1660 George Mott with his brother John patented in one tract 15,654 a. of land in present-day King George and Stafford Counties. The four daughters of Ann and George were Elizabeth, Margaret, Ann, and **Eleanor,** who in 1691 was married to Richard Shippey of Richmond County. George Mott died in 1674.

**Chart 12: Turner, Shippey, English, and Mott:
Families of the Northern Neck**

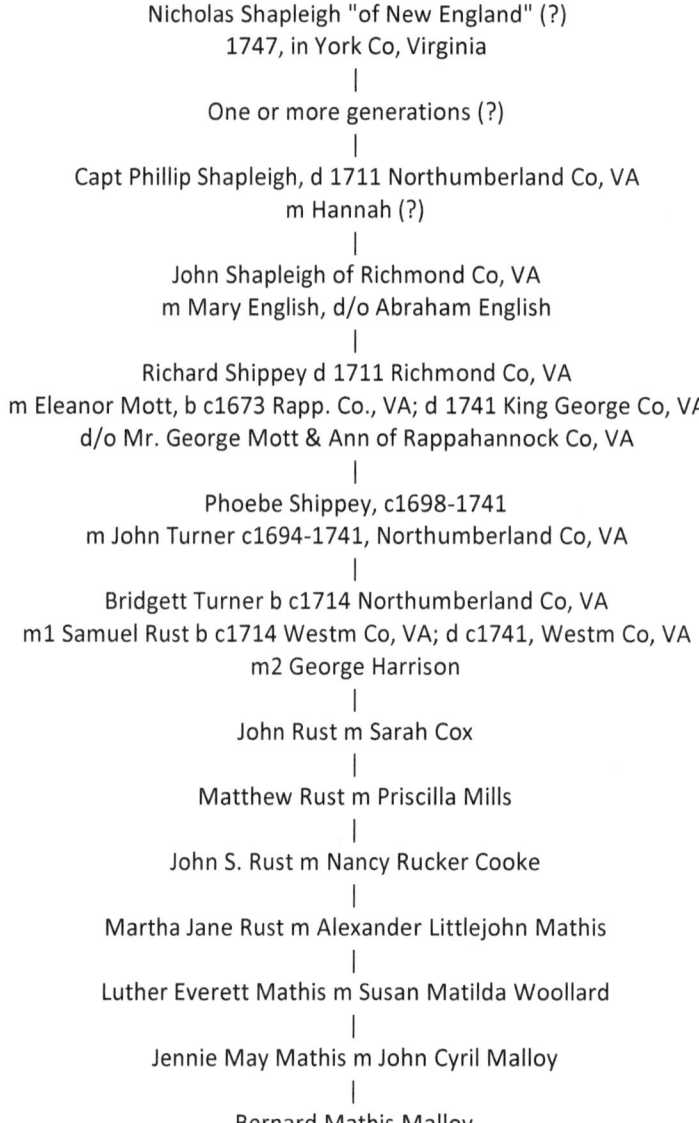

Nicholas Shapleigh "of New England" (?)
1747, in York Co, Virginia
|
One or more generations (?)
|
Capt Phillip Shapleigh, d 1711 Northumberland Co, VA
m Hannah (?)
|
John Shapleigh of Richmond Co, VA
m Mary English, d/o Abraham English
|
Richard Shippey d 1711 Richmond Co, VA
m Eleanor Mott, b c1673 Rapp. Co., VA; d 1741 King George Co, VA
d/o Mr. George Mott & Ann of Rappahannock Co, VA
|
Phoebe Shippey, c1698-1741
m John Turner c1694-1741, Northumberland Co, VA
|
Bridgett Turner b c1714 Northumberland Co, VA
m1 Samuel Rust b c1714 Westm Co, VA; d c1741, Westm Co, VA
m2 George Harrison
|
John Rust m Sarah Cox
|
Matthew Rust m Priscilla Mills
|
John S. Rust m Nancy Rucker Cooke
|
Martha Jane Rust m Alexander Littlejohn Mathis
|
Luther Everett Mathis m Susan Matilda Woollard
|
Jennie May Mathis m John Cyril Malloy
|
Bernard Mathis Malloy

Cox

Sarah Cox was the daughter of Eleanor **LAMKIN** and **George Cox** (son of **Mary PRESLEY** and **Charnock Cox**). For many years these families lived in the Northern Neck of Virginia, specifically Northumberland and Westmoreland Counties. The plantation of Sarah's parents was on the county line at the West Yeocomico River coast.

Sarah Cox married her cousin, **John Rust,** (son of **Bridgett TURNER** and 300-**Samuel Rust**) soon after he reached his majority. Within a year or two, they sold their plantation on the West Yeocomico River and in 1761 traveled to Granville County, North Carolina which at that time was attracting newcomers from the other colonies, including a recognizable group from Westmoreland County. Sarah's father George Cox had invested in land there, but in 1760 he died in Northumberland County without having made the move to North Carolina. As her part of his estate, Sarah received three negroes – Nan, Nell, and a boy named Ben – who went with them when they moved to Carolina.

Sarah and John Rust ad nine children: George, Samuel, John, Jeremiah, Sarah, **Matthew,** Mary (Polly), Vincent, and Lemuel. These were "Rust" names, except for Vincent and Lemuel, which were "Cox" names. Eventually, all their children moved away from Granville County.

Sarah's name appeared later on various deeds, the last time in 1786, so her death occurred after that year but before 1800, when the census showed her husband to be widowed. The line of descent of Sarah COX Rust is given below, from the earliest known American ancestor.

CHART 13: A line of Descent from Vincent Cox
of Westmoreland County, Virginia

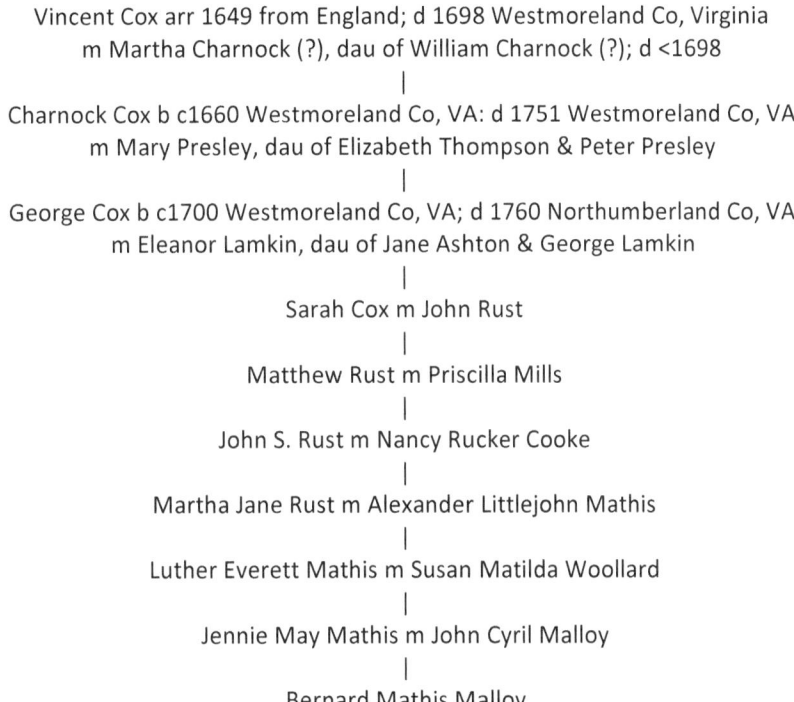

Vincent Cox arr 1649 from England; d 1698 Westmoreland Co, Virginia
m Martha Charnock (?), dau of William Charnock (?); d <1698
|
Charnock Cox b c1660 Westmoreland Co, VA: d 1751 Westmoreland Co, VA
m Mary Presley, dau of Elizabeth Thompson & Peter Presley
|
George Cox b c1700 Westmoreland Co, VA; d 1760 Northumberland Co, VA
m Eleanor Lamkin, dau of Jane Ashton & George Lamkin
|
Sarah Cox m John Rust
|
Matthew Rust m Priscilla Mills
|
John S. Rust m Nancy Rucker Cooke
|
Martha Jane Rust m Alexander Littlejohn Mathis
|
Luther Everett Mathis m Susan Matilda Woollard
|
Jennie May Mathis m John Cyril Malloy
|
Bernard Mathis Malloy

Mr Vincent Cox arrived in Virginia in 1649, leaving behind him in England the Civil Wars; his passage was bought through indenture. He completed the usual four years of servitude but had to go to court to establish the date of his arrival; it is interesting that he was referred to in the court records as "Mr" Cox. The surname of his wife **Martha** is not known but could have been **"Charnock,"** a surname found in parts of England but rare in Virginia, then (as now) except on the Eastern Shore; this distinctive name was given to their first-born son. Other children were Vincent, Thomas, Martha, Anne, and Elizabeth, named in the will of their father Vincent Sr.

He died (5 July 1698) a very wealthy man, holding extensive lands in Northern Neck at that time and bequeathing land to his sons and (most unusual) silver and cash (in the form of tobacco) to his four daughters.

The plantation of Vincent Cox was located between the Rust and Lamkin lands, all in Westmoreland County's Cople Parish.

Charnock Cox married **Mary Presley,** daughter of a distinguished family. Her father was Colonel Peter Presley (s/o Colonel William Presley and Jane Newman); her mother was Elizabeth Thompson (d/o Ursula Bysshe and Richard Thompson). Mary's father and both grandfathers were burgesses, the highest local honor of colonial Virginia. In 1744 Charnock Cox died; his will named his sons Presley, **George,** and William, his daughter Elizabeth Rust, and Peter Rust, his grandson. Like all members of the family, as well as his neighbors the Rusts and Lamkins, he was a member of Cople Parish Church and probably was buried in the Cople Parish Churchyard.

George Cox was listed as the fifth child of his father, who bequeathed him five Negroes. He married **Eleanor LAMKIN** (daughter of **Jane ASHTON** and **George Lamkin** [see Chart 14]. They resided in St Stephens Parish, across the line in Northumberland County. **George** died intestate in 1760, at which time his widow Eleanor and the children – **Sarah COX Rust**, Vincent, George Jr, Charnock, and Presley Cox – moved to Granville County, North Carolina.

Lamkin

Eleanor Lamkin was the daughter of **Jane ASHTON** and **George Lamkin**, Westmoreland County, Virginia. She is named in her father's will dated 1718. After marrying George Cox, Eleanor lived in Northumberland County. They had four known children: Sarah, George, Vincent, and Charnock Cox, and perhaps Presley Cox. In 1761 she administered the estate of her husband who died intestate. Thereafter, she also moved to Granville County, North Carolina. Their children, too, left Virginia and moved to North Carolina. Her line can be traced back to **Thomas Lamkin**, living in the Northern Neck by the 1650s, as shown below. [See chart 14]

Thomas Lamkin, was named as son-in-law in John Walker's will (1665) along with Walker's "eldest daughter" Connegan Lamkin. John Lamkin and George Lamkin were also named, presumably the sons of Connegan and Thomas Lamkin. The earliest evidence of Lamkins in the Northern Neck is a land patent to Capt Giles Brent in Westmoreland County for transporting David Lamkin, dated 6 July 1654.

George Lamkin, son of Connegan (or Commegan) and Thomas, married **Hannah,** surname not known, although there are many records of her presence in the Northern Neck. In 1672 land on Nominy River was conveyed by "Vincent Cox of Yoacomaco in Copley Parish" unto George Lamkin "and to the heirs of his body on the body Hannah Lamkin his wife." The will of George Lamkin, which named Hannah his executrix, was produced in court on 29th July 1691. [NOTE: At this same court, Capt Lawrence Washington and Andrew Munroe both appeared on routine matters.] Hannah and George Lamkin had a son who was also named **George.**

Hannah (Tucker?) Lamkin married (2) Dr Samuel Demourvel (Demovel/Damovel/Demourville/etc) who had emigrated from France. She appeared in court with reference to the estate of George Lamkin, dcd in February 1692/3, at which time she was identified as "Hanna Lamkin alias Demourville." In November of 1693, John Lamkin was summoned in a case between Samuel Magdalen, and Hannah. Samuel died in 1723 but Hannah lived on until 1744; her lengthy will named many grandchildren – including three Hannahs and two Magdalens.

George Lamkin, son of Hannah and George, married **Jane (Joan/Jean) Ashton** and had six children. George made a will in 1718 (when his health was poor) and named Peter, **Eleanor**, and George as his children; however, he did not die until 1727, by which time there were three additional children __ Samuel, Ashton, and Charles Lamkin [identified in Jane's will and many other records].

**CHART 14: A Line of Descent from Thomas Lamkin
of Westmoreland County, Virginia**

Thomas Lamkin b c1630 England; d Westmoreland Co, Virginia
m Connegan Walker, dau of Rachael Crawshaw (?) & Capt John Walker
|
George Lamkin b <1651 England? Virginia?; d 1691 Westmoreland Co, VA
m Hannah Tucker? Cox?
(who m2 Dr Samuel Demourvel and d 1744 Westmoreland, VA)
|
George Lamkin b c 1671 Westmoreland Co VA; d 1727 Westmoreland Co, VA
m Jane Ashton, d/o Col. Charles Ashton & Frances Burdett; d 1760
|
Eleanor Lamkin, b <1718 Westmoreland Co, VA; d >1789 Granville Co, NC
m George Cox, b c1700 Westmoreland Co, VA; d 1760 Northumberland Co, VA
|
Sarah Cox m John Rust
|
Matthew Rust m Priscilla Mills
|
John S Rust m Nancy Rucker Cooke
|
Martha Jane Rust m Alexander Littlejohn Mathis
|
Luther Everett Mathis m Susan Matilda Woollard
|
Jennie May Mathis m John Cyril Malloy
|
Bernard Mathis Malloy

Ashton

<u>Jane Ashton's</u> line of descent follows. The earliest members of this family were affluent and prominent all along the Potomac River, including the Virginia side (Northumberland, Westmoreland, and Stafford Counties) and the Eastern Shore (Accomac and Northampton Counties) as well as the Maryland shore on the east (Charles County). As tobacco merchants, they had much business across the river because at that time Port Tobacco in Maryland was the most important tobacco market in the world. Although much research of this family has been published, there are gaps. Some have speculated that a generation is missing; nevertheless, they are all considered to be related.

Jane Ashton (b. c1675, d.1760) was the daughter of **Colonel Charles Ashton** and his wife from Maryland, Miss Frances Burdett (Burditt). In 1698 Jane's father deeded land in Stafford County to Jane and her sister Sarah jointly. Jane Ashton married (1) **George Lamkin** and (2) Richard Partridge. The earliest known ancestors of Jane Ashton are shown below in the following pages. [See Chart 15.]

NOTE: The generations shown in Chart 15 represent one of several interpretations. An alternate theory is that Jane and Sarah Ashton were the grand-daughters of William Smith of Cople Parish, Westmoreland County, named in his will dated 1707.

Charles Ashton is said to have come to Maryland with Dr Thomas Gerrard from Lancashire, England. In Virginia, tobacco traders and planters conducted business with each other across the Potomac from the Virginia to the Maryland side. The earliest record of Charles ushton is the 1652 "Northumberland Oath of Loyalty to the Commonwealth." In 1658 "Mr Charles Ashton" held land in Cherry Point Neck adjoining William Medcalfe, among others. Evidently, engaged in exportation of tobacco, he was one of the Westmorelanders whose business affairs took them across the Potomac to Charles County, Maryland; in 1659 he witnessed a deposition there. In 1679 a Northumberland grant referred to land on "Mr Ashton's Creek" adjoining land of Thomas Gerrard. Charles died in 1672, leaving a widow Isabella who married (2) Dominick Rice. There indications that she had been the second wife of Charles Ashton.

Captain John Ashton was very prominent in Westmoreland County. Like his father, he too had business in Charles County across the river – in 1663 he and Thomas Burdett witnessed an assignment of property to "Gerrard ffowke of Portabaccoe Gent." Captain Ashton was one of the gentlemen justices of his time. In 1664 he owned land in Washington Parish (Northward on the Neck from Cople Parish which was in the extreme southern end; later, part of Washington Parish later would be in Stafford County when that county was created). He married twice and had five children; oldest son **Charles** and daughter Sarah were by the first wife and son Henry and daughters Prissilla, Grace Junior, and Mary were the children of second wife Grace. Both sons of John Ashton would be burgesses and justices. John Ashton's widow married (2) Mr James Key of Rappahannock County.

Colonel Charles Ashton was widely known up and down the river, in both colonies. For many years, his first wife was known to genealogists only as **"Miss Burdett."** She was the mother of his four children – Burdett, Charles, Jane, and Sarah, and though the surname "Burdett" was used in the family for many generations as a given name, the family had in time lost knowledge of its origin. It is now known that her name was **Frances,** and she was one of the four daughters **of Mr Thomas Burdett** of Charles County, Maryland; her sister Sarah married Mr Gerrard Fowke who held land in both colonies and was closely associated in Westmoreland and Stafford County affairs with Charles Ashton. After her death (c1698), Charles Ashton married (2) Ann WICKLIFFE Washington (widow of John, son of Coloenel John) and (3) Margaret FIELD Cossum Hart (widow of Henry Cossum and widow of Edward Hart). There were no children by these marriages. Colonel Charles died without a will in 1706.

Although the earliest Ashton referencese were in Northumberland (1648) and Westmoreland (1653) Counties, by the 1660s some of the family had moved northward up the Potomac River to the part that became Stafford County in 1664. Captain John Ashton held land on a branch of the Upper Machotic near Attopen Creek "near the path of the Nazaticos [Indians]." Colonel Peter Ashton had land in the same locale and also on Chappawansick in Stafford County.

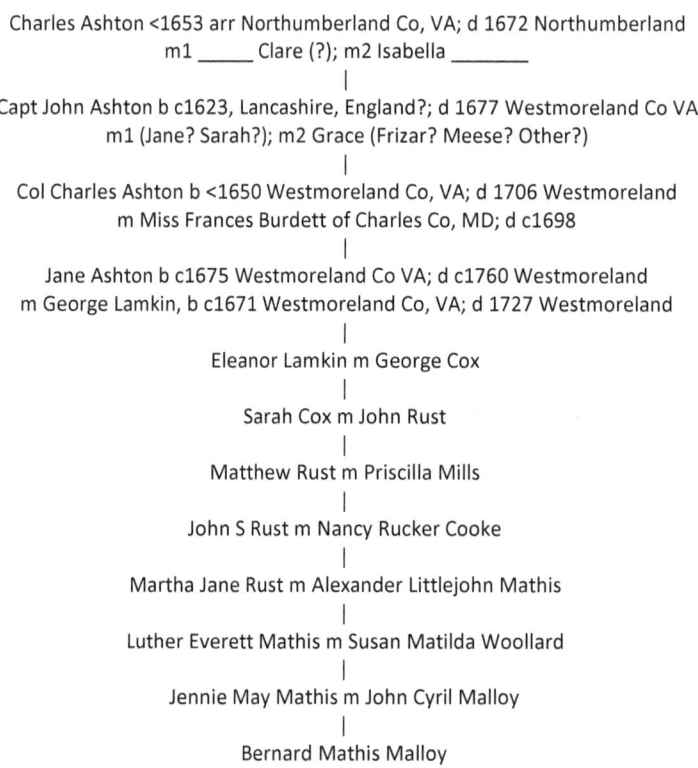

**CHART 15: A Line of Descent from the Ashtons
of Virginia's Northern Neck**

Charles Ashton <1653 arr Northumberland Co, VA; d 1672 Northumberland
m1 _____ Clare (?); m2 Isabella _____
|
Capt John Ashton b c1623, Lancashire, England?; d 1677 Westmoreland Co VA
m1 (Jane? Sarah?); m2 Grace (Frizar? Meese? Other?)
|
Col Charles Ashton b <1650 Westmoreland Co, VA; d 1706 Westmoreland
m Miss Frances Burdett of Charles Co, MD; d c1698
|
Jane Ashton b c1675 Westmoreland Co VA; d c1760 Westmoreland
m George Lamkin, b c1671 Westmoreland Co, VA; d 1727 Westmoreland
|
Eleanor Lamkin m George Cox
|
Sarah Cox m John Rust
|
Matthew Rust m Priscilla Mills
|
John S Rust m Nancy Rucker Cooke
|
Martha Jane Rust m Alexander Littlejohn Mathis
|
Luther Everett Mathis m Susan Matilda Woollard
|
Jennie May Mathis m John Cyril Malloy
|
Bernard Mathis Malloy

Burdett

Miss Frances Burdett, daughter of **Verlinda Cotton** and **Thomas Burdett**, was the granddaughter of two of America's earliest English colonists, namely **William Burdett** and his wife **Frances Lake**, who settled on Virginia's Eastern Shore by 1623. Frances' father relocated to Maryland with his foster parent, Governor William Stone, and later settled on Nanjemoy Creek; he died young, leaving his wife with four young daughters: Elizabeth, Frances, Parthenia, and Sarah. The girls grew up on the family manor named "Bird's Rest;" in 1668 when their mother remarried, the conveyed this property to the girls by prenuptial agreement. Both Frances and Sarah grew up to marry sons of their father's close associates, John Ashton and Gerrard Fowke. Frances Ashton, mother of Burdett, Charles, Jane, and Sarah Ashton, died about 1698. Her grandfather and father are briefly described below.

**CHART 16: Three Generations of Burdetts in the Colony of Virginia
Showing Continuance of Given Names in the Ashton Lineage:
Ashton – Burdett – Charles – Frances – Jane – John – Sarah**

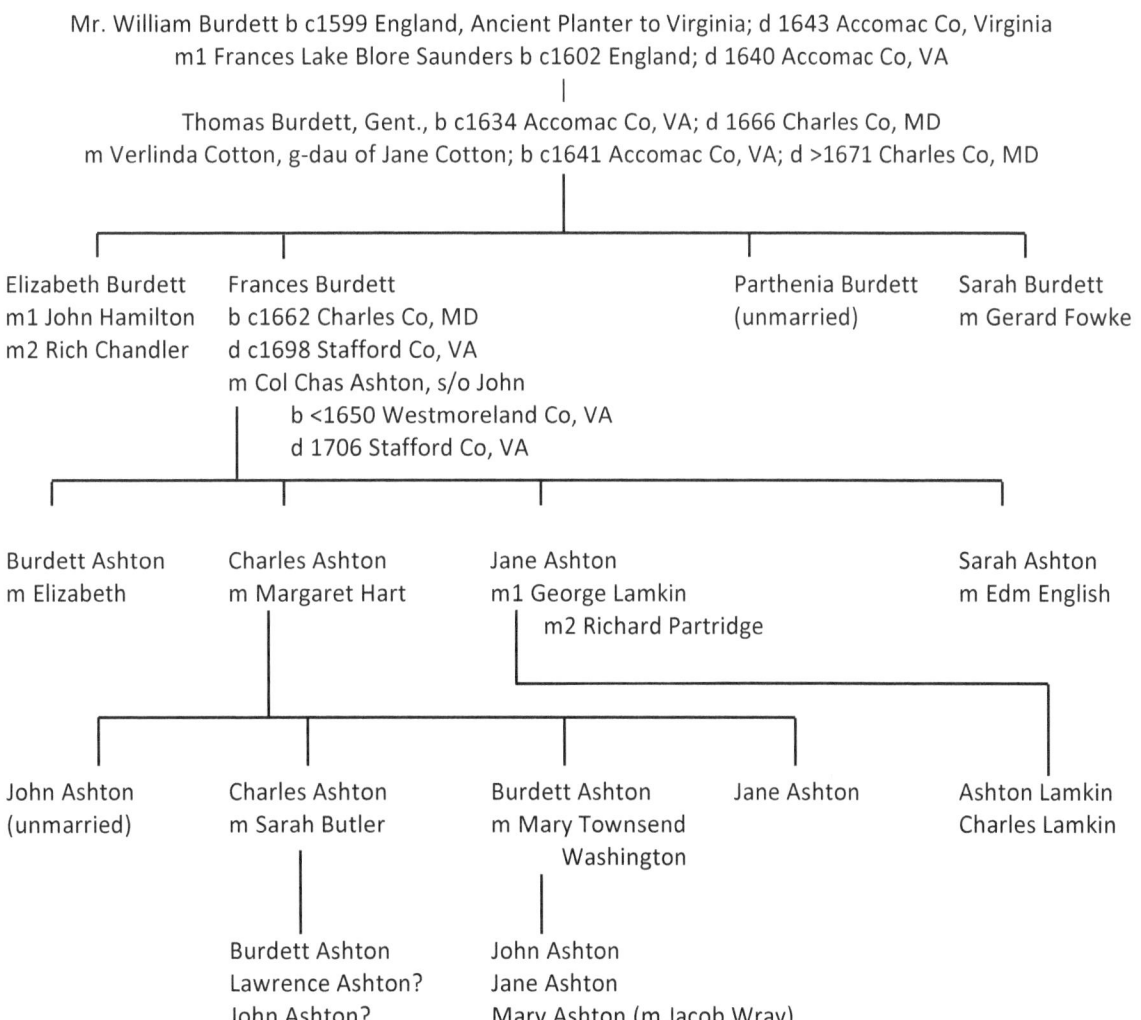

Mr. William Burdett b c1599 England, Ancient Planter to Virginia; d 1643 Accomac Co, Virginia
m1 Frances Lake Blore Saunders b c1602 England; d 1640 Accomac Co, VA

Thomas Burdett, Gent., b c1634 Accomac Co, VA; d 1666 Charles Co, MD
m Verlinda Cotton, g-dau of Jane Cotton; b c1641 Accomac Co, VA; d >1671 Charles Co, MD

Elizabeth Burdett
m1 John Hamilton
m2 Rich Chandler

Frances Burdett
b c1662 Charles Co, MD
d c1698 Stafford Co, VA
m Col Chas Ashton, s/o John
b <1650 Westmoreland Co, VA
d 1706 Stafford Co, VA

Parthenia Burdett
(unmarried)

Sarah Burdett
m Gerard Fowke

Burdett Ashton
m Elizabeth

Charles Ashton
m Margaret Hart

Jane Ashton
m1 George Lamkin
m2 Richard Partridge

Sarah Ashton
m Edm English

John Ashton
(unmarried)

Charles Ashton
m Sarah Butler

Burdett Ashton
m Mary Townsend
Washington

Jane Ashton

Ashton Lamkin
Charles Lamkin

Burdett Ashton
Lawrence Ashton?
John Ashton?

John Ashton
Jane Ashton
Mary Ashton (m Jacob Wray)

Mr William Burdett (born in England, c1599) came to Virginia in 1615 on the <u>Susan,</u> his age at about 15 or 16. He survived the Indian Massacre of 1622 and was listed in the Muster of 1624 by Captain William Eppes as living on the Eastern Shore. He was one of those earliest arrivals to be designated as "Auncient Planters." He has been referred to as a "principal merchant and devout Churchman" (Wise, 254) of his community, which he served as vestryman, Commissioner, and also as Burgess.

In 1633 he contracted a prenuptial agreement and married **Frances Lake,** already twice widowed. Born in 1598, she came to Virginia in 1620 aboard the London Merchant. She married John Blore (Blower), an Ancient Planter. They survived the Massacre and in 1623 were enumerated in the Muster of the Eastern Shore (their ages given as 25 and 27) with their two servants. John Blore's patent is the fifth listed in the earliest extant Patent Book; the following year he died, leaving an infant son William. As customary, Frances LAKE Blore remarried; her second husband was Captain Roger Saunders/Sanders. He died four years later, and Frances married William Burdett; they had one child **Thomas.** Frances Burdett died in 1640; her will provided for son Thomas Burdett [son William Blore having died] and mentioned her brothers and sisters in England.

William Burdett married (2) Alice Traveller (widow of George) in the early months of 1642 (between February and July); he himself died in July, making a will which named Captain William Stone (among others) as "faithful overseers … to take speciall Care for the education of my Tender Sonn."

Thomas Burdett, Gentleman, son of Frances LAKE and William Burdett, was born in Accomac County (c1634). Thomas was about six when his mother died, and his father survived her by only three years. Left by his father's will to the care of god-parents, chief among them Captain William Stone, Governor of Maryland, young Thomas Burdett grew up in St Mary's City (capital of Maryland). Thomas Burdett married **Verlinda Cotton** (d/o **Ann GRAVES** and **Wm Cotton)** and they lived in Charles County. As an exporter of tobacco, Burdett's friends included John Ashton of Westmoreland County, Virginia. Verlinda and Thomas had four daughters: Elizabeth (m. (1) John Hamilton, (2) Richard Chandler); **Frances** (m. Col Charles Ashton); Parthenis; and Sarah (m. Gerrard Fowke, Gent). In 1666 Thomas Burdett died intestate; his daughters inherited his lands.

Mills

Priscilla Mills married **Matthew Rust,** son of Eleanor Cox's daughter Sarah Cox Rust. Priscilla was probably the daughter of **William Mills** of Granville County, North Carolina. When Priscilla married Matthew Rust in 1791, William Mills signed the bond, so his accepted relationship would be that of father or brother to the bride. In 1802 Jeremiah Rust, brother died in 1806, Priscilla's children, Polly and John S., were bound to their Aunt Sarah and Uncle Jeremiah Rust. At the time of William Mills' death in 1828, Jeremiah Rust was coadministrator of the William Mills estate.

Priscilla and Matthew Rust had six Children, two of them carrying on the Cox names: Mary "Polly" Cox Rust, Charnock Cox Rust, John S. Rust, James Rust, George Boswell Rust. Priscilla Mills married (2) Harlon (Harlow/Harley) Priddy in 1809. She left Granville County later, and the 1830 census shows her living in Gibson County, Tennessee.

Rucker

Nancy Rucker Cooke, wife of **John S. Rust** (s/o Priscilla MILLS and Matthew Rust) was born in Granville County, North Carolina about 1805. Her parents were **Mary McGehee** (d/o **Benjamin)** and **William Cooke** (s/o **James Cooke)**. The Cookes of Granville County were descendants of Shem Cooke and his wife Ann Rucker. Who had moved there form Amelia County, Virginia, probably during the Revolutionary war.

On 31 March 1823, Nancy Cooke married John Rust. Nancy and John Rust had eight children, all born in Granville County: William B., James, Martha (m. Alexander Littlejohn Mathis), Sarah, John W., George M., Atlas, and Nancy Rust.

The family moved to Gibson County, Tennessee (along with other members of the Rust family). Nancy COOKE Rust died there 7 August 1877; she is buried with her husband in Rust Cemetery at Chapel Hill.

Nancy Cooke's antecedents, the Cookes, Ruckers, and the McGehees, are described briefly below, beginning with the earliest known. [See Chart 17.]

William Shemuel Cooke was born in Virginia, perhaps in Gloucester County. His parentage has not been proved, but it has been speculated that he was probably descended from **Mordecai Cooke,** an early arrival to the Virginia Colony who became quite influential, serving as Burgess, among other distinctions. Shem Cooke lived in Orange County when he married **Ann Rucker** (d/o **Elizabeth FIELDING** and **Peter Rucker).** Shem and Ann Cooke were named in the will of Peter Rucker; after the estate was settled, Shem and Ann lived in Amelia County where, presumably, all their children were -- Elizabeth (m.___Turpin); Will, James (d 1784, Amelia Co, VA), John D., Shem, Clayborn, Felicia (m. Jonathan Stone, Franklin Co, NC), and Delphia (m. Armistead Roberts).

Shem Cooke and John Cooke were patriots of the French & Indian War. In 1766, Shem sold land in Amelia County, Virginia; by 1778 he had received at least two land grants in Franklin County, North Carolina. He died 19 April 1792, survived by his wife Ann and six surviving children. Among his descendants, the name "Shem" was carried on, quite numerous within the next four generations.

James Cooke was a son of Ann Rucker and Shem Cooke of Orange County, Virginia. Very little is known about him. He owned a store in Amelia County, where he was fatally shot by a British solder during the Revolutionary War (in 1784). He left four orphans: **William**; Ann (m. Lemuel Rust); Shem; and Roland. All of them moved by 1786 to Granville County, along with the Cooke family and were named in Shem's will as his grandchildren in 1792.

James Cooke's wife may have been **Anna Ford**, daughter of **Captain Hezekiah Ford** and his wife **Elizabeth**, of Amelia County, Virginia,

William Cooke (s/o James, g-s/o Ann RUCKER & Shem Cooke) was born in Amelia County, Virginia, about 1750. An orphan, he moved with the Cooke family to Granville County, North Carolina . William Cooke married 22 August 1789 in Granville County **Mary McGehee** (d/o **Benjamin**). They lived on Middle Creek in Granville County, where they brought up their children, one of whom was Nancy Rucker COOKE Rust, who married John S. Rust.

Ann Rucker, wife of Shemuel Cooke, was the daughter of Elizabeth FIELDING and her husband Peter Rucker of Essex County, Virginia, near the Rappahannock River. Later, their home was in Orange County, where she maried Shem Cooke; they had eight children. Ann and Shem moved to Granville County, North Carolina. Ann RUCKER Cooke survived her husband.

Peter Rucker was traveling from France or Holland to Virginia with a party of Huguenots when their ship was wrecked in the storm just off the coast. He was naturalized in 1704, and in that year was living on Cockleshell Creek in Essex County. He married Elizabeth Fielding, perhaps a descendant of Colonel Ambrose Fielding, an early planter in Westmoreland County whose sons moved to Gloucester County. Elizabeth and Peter Rucker had ten children, well documented in Wood's published genealogy *The Rucker Family Genealogy, With Their Ancestors, Descendants, and Connections* by Sudie Rucker Wood, Richmond, 1932). Peter Rucker died in Orange County in 1743, and a final distribution was made in 1825, at which time, supposedly, his wife had died. Their neighbors were the James Madison and Zachary Taylor families. [NOTE: Several genealogies of Peter Rucker have been published; none agree as to the origins of Peter Rucker.]

CHART 17: Ancestry of Nancy Rucker Cooke
Showing Rucker-Cooke-McGehee Family Connections

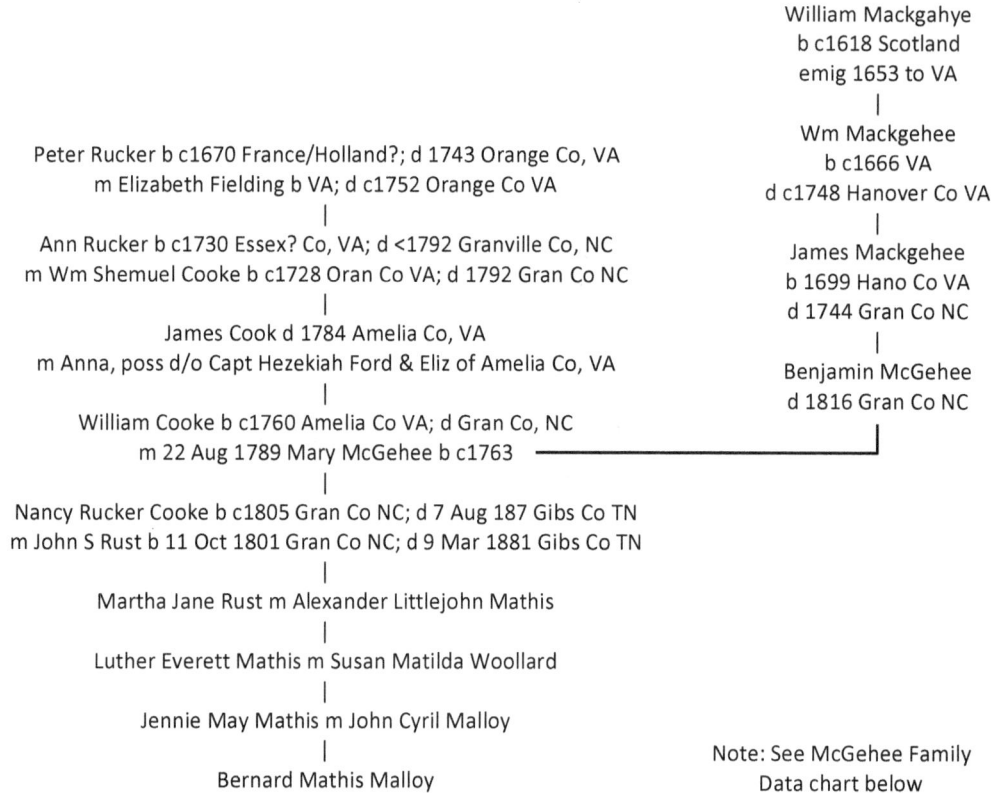

William Mackgahye
b c1618 Scotland
emig 1653 to VA

Wm Mackgehee
b c1666 VA
d c1748 Hanover Co VA

Peter Rucker b c1670 France/Holland?; d 1743 Orange Co, VA
m Elizabeth Fielding b VA; d c1752 Orange Co VA

Ann Rucker b c1730 Essex? Co, VA; d <1792 Granville Co, NC
m Wm Shemuel Cooke b c1728 Oran Co VA; d 1792 Gran Co NC

James Mackgehee
b 1699 Hano Co VA
d 1744 Gran Co NC

James Cook d 1784 Amelia Co, VA
m Anna, poss d/o Capt Hezekiah Ford & Eliz of Amelia Co, VA

Benjamin McGehee
d 1816 Gran Co NC

William Cooke b c1760 Amelia Co VA; d Gran Co, NC
m 22 Aug 1789 Mary McGehee b c1763

Nancy Rucker Cooke b c1805 Gran Co NC; d 7 Aug 187 Gibs Co TN
m John S Rust b 11 Oct 1801 Gran Co NC; d 9 Mar 1881 Gibs Co TN

Martha Jane Rust m Alexander Littlejohn Mathis

Luther Everett Mathis m Susan Matilda Woollard

Jennie May Mathis m John Cyril Malloy

Bernard Mathis Malloy

Note: See McGehee Family
Data chart below

McGehee

Mary McGehee was descended from the McGehee family who had settled on Middle Creek of Granville County, North Carolina about 1760. Mary's father was **Benjamin McGehee** (born c1699 and d. 1774 in Virginia); Mary was born about 1752, most likely in Virginia's Hanover County, where many McGehees are found in the county record books of that time.

Mary McGehee married **William Cooke** (s/o **James**) on 22 August 1789. One of their children, daughter **Nancy Rucker Cooke,** married **John S. Rust** (s/o **Priscilla MILLS & Matthew Rust**) and moved with him to Gibson County, Tennessee. The ancestors of Mary McGEHEE Cooke, described briefly below, were researched by Una W. Johnson, Genealogist (cited as UWJ) and George Rufus McGehee (GRM).

William Mackgahye has been identified as Mary's earliest ancestor in this country. He was a native of Scotland, born about 1618. He emigrated to Virginia in 1653.

William Mackgehee, son of William, was born about 1666 in Virginia. He died about 1748 in Hanover County, Virginia.

James Mackgehee, son of William, was born about 1699 in Virginia (Hanover Co?) and died in Granville County, North Carolina in 1774. His Granville County deeds are dated 1760 and 1762. From the deeds, it appears that he had sons James Jr, **Benjamin,** and Nathan.

Benjamin McGehee, son of James, was born in Virginia about 1721 but moved with his family to Granville County, North Carolina. The name of his wife (or wives) is not known. He lived on Middle Creek and Taylor's Creek, in near proximity to several of the Rust and Cooke families – Jeremiah Rust, Shem Cooke Jr, William Cooke Jr, Claborn Cooke, Shim McGehee, and Claborn McGehee, specifically, and surely others. Benjamin McGehee died in 1816.

McGEHEE FAMILY DATA
1760 – 1818

27 Nov 1760	Grant: Rt Hon John earl Granville to Jas McGehee, planter, of Gran co, 600 in the Par. of St John on both sides of a fork of Taylors Ck; wits Thos Jones, Will Hurst, Robt Eyre; pr by "the handwriting of William Hurst" (DB L:329)
Nov Ct 1761	Jas McGehee (with John Case(?) and Anne Priddy) wit: the will of Robt Priddy (Unrecorded Wills)
5 Aug 1762	Deed: Jas McGehee, planter to Benj McGehee, both of Gran Co, 200 a. adj Jas McGehee, the little fork of Taylor's Ck, Jas McGehee Sr's deed bearing date in March 1761; wits. Jas McGehee Jr, Nathan McGehe (DB E:340)
5 Aug 1762	Deed: Jas McGehee Sr, planter, of Gran Co to Benj McGehee, 200 a. on the little fork of Taylor's Ck; wits. Jas Mcgehee Jr, Nathan Mcgehee (DB E:340)
5 Aug 1762	Deed of Gift: Jas McGehee Sr, Gran Co, to Nathan McGehee "for the natural affection, good will, and divers good Causes & Considerations," 200 a. on a little Br of Taylors Ck, along Jas McGehee's line Benj McGehee's line," part of a Tract of land granted to the said Jas McGehee Sr by a Deed from the Earl of Granville bearing date in March 1761; wits. Benj McGehee, Jas McGehee Jr (DB E:343)
1769	Gran Co Tax List included Benj McGee, 2 whites; also Chas McGee, John, and Nathan McGee, 1 white each (Gwynn-1974, 277)
1774	Death of Jas McGehee
27 Apr 1808	Deed: Shem Cook Jr of Franklin Co, NC and Jeremiah Rust, 125 a E side of Middle Ck adj Wm Cook Jr & Shem Cook Jr, Person's line, Benj McGehee, Claborn Cook's spring branch; wits. John Nuttall, Saml Le May (DB T:321)
25 Dec 1808	Benj Mechee's will of this date gave his land to sons Crafford [Crawford], Shem, Banks, and Claiborn; cash bequests to sons Benjamin and Josiah; cash to daus Sarah Griffin, Haymon, Ann Parrott, Lucy Mcghee, Mary Cooke, Penelope Meghee, and Duke; his stock to son Claiborn; household furniture to son Claiborn and dau Polley; use of the dwelling house for his wife; extrs sons Shemual Maghee and ____ Maghee; wits. Thos Person, Nelson Nailing (WB 7:636)
Aug Ct 1816	Will of Benj McGehee, dcd was proved (WB 7:636)
Aug Ct 1818	Deed: Claborn Cook to Edmond G. Brodie, 350 a. Gran Co adj Jere Rust & THos Person... to Jos Megehees Spring branch... to Middle Ck, John Peace Jr, Blacknall's line, Wm Jeffreys Sr, along Claborn Megehee, Shim Megehee; wits. Shem Cook, Thos Person (DB Y:49)

Compiled from research by AWA, FFD, UWJ, and BMM

Malloy

CHART 18: Several Generations of the Malloy Family
of County Mayo, Ireland

John Molloy, b c1745 Buckfield, Kilmeena, Co Mayo, Ireland
|
Brian Molloy b c1768 m Mary Joyce
Ross, Kilmeena, Co Mayo
|
Manus Molloy, b btw 1815-1820 in Westport, Co Mayo, Ireland; d May 1861 Columbia PA
m1 c1845 Mary Moran? m2? c1855 Mary Paten
|
Bernard "Barney" Molloy b 4 May 1845 Westport, Co Mayo; d 6 May 1904 Chicago IL
m 3 Apr 1872 Mary Cass in Joliet IL;
she was bpt 19 Oct 1854 in Johnstown, Co Kilkenny, Ireland, d 14 May 1932 Chicago IL
|
John Cyril Malloy b 24 Dec 1887 Chicago IL; d 25 Feb 1974 Washington DC;
m Jennie May Mathis, b 29 Jan 1895 Jackson TN; d 12 Apr 1969 Washington DC
|
Bernard Mathis Malloy

John Cyril Malloy was born 24 December 1887 in Chicago, Illinois; he was christened on Christmas Day at the Church of the Annunciation. His parents were **Mary CASS** and **Barney Malloy**. Growing up in Chicago, John Cyril's boyhood friend was Avery Brundidge, who became the long-time president of the American Olympics. John Cyrl Malloy remembered seing the Iroquois Theatre fire as a youngster.

The year after the San Francisco earthquake, young John went to California,. After returning to Chicago, he studied law at Loyola Law School, and on 6 October 1916 John Cyril Malloy was admitted to the Illinois State Bar.

During World War I, he enlisted in May, 19018 at Chicago and was discharged in June, 1919 at Camp Grant, Illinois. He served as a private in the 315th Ammunition Train, 90th Division, American Expeditionary Forces; he went oversears and during the Occupation was stationed in Ohrbach, near Bernkastel, Germany.

On 8 February 1927 he married **Jennie May Mathis** at St. James Roman Catholic Church, Chicago. She was the daughter of **Susan Matilda WOOLLARD** and **Luther Everett Mathis** of Jackson, Tennessee. Their six children were **Bernard Mathis "Barney"**, John Cyril Jr., James Woollard, Martha Sue, William Paul, and Joseph Edward ("Luther").

In 1943 John Cyril Malloy retired and moved his family to Jackson, Tennessee. He joined the insurance business, working with the Metropolitan Life Insurance and Home Life Insurance companies. His wife died in 1969, and his death occurred on 25 February 1975 in Washington, DC at age 87. He is buried in Calvary Cemetery, Evanston, Illinois in the Malloy family burial plot.

John[1] Mulloy or Molloy was born about 1745 (based on estimated birth of son) in Buckfield, Killmeena, County Mayo, Ireland. He is the earliest known Malloy ancestor.[7] According to family lore, he was descended from a seventeenth-century forebear who was the proud father of twelve sons. He had been banished to Mayo from the interior of Ireland by Cromwell, who sent the native Irish "to Hell or to Connaught". The family name or motto means "never late." The name of his wife is unknown. Of his children, we know he had at least one son:

---

[7] Information about the Irish Mulloys is from Kitty Mulloy, of Kilmeena, Westport, Co. Mayo, Ireland, wife of Padraic and 4th cousin of Bernard Mathis Malloy.

Brian² Mulloy was born about 1768 (based on his estimated marriage); he married by 1790 Mary Joyce; they lived in Ross, Kilmeena, County Mayo, Ireland. Their children included Andrew, Manus (see next), Nancy, Mary, Kitty and Jan Molloy.

Manus³ Malloy, was born between 1815 and 1820 (based on ages reported in 1850 and 1860 census records) in Westport, County Mayo, Ireland. He married about 1845 (based on age of oldest known child) Mary Moran[8] and had at least two children before Manus emigrated to the United States. Family tradition holds that Manus emigrated with his son Barney, leaving the rest of the family behind. However, the 1850 census suggests that Manus may have come by himself: Manus Malloy, age 30, is enumerated without family in Columbia, Allegheny Co., Pennsylvania, a laborer living with a number of other Irish-born laborers in the household of Irish-born Ann Nowlin and Nowlin children:

The 1860 census for the same town finds Manus Malloy (enumerated as "Menace Meley") with Mary (34) and children Barney (14), William (12), and Mary (4). [Source: 1860 US Census, Columbia, Lancaster, PennsylvnaniaPage 50-51 (stamped); 14 (hand-written); lines 39-40, lines 1-3 [next page], Dwelling #109; family #109]. Malloy descendants had no knowledge of this family unit—believing that only Manus' son Barney came with his father from Ireland.

Additional findings suggest that the birthplace of daughter Mary may be inaccurate in the census. A baptism entry was found at St. Peter's Roman Catholic Church in Columbia, Pennsylvania that suggests she was actually born there:

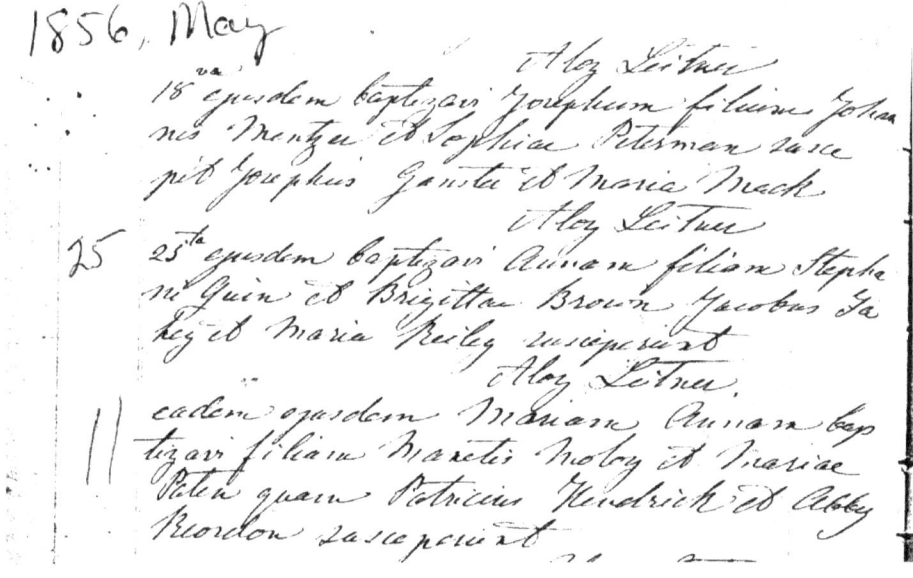

Transcription:

eodem [25 May 1856] ejusdem Mariam Annam baptizar filia Manetis Moloy et Mariae Paten quam Patricusu Hendrick et Abby Riordon susceptuint

Translation:

On 25 May 1856 was baptized Mary Ann, daughter of Manus Moloy and Maria Paten; with godparents: Patrick Hendrick and Abby Riordon

This identifies Manus's wife of 1856 as different from the Mary Moran that others have suggested. Either this tradition was inaccurate or Manus's first wife died – either in Ireland or shortly after emigrating – and Manus married second in Pennsylvania about 1855 one Mary Patton.

---

[8] Her maiden name is derived from family records; her given name from the 1860 census.

The best candidate for Manus's immigration is the ship "Bark William Kennedy" which arrived in Philadelphia 5 April 1849 from Westport, Ireland.[9] Manus Malloy, age 22 [b 1827], is listed immediately after a 48-year-old Pat Malloy [b 1801]. Given the timing, the Philadelphia arrival, and subsequent residence in Lancaster County, this Manus is a strong candidate for he of Columbia, PA. That said, we find no record of Pat anywhere nearby in the subsequent 1850 census. Passenger lists from Baltimore (a possible port of arrival) for this time period are missing. A search of passengers lists published on Ancestry.com finds no records for Manus' wife Mary, nor any of the children listed in the 1860 census.

According to family legend, Manus Malloy was killed in an explosion in the powder [or steel?] mill where he worked during the Civil War. A newspaper article subsequently found, clarifies the cause of death:

"Columbia Affairs."—The *Spy* gives the following account of accidents which occurred in Columbia last week: On Wednesday morning [i.e., 6 Nov 1861] an accident happened at the Columbia Rolling Mill, resulting in the death of Manus Malloy, one of the employees. Malloy was about adjusting the belting on one of the pulleys, when his clothing was caught and he was carried round the shafting, breaking both legs and an arm, besides inflicting internal injuries.—Drs. John and Hottenstein, were called in, but the case was hopeless. The injured man died in about two hours. He left a wife and family of several children." [*Lancaster Examiner and Herald*, Vol. XXXV, Lancaster, PA, Wednesday, November 13, 1861, No. 51.]

Family legend claims that on his body was found a ticket to Washington where, it is said, he hoped to retrieve Barney from the army.

A search of the 1870 census found no family unit matching that of the 1860 census. The older boys could have married or moved off (and indeed, Barney Malloy did; see below), but the daughter Mary should still be living with her mother, whether or not her mother remarried. There are no Malloys found in Lancaster County, PA in 1860 of any spelling. Did they return to Ireland shortly after the father's death? Such a return would support the family tradition that Barney sent money home to Ireland to bring his siblings (back) to the U.S.

Bernard[4] "Barney" Malloy was born 4 May 1845 in Westport, County Mayo, Ireland. A Kilmeenah Molloy cousin Joseph Mulloy wrote in the 1960s that "Bernard" was used instead of "Brian" because while it sounded like Brian, it was a saint's name, which the priest wanted.

No passenger list naming him has been found, but he is living with his father, Manus Malloy, in Columbia, Lancaster County, Pennsylvania in the 1860 census, along with a possible mother (or step-mother), Mary, and siblings William and Mary.

As a young man he worked as a boatman on the Susquehanna River. Family tradition holds that Barney, under age, first attempted to enlist in the US Army on 20 May 1861 as "Brian Maloy" (to evade his father's attempts to prevent his enlistment. No record supports this.[10] Failing in this, the story goes, he ran away again and enlisted on 31 May 1861 as "Barney Maloy" in Company E of the 41st Pennsylvania Volunteers. This enlistment is documented.[11] His son John C. Malloy later shared that Barney was good horseman, he became a courier and ranged behind Confederate lines in Virginia to gather intelligence.[12] Barney Malloy served in twenty battles during his three years, including battles at Mechanicsburg, Antietam, the 2nd Bull Run, and Gettysburg. At Gettysburg he was wounded in the shoulder by the bayonet of "a Confederate in a big hat." With his company, Barney Malloy was mustered out on 11 June 1864 in Harrisburg, Pennsylvania. His name is on the Pennsylvania State Memorial at Gettysburg as "Barney MALOY" because "the Dutchman said one heLL was enough.".

According to family tradition, Barney sent the money he received for enlisting to his brother in Ireland to bring him and their sister, Rose. The unnamed brother emigrated with his girlfriend however, and Rose never came to America. Years later, Barney had a knock on the door and it was his erstwhile brother. Barney simply shut the

---

[9] Philadelphia, Pennsylvania. *Passenger Lists of Vessels Arriving at Philadelphia, Pennsylvania, 1800-1882*. Washington, D.C.: National Archives and Records Administration. Micropublication M425, Roll 68, list 42.

[10] The story has also been told through the generations that Barney was paid to enlist on behalf of another. A later researcher challenged this story, arguing that bounties of this nature did not commence until 1864 by which time Malloy was almost out of the service.

[11] Organization Index to Pension Files of Veterans Who Served Between 1861 and 1900. Record group 15, NARA T289, Roll 463. See also *American Civil War Soldiers* [database on-line]. Provo, UT, USA: Ancestry.com Operations Inc, 1999.

[12] Bernard Mathis Malloy, Typescript, 1978, recording stories told him by his father, John C. Malloy.

door.

In the 1870 census, Barney is found enumerated in Yonkers, Westchester County, New York, as a laborer, living in the household of Mich[ael] Callahan, Irish-born "rail iron straightener," an occupation Barney will later join.

According to family tradition, Barney then went to Joliet, Illinois where he began to attend church. One Sunday as he was taking his First Communion with a group of children, he was observed by "Aunt Nell" who introduced him to his future bride, **Mary Cass**. They were married 3 April 1872 in St. Mary's Church, Joliet, Illinois by the Reverend Father Mackin.[13]

Between 1874 and 1877, the family moved to Chicago where Barney worked as foreman in the Blue Island Steel Mills. The family built a business/residence at 23 West North Avenue, in Chicago, where Mary ran a grocery store and a saloon—"Barney Malloy's Place." Barney also worked as a mechanic in a bicycle factory.

In 1880, Barney and Mary and their first four sons (all born in Illinois) lived in Chicago, Cook County, Illinois:

On 23 August 1890, the family gave up the store and moved to 1810 North Spalding Avenue in Chicago. The following October 20, Barney applied for a Federal pension on the basis of rheumatism acquired during his Civil War service. Around this time, the sons of Barney and Mary Malloy had their photograph taken:

In 1900, Barney and Mary lived in Jefferson, Chicago, Cook County, Illinois with seven of their ten sons, one of whom was deceased by this time. Barney was a watchman. Barney and Mary's immigration is incorrectly listed as 1878. (1858 is a more likely year for Barney.)

Bernard "Barney" Malloy died 4 May 1904, at which time he was living at 1810 N. Spaulding in Chicago. Cause of death was "exhaustion following laparotomy for perforative appendicitis and septic cholangitis five days before." He is buried at Calvary Cemetery in Evanston, Illinois.

Mary (Cass) Malloy was living at 4716 North Magnolia when she died 14 May 1932; she was buried 17 May 1932 in Calvary Cemetery, Evanston, Cook, Illinois. Four of her ten sons pre-deceased her.

Their children: Edward "Eddy" Malloy (1873); William G. Malloy (1874); Bernard "Barney" Malloy, Jr. (1876); Charles C. Malloy (1878); Manus Malloy (1880); Richard Malloy (1881); James Malloy (1882); Sylvester Malloy (1885); **John[5] Cyril Malloy** (1887); Frances Malloy (1890).

---

[13] This marriage date was recorded in a 23 June 1904 affidavit by Jon O'Neil and Annie Moriarty, "well acquainted with Mary Malloy" who claimed that the marriage was solemnized by Rev. John Mackin, then Parish Priest of Saint Mary's Roman Catholic Church, Joliet, Illinois. However, a 1993 inquiry to that church resulted in finding no such entry in their marriage register. This affidavit was no doubt made in support of Mary obtaining a widow's pension.

Cass

Mary Cass, wife of Barney Malloy, may have been born as early as 1848; she was baptized 19 October 1854 in Ossory Parish, Johnstown, County Kilkenny, Ireland, daughter of **Richard Cass** and **Margaret Hely** (Healy or Haley). According to family tradition, her father was apparently a University professor of Latin who had married a much younger woman. He died before or shortly after she was born. Mary's mother married (2) Michael Fleming on 20 June 1856, and they had seven children: Charles, Thomas, Margaret, Eliza, Ellen, Winifred, and Martin Fleming.

In 1855 the child Mary Cass traveled on a free boat to Canada by English mail, landing at St Helen's Isle near Montreal; she always remembered wearing a mail tag with her name and destination. During the passage, auburn-haired and blue-eyed Mary took her meals at the Captain's table. She was being sent to live with her maternal Grandmother O'Neill, who lived in Joliet, Illinois. There, she grew up in her grandmother's home, tended also by her Aunt Nell.

At age fifteen, Mary Cass took a competitive examination and was selected to be a teacher in Joliet. Aunt Nell saw a man at church and introduced him to Mary – his name was Barney Malloy, and on 3 April 1872 they were married at St Mary's Church. They became the parents of ten sons. By 1877 the family had moved to Chicago, where they built at 231 (now 1500) West North Avenue; they operated a store and saloon in the same building, until 23 August 1890 when the family moved to 1810 North Spalding Avenue (now 3200 N. Belmont).

Mary CASS Malloy's husband died on 6 May 1904. A true matriarch, Mary Malloy's ten sons brought their earnings to her each week. Because of her stately carriage, in her later years she was known as "the Dutchess." She was living at 4716 North Magnolia in Chicago when she died on 14 May 1932, about 80 years of age; she was buried with her husband Barney Malloy at Calvary Cemetery in Evanston.

Joh Richard Cass, father of Mary CASS Malloy, was said to have been a professor of Latin at the university of (Dublin?). In 1826 John Richard Cass was the school teacher in Johnstown. The "Primary Valuation" for Kilkenny shows that John Cass leasing the same property. Unfortunately, dates are not supplied; by inference, dates were earlier than 1861. John Cass married **Margaret** (or **Mary A.**) **Haley (Healey),** who was considerably younger. He died before the birth of their daughter Mary. The records show that on 20 June 1856 the Widow Cass married (2) Michael Fleming in Jamestown.

NOTE: Research on the Moran, Healey, and O'Neill lines has been cursory, not yielding definite information. (Researched by Hibernian Research Company, Limited of Dublin)

CHART 19: All that is Known of the Fmaily of Mary Haley/Heley
of County Kilkenny, Ireland

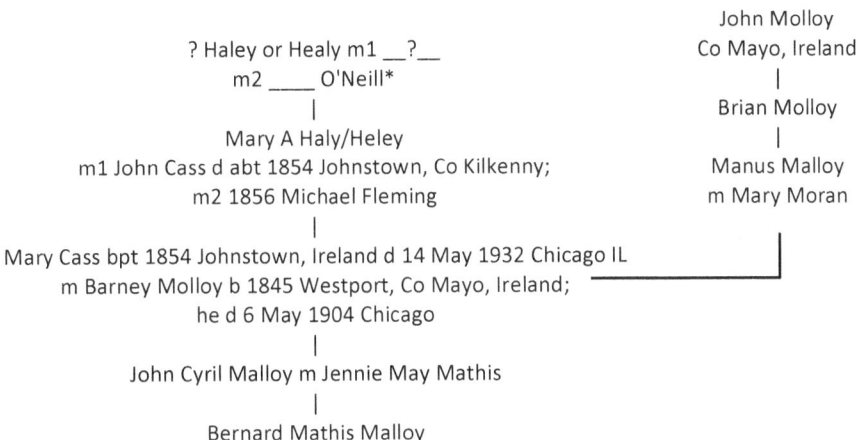

```
                                                    John Molloy
   ? Haley or Healy m1 __?__                        Co Mayo, Ireland
       m2 ____ O'Neill*                                   |
            |                                        Brian Molloy
      Mary A Haly/Heley                                   |
m1 John Cass d abt 1854 Johnstown, Co Kilkenny;      Manus Malloy
     m2 1856 Michael Fleming                          m Mary Moran
            |
Mary Cass bpt 1854 Johnstown, Ireland d 14 May 1932 Chicago IL
  m Barney Molloy b 1845 Westport, Co Mayo, Ireland;
              he d 6 May 1904 Chicago
            |
   John Cyril Malloy m Jennie May Mathis
            |
      Bernard Mathis Malloy
```

* It has been speculated that Mary Haley's mother was widowed
and the remarried, to someone whose surname was "O'Neill"

155

REFERENCES
Listed Alphabetically by Author, Short Title, Acronym, Initials

Adam, Blanche [also Adams-Chapman]. Marriages of Isle of Wight County, Virginia: 1628-1800. Smithfield, 1938.

_____. Wills and Administrations of Isle of Wight County, Virginia: 1647-1800. Smithfield, 1958.

_____. Wills and Administrations of Southampton County, Virginia, 1749-1800. Baltimore, 1980.

Adventurers of Purse and Person, Virginia, 1607-1624/25. Jester & Hiden, eds. Richmond, 1964.

AIS. Accelerated Indexing Systems, Inc. See Latter-day Saints; chronological and geographical index for American surnames, c1608 to c1885, based primarily on census records.

Allston, Susan Lowndes. Brookgreen, Waccamaw. Charleston, SC, 1935.

Alston-Williams-Boddie-Hilliard Society. Society and Family Book. Vol 1. Winston-Salem, NC, 1961.

Ardery, Julia Spencer. Kentucky Court and Other Records. Vol 2. Baltimore, 1971.

Baker, Lucy Harrison Miller & Hazel Letts Williamson. Marriages of Campbell County, Virginia: 1782-1810. Lynchburg, 1971.

Banks, James Jones. Descendants of Captain James Jones. Rome, GA, 1971.

Banta, D.D. A Historical Sketch of Johnson County, Indiana. Chicago, 1881.

Barber, Henry. British Family names: Their Origin and Meaning. London, 1903.

Bardsley, Charles Wareing. A Dictionary of English and Welsh Surnames. Baltimore, 1980.

Barnhart, Clarence L. New Century Cyclopedia of Names. New York, 1954.

Bell, Annie Walker Burns. Abstracts of Pension Papers of Soldiers of the Revolutionary War, War of 1812 and Indian Wars Who Settled in the County of Nelson, Kentucky. Washington, DC, 1934.

_____. Nelson County, Kentucky Record of Wills, 1784-1851. Seat Pleasant, MD, 1934.

_____. Jefferson County, Kentucky Marriages, 1780-1813. LDS # 08711569.

_____. Kentucky Brides Index. Undated.

Bell, Landon C. Sunlight on the Southside: Lists of Tithes, Lunenburg County, Virginia, 1748-1783. Baltimore, 1974.

Bergen, John V. Illustrated Historical Atlas of Johnson CO, Indiana, 1820-1900. 1984.

Boddie, John Bennett. Seventeenth Century Isle of Wight County, Virginia. Chicago, 1938.

_____. Colonial Surry. Richmond, 1948.

_____. Albemarle, Virginia. Baltimore, 1958.

_____. Births, Deaths, and Sponsors, 1717-1778: From the Albemarle Parish Registers of Surry and Sussex Counties, Virginia. Baltimore, 1964.

_____. Southside Virginia Families. Baltimore, 1966.

_____. Historical Southern Families. Baltimore, 1967.

_____. Virginia Historical Families. Redwood City, CA, 1975.

Boedecker, Edward. Inscriptions of Shelby Co, Illinois. Vol 9. Shelbyville, 1984.

Brookes-Smith, Joan E. Master Index of Virginia Surveys and Grants, 1774-1791. Frankfort, 1976.

Brumbaugh, Gaius Marcus. Revolutionary War Records. Vol 1. Washington, DC, 1936.

Burgess, Louis A. Virginia Soldiers of 1776. Baltimore, 1973.

Burgner, Goldene Fillers. North Carolina Land Grants in Tennessee, 1778-1791. Memphis, 1981.

Burns, Annie Walker. See Bell, Annie Walker Burns.

Cal. See Calendar of State Papers [Virginia].

Calendar of Virginia State papers and Other Manuscripts. 11 vols. Richmond, 1968. Cited as Cal.

Carlton, William M. The Family of John Carleton of Craven and Duplin Counties, NC. Athens, GA, 1967.

Carlton Family of Wilkes County, North Carolina, 1750-1860. LDS Film# 1035987.

Carpenter, Evelyn Y. John Yates, 1712-1779, and His Descendants to 1989. Clarksville, TN, 1989.

Catton, Bruce, ed, and narr. The American Heritage Picture History of the Civil War. New York, 1960.

Certificate Book of the Virginia Land Commission, 1779-1780: Register, Kentucky State Historical Society. Vol 21. Easley, SC, 1981.

Clark, Clarence Edin. Territorial Papers of the United States. Vol 4. Washington, DC, 1936.

Clark, Walter. The State Records of North Carolina. 19 Vols. New York, 1970.

Clift, G. Glenn. Kentucky Sodiers in the War of 1812. Anchorage, Ky, 1964.

_____. "Second Census"of Kentucky: 1800. Baltimore, 1966.

_____. Kentucky Marriages, 1797-1865. Baltimore, 1966.

Coldham, Peter Wilson. The Complete Book of Emigrants, 1607-1660. Baltimore, 1987.

Colonial Dames XVII Century, The National Society. Washington, DC. Cited as NSCD.

Cook, Michael L. & Bettie A. Cummings Cook. Kentucky Court of Appeals Deed Books. Evansville, IN, 1985.

_____. Fincastle & Kentucky County, Virginia-Kentucky, Records and History. Evansville, IN, 1987.

_____. Jefferson County, Kentucky Records. 5 vols. Evansville, IN. 1987.

_____. Lincoln County, Kentucky Records. 3 vols. Evansville, IN, 1987.

_____. Virginia Supreme Court, District of Kentucky Order Books, 1783-1792. Evansville, IN, 1988.

C&P. Cavaliers and Pioneers. See Nugent.

Corbitt, David Leroy. The Formation of North Carolina Counties, 1663-1943. Raleigh, 1975.

Crozier, William Armstrong. Westmoreland County Wills. Baltimore, 1962.

_____. Virginia County Records. 11 vols. Baltimore, 1971 cited as VCR.

_____. Virginia Colonial Militia, 1651-1776. Baltimore, 1986.

Currer-Briggs, Noel. Virginia Settlers & English Adventures: Abstracts of Wills, 1484-1798. Baltimore, 1970.

_____. English Wills of Colonial Families. Cottonport, LA, 1972.

DAR. See Daughters of the American Revolution.

Daughters of the American Revolution, National Society of (NSDAR). This organization has published much research over the years, far too numerous to cite individually; hence, "DAR" will be used to indicate any source identified under their system of classification.

Davidson County, Tennessee Minute Book – Vol A, Part 2: 1788-1790. DAR.

Davidson, Eva Cutts Rucker, comp. Rucker Kinsmen. Arlington, VA, 1974.

Davis, Eliza Timberlake. Surry County, Virginia Records, 1652-1684. Berryville, 1956.

_____. Wills & Administratons of Surry Co, Virginia: 1671-1750. Berryville, 1980.

Dean, Frances Forsythe & Bernard Mathis Malloy. Rust of North Carolina. 14 vols. Washington, DC, 1958.

Des Congnets, Louis. English Duplicates of Lost Virginia Records. Princeton, 1958.

Dolan, J.R. English Ancestral Names. New York, 1972.

Dorman, John Frederick. Virginia Revolutionary Pension Applications. 14 vols. Washington, DC, 1958.

____. Orange County, Virginia Will Book I: 1735-1743. Washington, DC, 1958.

____. Essex County, Virginia Records, 1717-1722; Deeds, Etcetera NO. 16, 1718-1721; Wills, Inventories & Settlements, No.3 1717-1722. Washington, DC, 1959.

____. Orange County, Virginia. Washington, DC, 1961.

____. Essex County, Virginia Wills, Bonds, Inventories, Etcetera, 1722-1730. Washington, DC, 1961.

____. Essex County, Virginia Records 1706-1719; Deeds & Wills No.12, 1704-1707; Deeds & Wills No. 15, 1716-1718. Washington, DC, 1963.

____. Essex County, Virginia Deeds & Wills No.13, 1707-1711. Washington, DC, 1965.

Draughon, Wallace R. & William Perry Johnson, North Carolina Genealogical Reference. Durham, 1966.

Duvall, Lindsay O. Northumberland County, Virginia: 1678-1713. Easley, SC, 1978.

____. Virginia Colonial Abstracts, Series 2. Easley, SC, 1978. Cited as VCA(2).

Early Green County, Kentucky Survey Depositions, 1783-1828. DAR, 1959.

Early Kentucky Tax Records. Register of the Kentucky Historical Society. Baltimore, 1987.

Eckenrode, Hamilton James. Revolutionary Soldiers of Virginia. Richmond, 1912.

____. Virginia Soldiers of the American Revolution. Richmond, 1989.

Everton, George B. & Gunnar Rasmussen. Handy Book for Genealogists. Logan, UT, 1962.

Family Findings. Published by Mid-West Tennessee Genealogical society, Jackson, TN. Cited as FF.

FF. See Family Findings.

Field, Thomas P. A guide to Kentucky Place Names. Lexington, 1961.

Fleet, Beverly. Virginia Colonial Abstracts. 34 vols. Baltimore, 1937-1949. Cited as VCA (1).

____. Virginia Colonial Abstracts. 3 vols. Baltimore, 1988. Cited as Fleet.

Ford, Carol Lee. Early Kentucky Tax Records. Baltimore, 1984.

Fothergill, Augusta B. & John Mark Naugle. Virginia Taxpayers, 1782-87: Other Than Those Published by the us Census bureau.

Franklin, Charles M. Lincoln County Kentucky Wills& Estates. Vol 1 (1781-1807) and vol 2 (108-1822). Indianapolis, 1986.

Fullerton, Jane H., genealogist. Nashville, TN. Correspondence with BMM.

Furneaux, Rupert. Invasion 1066. Englewood Cliffs, NJ, 1966.

Garner, Grace Kelso & Ralph L. Tripplett. Early Marriages: Western Frederick County, Virginia and Eastern Hampshire County, West Virginia. 1975.

Garrett, Jill Knight & Iris Hopkins McClain. Sacred to the Memory: Hickman County, Tennessee Cemetery Records. Columbia, TN, c1966.

GCHS. See Green County Historical Society.

GCR. See Green County Review.

Genealogies of Virginia Families. 5 vols. Baltimore, 1982. Cited as GVF.

Goodspeed's General History of Tennessee. Columbia, TN, 1887.

Green County, Kentucky Marriages: 1793-1836. Greensburg, KY. Cited as GCHS.

Green County Review. Green County Historical Society Quarterly. Greensburg. Cited as GCR.

Greer, George Cabell. Early Virginia Immigrants, 1623-1666. Richmond, 1912.

Grider, Ethel C. Woodall. McGehee Descendants. Vol 1. Winder, GA, n.d.

Grimes, J. Bryan. Abstracts of North Carolina Wills. Baltimore, 1967.

Groves, Joseph A., MD. The Alstons and Allstons of North and South Carolina. Atlanta, 1901.

GVF. See Genealogies of Virginia Families.

Gwathmey, John H. Historical Register of Virginians in the Revolution, 1775-1783. Baltimore, 1973.

Gwynn, Zae Hargett. Abstracts of Wills, Granville County, North Carolina: 1746-1808. Rocky Mount, 1973.

_____. Abstracts of Early Deeds, Granville County, North Carolina: 1746-1765. Rocky Mount, 1974.

_____. Kinfolks of Granville County, North Carolina. Rocky Mount, 1974. Cited as Kin.

_____. Abstracts of Wills, Granville County, North Carolina: 1808-1833. Rocky Mount, 1976.

_____. Abstracts of Court Minutes, Granville County, North Carolina: 1746-1820. Rocky Mount, 1977.

_____. Abstracts of Guardian Accounts, Granville County, North Carolina: 1810-1856. Rocky Mount, 1978.

Hadfield, Kathleen Halverson & W. Cary McConnaughey. Historical Notes on Amelia County, Virginia. Amelia, 1982.

Hardin County, Kentucky Records Book 1. DAR.

Hart, Lyndon H., III. Surry County, Virginia Wills, Estate Accounts & Inventories: 1730-1800. Easley. SC, 1985.

Hathaway, J.R.B. The North Carolina Historical and Genealogical Register. Edenton, 1901.

Hatton, Lillian. Marriage Licenses of Northumberland County, Virginia: 1735-1795. Richmond, 1939.

Haun, Weynette Parks. Surry County, Virginia Court Records: 1664-1671 (DB 1), Bk 2. Durham, NC, 1987.

Headley, Robert K., Jr. Wills of Richmond County, Virginia: 1699-1800. Baltimore, 1983.

Hening, William Waller. The Statutes at Large: Being a Collection of All the Laws of Virginia. 13 vols. Richmond, 1823.

Hicks, John D. & George E. Mowry. A short History of American Democracy. Boston, 1956.

Hiden, Martha Woodroof. See Adventurers.

Hodges, Sarah Milliken. Wagoner, OK. Correspondence with BMM.

Hofmann, Margaret M. Province of North Carolina 1663-1729, Abstracts of Land Grants. Weldon, 1977.

_____. Colony of North Carolina 1735-64, Abstracts of Patents. Vol. 1. Weldon, 1982

_____. Colony of North Carolina 1764-75, Abstracts of Land Patents. Vol 2. Raleigh, 1984.

_____. Granville District of North Carolina, 1748-1763: Land Grants. Weldon, 1986.

_____. Deeds of Edgecombe Precinct, North Carolina: 1732-1758. Weldon, 1987.

_____. Granville Grantees, Halifax County, North Carolina Public Registry. Weldon, n.d.

Holcomb, Brent. Bute County, North Carolina Land Grant Plats & Land Entries. Chapel Hill, 1974.

_____. Marriage and Death Notices from the Southern Christian Advocate. Easley, SC, 1979.

_____. Marriages of Granville County, North Carolina, 1753-1868. Baltimore, 1981.

_____. Marriages of Rowan County, North Carolina: 1753-1868. Baltimore, 1981.

_____. Marriages of Orange County, North Carolina 1779-1868. Baltimore, 1983.

____. Marriages of Wake County, North Carolina: 1770-1868. Baltimore, 1983.

____. Bute County, North Carolina Minutes of the Court of Pleas & Quarter Sessions, 1767-1779. Columbia, SC, 1988.

Hotten, John Camden. The Original Lists of Persons of Quality, 1600-1700. London, 1874.

Humel, Elizabeth Hicks. History of Granville County, North Carolina: Marriage Bonds. Vol 1. Oxford, NC, 1965.

Hunt, C.S. Linden, TN. Correspondence with BMM.

Hutchison, Louisa. 1810 Census Index. Leesburg, typescript.

IGI. International Genealogical Index. See Latter-Day Saints.

Indiana Source Books 1 and 2. Indiana Historical Society, Family History Section. Indianapolis.

Jefferson County, Kentucky Marriages, 1780-1813. [See Annie Bell.]

Jester, Annie Lash. See Adventurers.

Jewell, Aurelia M. Loudoun County, Virginia Marriages Bonds, 1762-1850. Berryville, 1962.

____. Loudoun County, Virginia Marriage Records to 1881. Alexandria, 1975.

____. Cemeteries of Loudoun County, Virginia. Leesburg, n.d.

Jillson, Willard Rouse. The Kentucky Land Grants: A Systematic Index to All of the Land Grants recorded in the State Land Office at Frankfort, Kentucky, 1782-1924. Louisville, 1925.

____. Old Kentucky Entries & Deeds: Complete Index to All Earliest Land Entries, Military Warrants, Deeds & Wills of the Commonwealth of Kentucky. Baltimore, 1969.

Johnson, June Whitehurst. Fairfax County, Virginia: Will Bk A 1742-52 and Will Book B, 1752-1767. Fairfax, 1982.

Johnson, Robert C. A History of Early Jeffersontown and Southeastern Jefferson County, Kentucky. Baltimore, 1977.

Johnson, William Perry. Index to North Carolina Wills, 1663-1900. Reigh, 1963.

Johnston, Hugh Buckner. "Williford – Wilford – Willford of Southhampton, Warren, and Edgecombe Counties" [Chapter Three of unidentified book].

Johnston, Ross B. West Virginia Estate Settlements to 1850. Baltimore, 1978.

Journals of the House of Burgesses, Province of North Carolina, 1749. Raleigh, 1949.

Journals of the House of Burgesses of Virginia, 1619-1776. 13 vols. Richmond, 1905-1915.

Joyner, Peggy Shomo. Abstracts of Virginia's Northern Neck Warrants & Surveys, 1697-1784. Vol 4. Portsmouth, 1985.

____. Abstracts of Virginia's Northern Neck Warrants & Surveys: Orange and Augusta Counties, 1730 to 1754. Vol 1. Portsmouth, 1985.

____. Abstracts of Virginia's Northern Neck Warrants & Surveys: Dunmore, Shenandoah, Culpeper, Prince William, Fauquier, and Stafford Counties, 1710-1780. Vol 3. Portsmouth, 1987.

KA. See Kentucky Ancestors.

Kegley, Mary B. Soldiers of Fincastle County, Virginia: 1774. Roanoke, 1974.

Kentucky Ancestors. Kentucky Historical Society Quarterly. Frankfort, since 1903.

Kentucky Vital Records: Wills & Marriages. LDS# 051777 (from Ardery).

Kerr, Mary Hinton, genealogist. Warrenton, NC. Correspondence with BMM.

____. Warren County, North Carolina Records. Vol 3. Warrenton, 1969.

Kilgore, Ruth Fay Wright. Lancaster Ancestors. Berryville, VA. 1982.

King, Estelle Stewart. Abstract of Wills and Inventories, Fairfax County, Virginia: 1742-1801. Baltimore, 1959.

King, George Harrison Sanford. St Paul's Parish, Stafford County, Virginia: 1715-1798. Fredericksburg, 1960.

_____. The Register of Overwharton Parish, Stafford County, Virginia: 1723-1758. Fredericksburg, 1961.

_____. Marriages of Richmond County, Virginia: 1668-1853. Fredericksburg, 1964.

_____. The Registers of North Farnham Parish, 1663-1814, and Lunenburg Parish, 1783-1800, Richmond County, Virginia. Fredericksburg, 1966.

Kirkham, E. Kay. Counties of the United States and Their Genealogical Value. Salt Lake City, UT.

Kozee, William C. Early Families of Easter and Southeastern Kentucky. Baltimore, 1973.

Landrum, John Belton O'Neal. History of Spartanburg, South Carolina. Greenville, 1897.

Latter-day Saints, The Church of Jesus Christ of. The Genealogical Department of the LDS publishes the International Genealogical Index, available on microfiche; many other records have been microfilmed (Listed by catalog number), including the AIS and IGI. Cited as LDS.

Laurance-Dow, Elizabeth. Virginia Rent Rolls, 1704. New York, 1979.

LDS. See Latter-day Saints.

Lee, Ida Johnson. Lancaster County, Virginia Marriages, 1652-1850. Baltimore, 1972.

_____. Lancaster County, Virginia Will Abstracts, 1653-1850. Baltimore, 1973.

Leeper, Kate. Hickman County [Tennessee] Court Minutes. n.p., 1968.

Legislative Journals of the Council of Colonial Virginia. Vol 1. H.R. McIlwaine, ed. [Which see.]

Lewis, James F. & J.Motley Booker. Northumberland County, Virginia Wills and Administrations, 1713-1749. Vol 4. Callao, 1967.

Loveless, Richard W. Records of the District of West Augusta, Ohio County, and Yohogania County, Virginia. Columbus, OH, 1970.

Lucas, Silas Emmett, Jr. Genealogy of Dodson, Lucas, Pyles, Rochester. Birmingham, AL, 1959.

Lyle, Virginia Reavis. Granville County, North Carolina Potpourri. Nashville, 1969.

Magazine of Virginia Genealogy. Quarterly publication of Virginia Genealogical Society, Richmond.

Malloy, Bernard Mathis & Frances Forsythe Dean. Rust of North Carolina. Unpublished MS. Cited as R/NC. . Denver, 1973.

Mason, Olivia Gouger. The James Alston Line. Forth Worth, TX, 76107.

Master Index to Virginia Surveys and Grants, 1774-1791. See Brookes-Smith.

Matthews, C.M. English Surnames. New York, 1967.

McAllister, Joseph Thompson. Virginia Militia in the Revolutionary War. Bowie, MD.

McBride, Ransom, genealogist. Cary, NC. Correspondence with BMM.

McBride, Robert M., ed. Eastin Morris' Tennessee Gazetteer. Nashville, 1971.

McIlwaine, H.R. Minutes of the Council and General Court of Colonial Virginia. Richmond, 1979.

McNeely, James B. Reminiscent Reflections. Farmington, KY, 1917.

Meade, Bishop William. Old Churches, Ministers, and Families of Virginia. 2 vols. Philadelphia, 1857.

Mesmer, Eunice Plunkett. Rust and Allied Families. Lynchburg, VA. 1939.

MVG. See Magazine of Virginia Genealogy.

NCGSJ. See North Carolina Genealogical Society Journal.

Norris, Walter Biscoe Jr. Westmoreland County, Virginia: 1653-1983. Montross, 1983.

North Carolina Genealogical Records. DAR, 1935.

North Carolina Genealogical Society Journal. Published by the North Carolina genealogical Society, Raleigh, since 1975. Cited as NCGSJ.

North Carolinian, vol 6(3), Sep 1960. Cited as VC.

Nottingham, Stratton. Marriage Bonds of Lancaster County, Virginia: 1701-1848. Onancock, VA, 1927.

Nugent, Nell Marion. Cavaliers & Pioneers: Abstracts of Virginia Land Patents and Grants. 3 vols. Richmond, 1934. Cited as C&P.

Patterson, Margaret Ann. Abstracts of Hardin County, Kentucky Will Books A, B, D, and E, 1793-1838. Salt Lake City, 1971. LDS Film#0855031.

Pickard, Howard. Letter to Susan M. Woollard Mathis. Nashville, 20 May 1931.

Pierce's Register: Certificates Issued by John Pierce, Esquire, Paymaster General and Commissioner Army Accounts for the United States, to Officers and Soliders of the Continental Army Under Act of July 4, 1783. DAR, 1984.

Pickerton, W.L. Letter to D.M. Cooper. Centerville, TN, 3 Mar 1948.

Powell, William S. North Carolina Gazetteer. Chapel Hill, 1976.

Rankin, Hugh F. North Carolina Continental Line in the American Revolution. Raleigh, 1959.

_____. The North Carolina Continental Line in the American Revolution. Raleigh, 1977.

_____. Revolutionary Pensioners: A transcript of the Pension list on the United States for 1813. Baltimore, 1959.

Ratcliff, Clarence E. North Carolina taxpayers, 1701-1786. Baltimore, 1984.

Ray, Worth S. Colonial Granville County and its People. Austin, 1945.

Reaney, Percy Hide. A Dictionary of British surmandes. London, 1976.

Register of the Kentucky State Historical Society. Vol 21. Frankfort, 1923.

Register, Alvaretta K. State Census of North Carolina, 1784-1787. NA 1971.

Richards, Gertrude R.B. Register of Albemarle Parish, Surry and Sussex Counties, Virginia: 1739-1778. Richmond, 1958.

Richmond County, Virginia. See Ryland.

Riedel, Mildred H., genealogist. Frankfort, KY. Correspondence with BMM.

R/NC. Rust of North Carolina. See Dean or Malloy.

Rucker, Lauralee Bush. The Genealogy of the Rucker Family. New York, 1963.

Rust, Albert D. Records of the Rust Family. Waco, TX, 1891.

Rust, Ellsworth Marshall. Rust of Virginia. Washington, DC, 1940. Cited as R/V.

R/V. Rust of Virginia. See Rust, Ellsworth Marshall.

Ryland, Elizabeth Lowell. Richmond County, Virginia. Warsaw, VA, 1976.

Salley, Alexander S. Stub Entries to Indents Issued in Payment of Claims Against South Carolina, Growing out of the War of the Revolution. Book 10, Part 2. n.p., 1939.

Sames, James W. Index to Kentucky and Virginia Maps. Frankfort, 1976.

Saunders, William L. The Colonial Records of North Carolina. 10 vols. Raleigh, 1886.

Scheer, George F. & Hugh F. Rankin. Rebels and redcoats. Cleveland, OH, 1957.

Schreiner-Yantis, Nettie & Florence Speakman Love. The 1787 Census of Virginia. 3 vols. Springfield, 1987.

Scott, Hattie M. Green County, Kentucky Marriages. Books 1 and 2. DAR, 1932.

Selby, Robert S. & Phyllis J. Selby. Grant County, Indiana Marriage Records, 1831-53. Kokomo, 1983.

Mary Louise Marshall Hutton, comp. Seventeenth Century Colonial Ancestors. Ann Arbor, 1976. Cited as NSCD [Natl Society Colonial Dames XVII Century]

Shields, Ruth Herndon. Wills Recorded in Orange County, North Carolina: 1800-1850. Vol 2. Chapel Hill, 1958.

Smith, Agnes Rust Gordon. Back When and Now. San Angelo, TX, 1976.

Smith, Elsdon C. New Dictionary of American Family Names. New York, 1973.

Spalding, Mattingly. Biography of a Kentucky Town. Baltimore, 1942.

Sparacio, Ruth L. & Sam Sparacio. Deed Abstracts of Orange County, Virginia: 1743-1759. Mclean, 1985.

_____. Deed Abstracts of Orange County, Virginia: 1759-1778. McLean, VA. 1985.

_____. Will Abstracts of Orange County, Virginia: 1778-1821. McLean, VA, 1985.

Spence, Jerome D. & David L. Spence. A History of Hickman County, Tennessee. Nashville, 1900.

Stanard, William Glover. Some Emigrants to Virginia. Richmond, 1911.

_____. The Colonial Virginia Register. Albany, NY, 1902.

Stancliff, Mary Harrel. Marriage Bonds of Nelson County, Kentucky: 1785-1832. Houston, 1960.

Standfield, Mrs E.L. Jackson, TN. Contributor.

Stanfill, Mary H. Hardin County, Kentucky Marriages: 1792-1812.

State Gazette of North Carolina: 1792-1799, Abstracts from. LDS Microfilm.

Stephenson, Jean & Ms John S. Cannon. Kentucky Records: Jefferson County Miscellany. DAR, 1943.

Stewart, Robert Armistead. Index to Printed Virginia Genealogies. Baltimore, 1970.

Summer, Lewis Preston. Annals of southwest Virginia, 1769-1800. Baltimore, 1970.

Sweeny, William Montgomery. Wills of Rappahannock County, Virginia: 1656-1692. Lynchburg, 1947.

Swem, E.G. Virginia Historical Index. 2 vols. Roanoke, 1936.

TQ. See Tyler's Quarterly Magazine.

Taylor, Henry. Index to Yardley Taylor's Map of Loudoun. Leesburg, VA, 1985.

Taylor, Phillip Fall. A Calendar of Warrants for Land in Kentucky Granted for Service in French & Indian War. Baltimore, 1967. LDS # 6019959.

Teigan, Bayard L. The Lancasters: 300 years in America. Orange, CA, 1984.

Tennessee Genealogical Records. DAR, 1972-82. [Helen Crawford Marsh].

Thruston, R.C. Ballard. Jefferson County, Virginia-Kentucky Early Marriages, Book 1: 1781 to July 1826. Owensboro, KY. 1981.

Torrence, Clayton. Virginia Wills and Administrations, 1632-1800. Baltimore, 1965.

Tyler, Kenneth. McNeely Family Genealogy. Mountain View, CA. 1986.

Tyler's Quarterly Historical and Genealogical Magazine. 21 vols. Richmond, 1920-1952. Cited as TQ.

VCA (1). Virginia Colonial Abstracts, Series 1. See Fleet.

VCA (2). Virginia Colonial Abstracts, Series 2. See Duvall.

VCR. Virginia County Records. See Crozier.

VG. See Virginia Genealogist.

Virginia Colonial Records. See Crozier.

Virginia Genealogist. J.F. Doman, ed. Quarterly, since 1951. Washington, DC. Cited as VG.

Virginia Magazine of History and Biography. Quarterly publication of the Virginia Historical Society, Richmond. Cited as VMH.

Virginia Land Records. 3vols. Baltimore, 1982.

VLR. See Virginia Land Records.

VMH. See Virginia Magazine of History and Biography.

Vogt, John & T. William Kethley, Jr. Virginia Historic Marriage Register: Rappahannock County, 1823-1850. Athens, GA, 1984.

____. Loudoun County Marriages, 1760-1850. Athens, GA, 1985.

Waldemaier, Inez. A Finding List of Virginia Marriages Before 1853. Washington, 1957.

Walker, John T. Correspondence with BMM. Union City, TN, 10 Jun 1929.

Wallace, Lee A., Jr. The Orderly Book of Captain Benjamin Taliaferro: 2nd Virginia Detachment, Charleston, South Carolina, 1780. VA State Library, 1980.

Wardell, Patrick G. Timesaving Aid to Virginia-West Virginia Ancestors. Athens, GA, 1987.

Warner, Thomas Hoskins. History of Old Rappahannock County, Virginia: 1656-1692. Tappahannock, 1965.

Waters, Henry F. Genealogical Gleanings in England. Baltimore, 1981.

Watson, Joseph W. Kinfolks of Franklin County, North Carolina, 1788-1855. Rocky Mount, 1969.

____. Kinfolks of Franklin County, North Carolina, 1793-1844. Rocky Mount, 1985.

Watson, Ruth Lancaster Trowell. Lancaster and Related Families. Greenville, SC, 1986.

Weisiger, Benjamin B. Prince George County, Virginia Wills and deeds, 1713-1728. Richmond, 1973.

Wellman, Manly Wade. The County of Warren, North Carolina, 1586-1917. Chapel Hill, 1959.

Wells, Carol. Davidson County, Tennessee Court Minutes, 1783-1792. Bowie, MD, 1990.

Wertz, Mary Alice. Marriages of Loudoun County, Virginia: 1757-1853. Baltimore, 1985.

Westmoreland County, Virginia. See Norris.

Wheeler, John H. Reminiscences and Memoirs of North Carolina and Eminent North Carolinians. Baltimore, 1966.

____. Historical Sketches of North Carolina, 1584-1815. New York, 1925.

Whitley, Edyth Johns Rucker. Ruckers and Connections. n.p., 1927.

Wiley, S.T. Indexes to History of Preston County, West Virginia. Parsons, 1971.

Wilkerson, Eva Eubank. Index to marriages of Old Rappahannock and Essex Counties, Virginia, 1655 to 1900. Richmond, 1953.

William & Mary Quarterly Magazine, Series 1 and 2. Quarterly published by the Institute of Early American History and Culture. Williamsburg, since 1966. Cited as W&M (1) and (2).

Williams, Emma Inman. Historic Madison: The Story of Jackson and Madison County, Tennessee. Jackson, 1946.

Williams, Sherril. The Dodson Family of North Farnham, Richmond County, Virginia. Easley, SC, 1946.

Wilson, Samuel Mackay. Catalogue of Revolutionary Soldiers and Sailors of Commonwealth of Virginia, Land

Bounty Warrants. Baltimore, 1953.

Winslow, Ellen Goode Rawlings. History of Perquimans County. Raleigh, 1931.

Winstead, Thomas D. Chronicles of Hardin County, Kentucky: 1766-1974. Elizabethtown, 1976.

Withington, Lothrop. Virginia Gleanings in England: Abstracts of 17th and 18 century English Wills and Administration Relating to Virginia and Virginias. Baltimore, 1980.

W&M. See William &Mary Quarterly.

Wood, Michael. Domesday: A search for the Roots of England. New York, 1986.

Wood, Sudie Rucker. The Rucker Family. Richmond, 1986.

WPA. Work's Progress Administration, Historical Records Project; Cited by Office Project: cited by Official Project Number.

Wright, Louis B. First Gentlemen of Virginia. San Marino, Ca, 1940.

Young, Florence Nelson & Virginia D. Young. Fleming County, Kentucky Deed Books A – G: Abstracts, 1797-1818. Vol 1. Denver, Western Heraldry Organization, 1974.

www.ingramcontent.com/pod-product-compliance
Lightning Source LLC
Chambersburg PA
CBHW051957280526
45793CB00005B/752